Principles of E-learning Systems Engineering

Chandos
Information Professional Series

Series Editor: Ruth Rikowski
(email: Rikowskigr@aol.com)

Chandos' new series of books are aimed at the busy information professional. They have been specially commissioned to provide the reader with an authoritative view of current thinking. They are designed to provide easy-to-read and (most importantly) practical coverage of topics that are of interest to librarians and other information professionals. If you would like a full listing of current and forthcoming titles, please visit our web site **www.chandospublishing.com** or contact Hannah Grace-Williams on email info@chandospublishing.com or telephone number +44 (0) 1993 848726.

New authors: we are always pleased to receive ideas for new titles; if you would like to write a book for Chandos, please contact Dr Glyn Jones on email gjones@chandospublishing.com or telephone number +44 (0) 1993 848726.

Bulk orders: some organisations buy a number of copies of our books. If you are interested in doing this, we would be pleased to discuss a discount. Please contact Hannah Grace-Williams on email info@chandospublishing.com or telephone number +44 (0) 1993 848726.

Principles of E-learning Systems Engineering

Lester Gilbert
and
Veronica Gale

CP
Chandos Publishing
Oxford · England

Chandos Publishing (Oxford) Limited
TBAC Business Centre
Avenue 4
Station Lane
Witney
Oxford OX28 4BN
UK
Tel: +44 (0) 1993 848726 Fax: +44 (0) 1865 884448
Email: info@chandospublishing.com
www.chandospublishing.com

First published in Great Britain in 2008

ISBN:
978 1 84334 290 8 (paperback)
978 1 84334 291 5 (hardback)
1 84334 290 1 (paperback)
1 84334 291 X (hardback)

British Library Cataloguing-in-Publication Data.
A catalogue record for this book is available from the British Library.

Typeset by Domex e-Data Pvt. Ltd.
Printed in the UK and USA.

Contents

List of figures and tables

Figures

Tables

List of acronyms

BVA	boundary value analysis
CBA	cost-benefit analysis
CBT	computer-based teaching/training
CDT	component display theory
CER	cause-effect relationship
CMM	capability maturity model
CPM	critical path method
ELSYE	e-learning systems engineering
FE	further education
HE	higher education
IRR	internal rate of return
ITT	instructional transaction theory
IV	interactive video
KR-20	Kuder-Richardson formula 20
LCV	learned capability verb
MCQ	multiple-choice question
NPV	net present value
PERT	project evaluation and review technique
PPF	primary presentation form
QA	quality assurance
SME	subject matter expert
SPF	secondary presentation form
SSADM	structured systems analysis and design methodology
SSM	soft systems methodology
TBLT	technology-based learning and teaching

TEL	technology-enhanced learning
TNA	training needs analysis
WIFM	'What's in it for me?'

About the authors

Lester Gilbert has an MSc in psychology from the University of Cape Town, specialising in cognition and learning, and subsequently spent about ten years working as an academic in departments of psychology in South Africa. In the 1980s he was a programmer and manager in UK commerce and industry, among many other roles leading and managing the development and delivery of commercial CBT, CAI and interactive video training solutions for customers such as Midland Bank, British Aerospace, Abbey National and the UK Atomic Energy Authority. He re-entered academia in 1992 as a lecturer in IT subjects, and now works at the University of Southampton School of Electronics and Computing Science on the IT in Organisations degree programme, jointly presenting introductory and advanced modules on e-learning and technology-enhanced learning.

Lester is particularly interested in the use of technology in teaching and learning in adult and higher education, and has completed two textbooks dealing with IT at Advanced GNVQ level. He is currently involved in a number of funded projects in the field of technology-enhanced learning, and has presented various conference and workshop papers, most recently in the area of e-learning and service-oriented architectures for virtual learning and research environments. His extramural interests include radio-controlled racing yachts: he is a regular competitor, has been selected for the Great Britain team at recent world and continental championships and is an accredited national judge.

Veronica Gale has a BSc in banking and finance and an MSc in training. She is an experienced learning consultant: conducting research and analysing needs, then designing and implementing education and training solutions using a mix of media, including technology-enhanced learning, coaching and paper-based self-study. Veronica has more than 20 years' experience in needs analysis, instructional and performance tool design, coaching, assessment and evaluation.

Preface

The purpose of this book is to integrate the principles of software engineering with those of educational theory, and to apply these principles to the problems of e-learning development, thus establishing the discipline of e-learning systems engineering. For the first time these principles are collected and organised into the coherent framework that this book provides. Both newcomers to and established practitioners in the field now have an integrated and grounded source of advice on theory and practice.

Developing any system is risk- and error-prone. Almost since the very first commercially available digital computer, programmers and managers have grappled with the problems of how to specify what a system should do, how to design the system to do it, how to implement the design as software and hardware, how to test the implementation and how to manage the whole process of development. This enterprise is known as software engineering, and is now a well-developed branch of information technology.

In the early days of computers, software was developed in an *ad hoc* amateur fashion; there was little recognition, for example, that it made sense to design the system before writing the software, or that introducing apparently innocuous changes to requirements during the coding phases could cause huge project over-runs. A very large number of lessons have been learned since those early days, and the professional software engineer is now as well equipped as the professional civil engineer to undertake all manner of small- and large-scale projects effectively and efficiently.

We are, however, in the early days of teaching, training and learning technologies. These are not early days chronologically, since computers have been applied to teaching and training problems for almost as long as to commercial and scientific problems, but in terms of the professional maturity with which e-learning projects are currently developed.

The book presents both strong practical and strong theoretical frameworks for the design and development of technology-based materials and environments which have teaching, training or educational value. It brings together for the first time a complete range of the specific theories and detailed techniques involved in the design and development of materials such as business presentations, web-based presentations, training courses and academic lessons. Although the methods and theories discussed are generally appropriate to all forms and levels of learning and teaching, the book illustrates their use in and focuses its approach upon e-learning with adults.

The book is primarily aimed at developers of e-learning systems from two communities: those who may be familiar with principles of pedagogy but are new to or inexperienced in the use of information technology media – business trainers, professionals, lecturers and teachers – who now need or wish to use new technology to deliver their message, lesson or training; and those who may be familiar with information technology but are new to or inexperienced in principles of pedagogy – programmers, analysts, technicians – who now need or wish to use their skills to provide educational or training experiences for students.

The book would be particularly useful as a student textbook to accompany any college or university course concerned with teaching, training and the effective communication of information using new technology.

Experienced e-learning developers will hopefully find the book useful both as a reference source in bringing together the major techniques of e-learning systems design in one place and as a source of some of the more specialised techniques that might be found useful.

1

Introduction

The principles of 'e-learning systems engineering' or ELSYE are concerned with the structured development of materials and environments for learning and teaching. The term 'e-learning' is used throughout the text to denote learning and teaching materials, courses and environments with significant information technology components. Currently gaining favour in the UK and Europe is the term 'technology-enhanced learning', or TEL, covering the same area but also including social aspects of learning. In other parts of the world the term 'instructional' is preferred, and covers much the same ground as 'learning and teaching'. Although some distinction can be made between education on the one hand and training on the other, the distinction is not a useful one from the point of view of the engineering of learning and teaching materials and environments. The focus of the text is on the development of learning and teaching systems for technology-based rather than lecturer-, teacher- or instructor-based delivery, but the principles of such development remain the same.

Underpinning and unifying this broad and comprehensive approach to the engineering of learning and teaching is a systems or systemic approach. The systems approach informs both the way in which instructional materials may be developed and the design and structure of the materials themselves. The approach thus offers a methodology for the engineering of learning and teaching systems on the one hand, and a theory for the content of learning and teaching on the other. Figure 1.1 illustrates these two central themes arising from a systems point of view.

Materials that are intended for information or entertainment, rather than learning, may also be usefully developed from an ELSYE perspective. In particular, the development of webpages and websites can be successfully approached as ELSYE projects. For such environments, not all the components and techniques of ELSYE are applicable. The relevant differences are pointed out in the text as they occur.

The concept of an 'engineered system' is intended to suggest something rather more than a set of 'crafted' or even 'designed' materials. An ELSYE project gives attention to the environment in which the materials are to be used, to the business case which must underlie a realistic and

Figure 1.1 General systems theory informing e-learning development and content

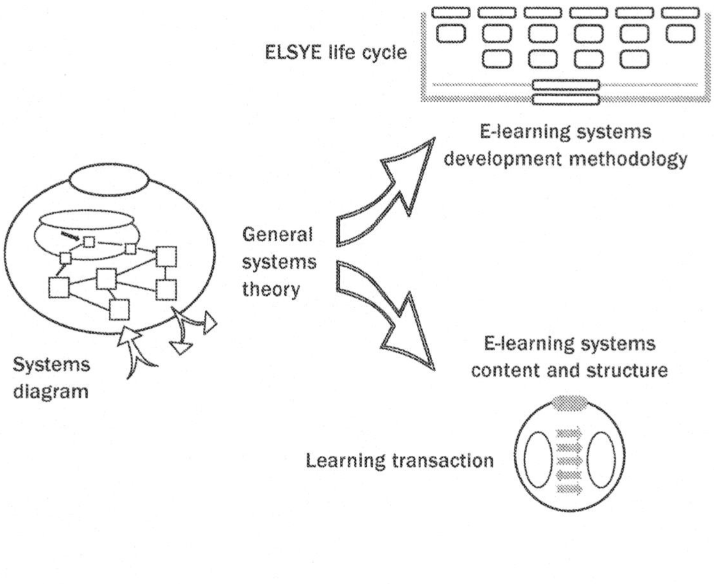

cost-effective project, to the project management and quality assurance issues which arise during development and to a complete set of structured techniques which ensure satisfactory design and implementation. In addition to these 'process' concerns, the text pays explicit attention to 'content': the nature and structure of e-learning systems and materials themselves.

Following an introduction to systems theory in Chapter 2, Chapter 3 establishes a methodology or framework for e-learning design and development. The theory of effective project management is illustrated in terms of systems control theory, and this provides the basis for the overall method and approach of e-learning design and development that characterises this book. Figure 1.2 gives a key overview illustration of this development methodology. In summary, the development of an ELSYE project proceeds in phases (feasibility, analysis, design, construction, operation and evaluation) that are underpinned by project management and quality management tasks.

Chapter 4 considers the nature of learning and teaching, beginning with Pask's theory of a learning system, itself based upon systems theory. Laurillard (2001) has developed Pask's approach into a particular and pertinent view of the structure of learning and teaching environments. The end product of ELSYE, an e-learning system or environment, is an example of a learning and teaching situation which Laurillard calls a 'conversational framework'. The chapter concludes with an outline of the content and structure of learning and teaching materials, developed from Laurillard's 'conversational framework'.

Chapter 5 introduces the start of the ELSYE methodology, the feasibility phase, while Chapters 6 and 7 introduce the analysis phase, comprising the stages of front-end analysis and project plan respectively. The design phase is considered

Figure 1.2 ELSYE development stages

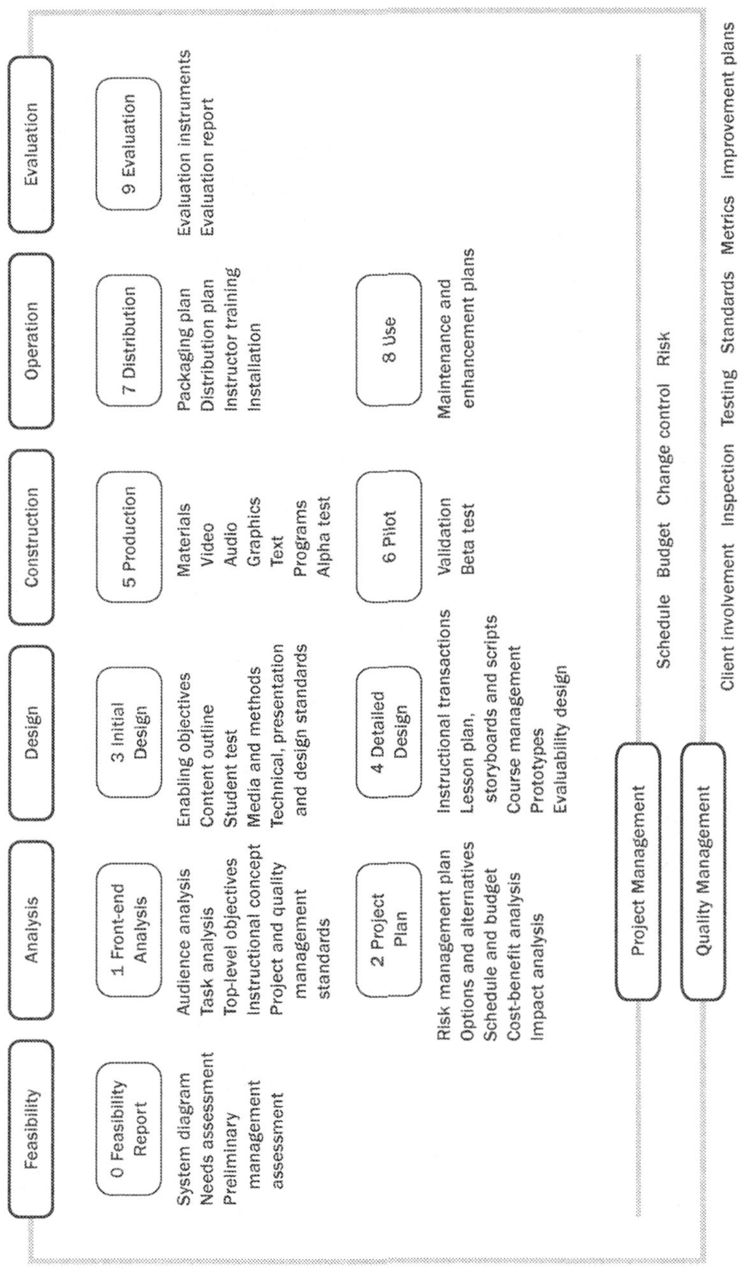

in Chapter 8 for initial design; Chapters 9, 10 and 11 cover detailed design.

The detailed design phase is particularly concerned with the central component of any learning and teaching situation, illustrated in Figure 1.3, the e-learning transaction. This shows the abstracted elements of an e-learning transaction, the lowest-level 'unit' of learning and teaching, involving the teacher in 'showing', 'telling' and, crucially, 'asking' the student in using or applying their knowledge or skills, and the teacher in giving feedback to the student on how they did. Equally crucially, the transaction is contextualised and embedded within some question or problem that the teacher and student are

Figure 1.3 E-learning transaction

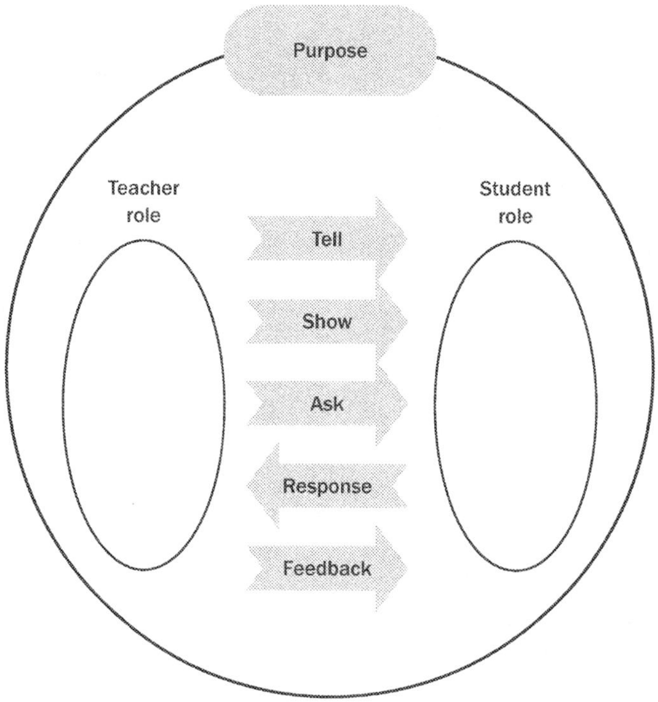

addressing. This context is what gives the learning and teaching point or purpose, and is the major means by which student motivation is maintained.

A set of e-learning transactions is assembled into a learning and teaching session, typically a lesson. An e-learning session involves transactions which both 'set up' and 'round off' the lesson, as well as transactions which deal with the subject matter (the knowledge and skills relevant to the student's learning, focused upon a particular problem). The introductory and terminating transactions are drawn from the work of Gagné (Gagné et al., 2004) and others, and include gaining the student's attention, informing them of the session objectives, stimulating and assessing prior learning, supporting reflection and retention, giving formative assessment and evaluating the session.

In summary, the first four chapters identify and introduce the content and structure of learning and teaching, as well as the methods to be employed in the engineering of learning and teaching, each derived from systems theory. Following from these, later chapters take the engineering steps in turn and expand upon them, showing how the content (e-learning transactions) and structure (sessions, lessons, modules, units and programmes) of the proposed e-learning are developed through the ELSYE stages of analysis and design. The remaining ELSYE phases and stages of production are discussed in Chapter 12, and piloting, distribution, use and evaluation are summarised in Chapter 13.

The final two chapters, 14 and 15, respectively introduce the quality management and project management issues relevant to ELSYE.

2

General systems theory

People often discuss an e-learning system without giving much attention to the accuracy of their description of something as a 'system', and this chapter provides some background which might help correct this. According to systems theory, something that is properly called a 'system' should have certain characteristics. Figure 2.1, a classic system diagram, illustrates these major characteristics.

The characteristics of a 'system' are that it:

- is embedded and operates in an environment;
- is distinguished from its environment by a clear system boundary;
- takes input from its environment and processes or transforms it;
- provides resulting output into its environment;
- involves internal processes;
- contains a control subsystem;
- has emergent properties;
- uses resources;
- involves authorisation to operate.

In order to take a systems approach to the engineering of an e-learning project, it is useful to be able to identify and analyse these characteristics in the particular system

Figure 2.1 System diagram

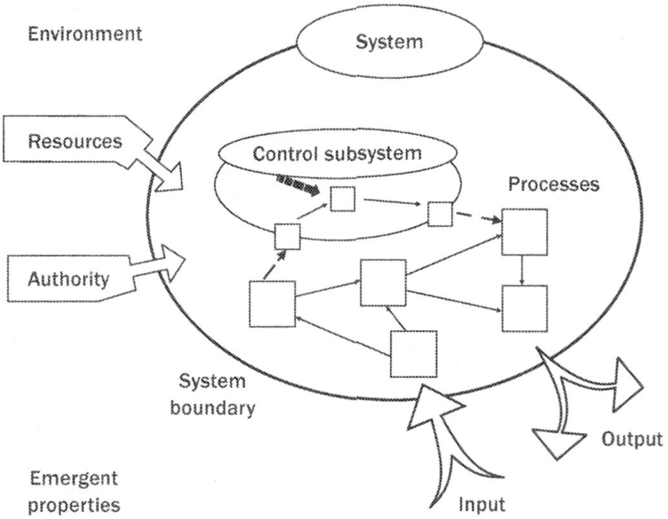

involved. This idea is taken up in the chapter on the feasibility report.

Perhaps the most unfamiliar of these system characteristics is the notion of emergent properties. Taking the example of an aircraft as a system, its emergent property is that it flies, a property possessed by none of its parts. Another conventional example of a system with emergent properties is any living organism, whose emergent property, life, is not found in any of its separate parts.

The control subsystem

What is particularly interesting for ELSYE is the control subsystem, that component of a complete system which enables it to function correctly. The control subsystem is illustrated in detail in Figure 2.2. A consideration of control

Figure 2.2 Control subsystem

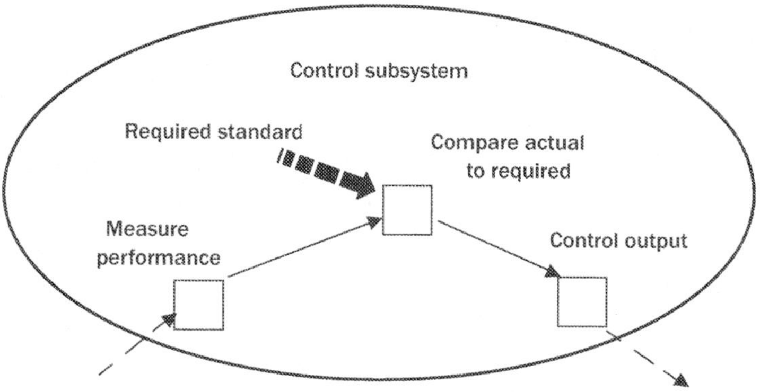

theory provides suggestions for ELSYE as to the arrangement of methods and procedures for the development of e-learning, and on the components that should be designed into e-learning. The control subsystem has four components.

- First, the control subsystem measures some information of interest about the current, actual state of the system being controlled.
- Second, the control subsystem itself has some information about what these measures should be, called the required standard.
- Third, the actual measured system information is compared to the required standard.
- Fourth, the control subsystem generates a correction or control output which acts on the system.

The goal of this arrangement is that the system's resulting effects upon the environment, its outputs, are adjusted according to the required standard embedded in the control subsystem.

A concern in the analysis of any system, and particularly in the analysis of the failure of any system to function correctly, is to be able to identify clearly the components of the control subsystem – that is, to be able to identify where measures of performance are obtained, where relevant standards are established, where performance is compared to the required standards and where action is taken to address any discrepancies between what is required and what actually happens.

Notice, from Figure 2.1, that the control subsystem is part of a loop that must pass through the environment as well as through other components of the system. That is, the measured system information that the control subsystem takes as its input is the measured consequence of how effectively the system operates upon the environment as a result of the control subsystem's control output. This is a somewhat long-winded way of saying that the control subsystem depends upon feedback in order to achieve its purpose and function correctly, and that this feedback results from the system as a whole operating upon and within its environment.

Notice also that the interesting properties of a system capable of maintaining some consistent operation upon its environment are really expressed by that system's control subsystem. Because of this, it may be possible to omit the various other details of a system and deal only with the control subsystem when modelling the quality of its performance.

Control theory in management

Another way of portraying a control subsystem derives from management theory. Figure 2.3 illustrates a very common generic approach to the management and control of any

Figure 2.3 Management project control

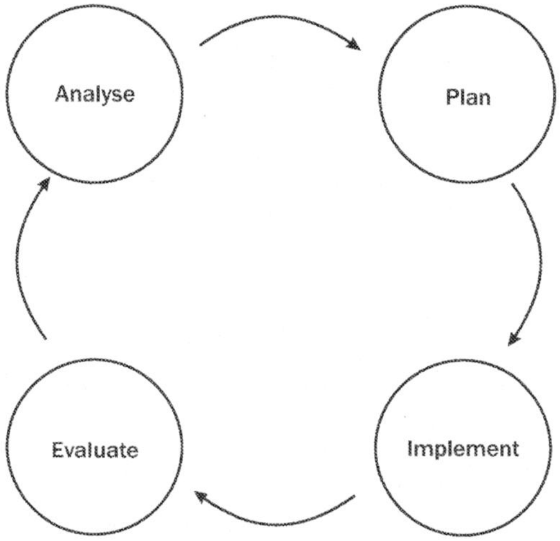

project, and is often presented as a system of project management. It has four parts: analyse; plan; implement, execute or act; and evaluate results. This portrayal provides a direct and natural model of procedures for the development of learning and teaching materials. It also gives a basis for managing and maintaining learning and teaching materials once developed.

This management approach is an analogue of a control subsystem. The 'analyse' component corresponds to the 'desired standard' of the control subsystem. The 'plan' component corresponds to the 'comparator' of the control subsystem: something capable of bringing about the required outcome is identified, specified or designed. The 'implement, execute or act' component corresponds to the 'control output' of the control subsystem: a mechanism designed to bring about the required outcome is activated. Finally, the 'evaluate' component corresponds to the 'measure performance' of the control subsystem, where measures are taken in order to find out whether the intended

Figure 2.4 Management project control arranged linearly

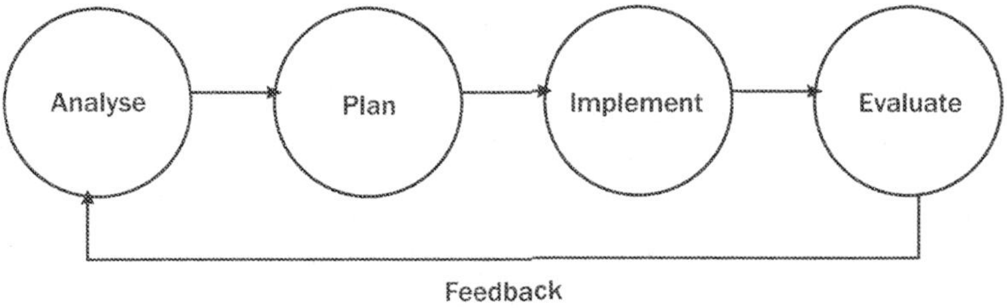

outcome was achieved. The loop is closed by feedback from the evaluation into the next analysis stage, as illustrated in Figure 2.4, where the components are laid out in linear sequence rather than a circle. The way these ideas can be extended to provide for a methodology for developing e-learning systems is outlined in Chapter 3. In particular, the development methodology of e-learning will focus upon analysis, design, production and evaluation processes.

These ideas can also be extended to provide for the specification of e-learning, and for the methods of management of such e-learning. Chapter 4 and subsequent chapters identify elements of e-learning transactions, sessions, units and programmes which are suggested by control theory. In particular, attention is given to ensuring the e-learning contains elements which aid evaluation, and that the management of the e-learning involves review and reflection.

3

Project development framework

The considerations of management and systems control theory provide the basic model of the technical components of the ELSYE process, as illustrated in Figure 3.1. The 'non-technical' components of ELSYE, project management and quality management, are added subsequently.

The 'analyse' component is concerned with establishing the 'what' of an e-learning project – what is required, what are the objectives, what are the constraints and so on. This will be called 'analysis' in ELSYE – 'front-end analysis' in particular.

The 'plan' component is concerned with establishing the 'how' of an e-learning project – how can the objectives and requirements be met? This is called 'design' in ELSYE – in particular, initial design and detailed design.

The 'implement' component is concerned with producing the materials and environment of an e-learning project, and then using the materials in learning and teaching. This is called construction and operation in ELSYE.

The 'evaluate' component is concerned with checking whether the objectives and requirements have been met – did the e-learning work? Evaluation would be done after a period of operation.

These basic components are expanded and extended into a complete model of the phases and stages of an e-learning project in the following discussion.

Figure 3.1 Basic technical components of the ELSYE process

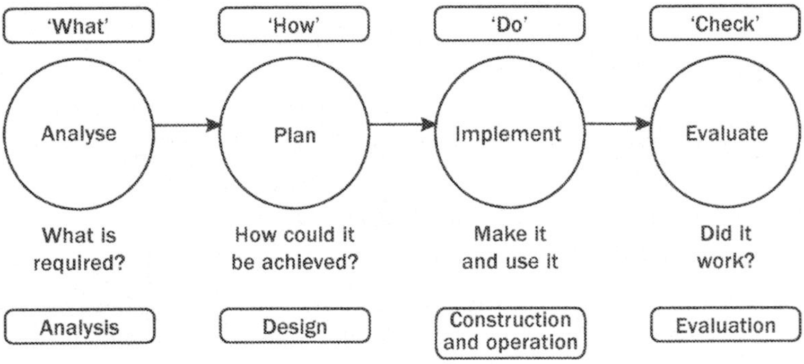

ELSYE project phases and stages

First, a prior component of 'feasibility' is required for the technical phases. The feasibility phase is concerned with establishing whether the requirement for e-learning is likely to meet the needs of the student and the customer, and whether it is likely to meet the financial and organisational constraints of the e-learning project. In short, the feasibility phase asks 'Is this worth doing?' The addition of the feasibility phase gives the six basic phases of an e-learning project, as shown in Figure 3.2.

Second, project management and quality management phases need to be added to complete the ELSYE model. Project management and quality management activities occur throughout an e-learning project, so these are shown as running in parallel with the technical phases in Figure 3.3. Quality management is considered to 'embrace' the entire

Figure 3.2 The basic ELSYE model technical phases

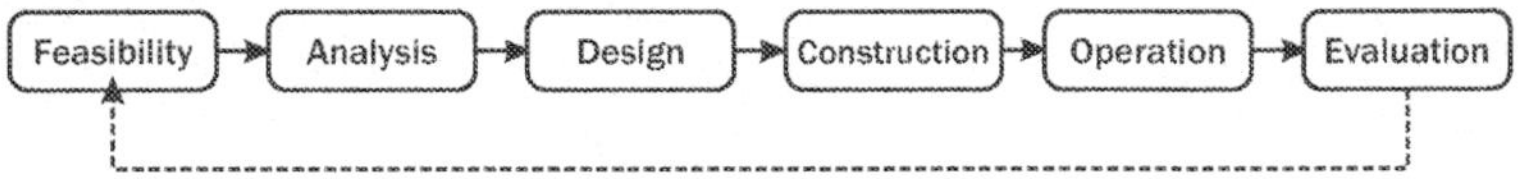

Figure 3.3 **Overview of the complete ELSYE project**

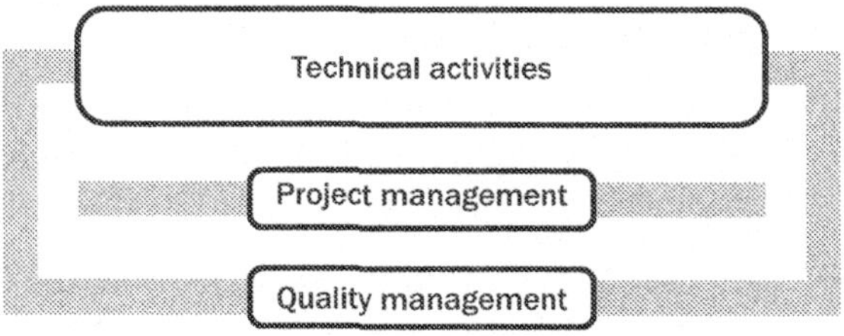

project, so this component is shown as covering both project management and the technical activities.

The phases of a complete ELSYE project are shown in Figure 3.4, which expands upon the overview of Figure 3.3. This figure is the 'standard icon' of the principles of e-learning systems engineering, and expresses a summary of these principles. The remainder of the text is devoted to amplifying and explaining them.

There is nothing particularly new in this ELSYE model. Other authors (e.g. Dick et al., 2004; Gery, 1987) have proposed similar models, and reviews have identified 80 or more other variants. The ELSYE model has strong similarities to the ADDIE model (Molenda, 2003), which is said to exist in over 100 variants. What is important, however, is to note that the ELSYE model is very similar to those used in the systems analysis and design of information systems. This similarity serves to inform the practice of ELSYE with the experience and best practice of one of the

Figure 3.4 **ELSYE phases**

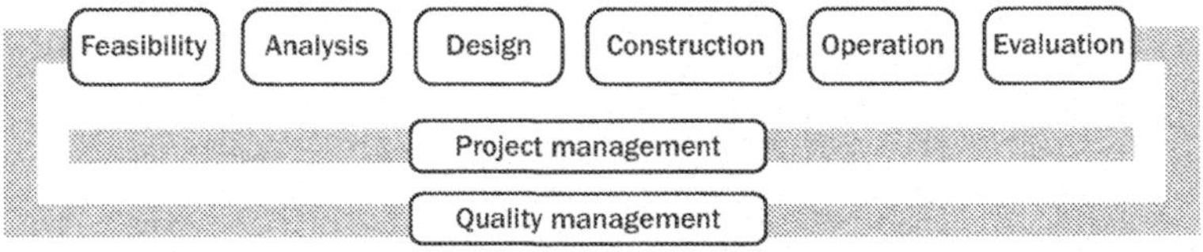

largest international industries currently operating in the world, that of information technology and systems development. In the discipline of software engineering, the common systems analysis and design model (e.g. Pressman, 2004) is illustrated in Figure 3.5 in a way that brings out its similarities to the ELSYE process of Figure 3.4.

The simple (SSADM) model of software engineering of Figure 3.5 is known to have a number of deficiencies, and hence has been improved and elaborated in a variety of ways. The most important of these improvements has been the provision of checkpoints or reviews at the beginning and end of each of the stages, to ensure the project remains on course and under control (Boehm, 1981). Similarly, the simple linear ELSYE model's technical phases of 'feasibility', 'analysis', 'design', 'construction', 'operation' and 'evaluation' require improvement, and this is addressed in the chapters which deal with these phases individually.

Within the phases of Figure 3.4 there are various activities that can be conveniently assembled into stages. These are introduced in Figure 3.6. Most of the project technical phases involve two stages of technical work. The technical stages are numbered for reference. Each of the project stages is shown as being enclosed by project management and quality management activities, as well as the project as a whole. These project and quality management activities are mentioned in Figure 3.8; more detail is provided in Chapters 14 and 15.

Figure 3.5 **Software engineering development model based on SSADM**

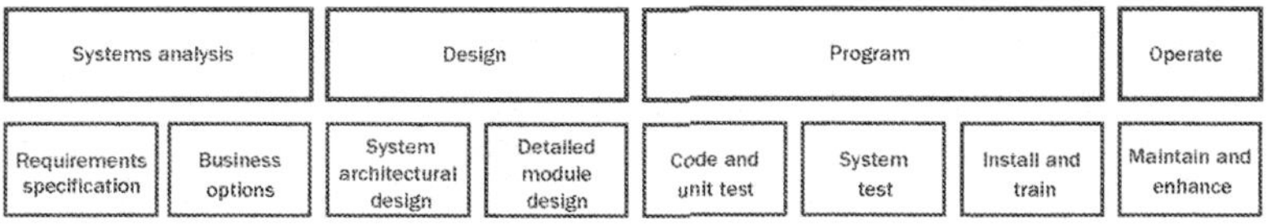

Figure 3.6 ELSYE project technical stages

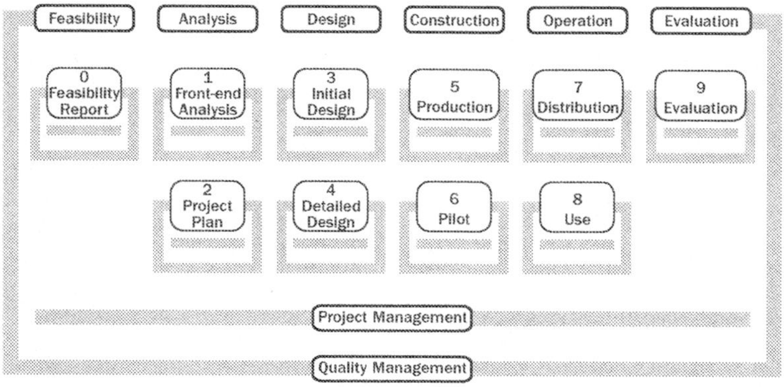

The technical stages are elaborated in Figures 3.7 and 3.8 to show the technical steps that make up the stages. The specific details of the activities of each step are covered in Chapters 5–13.

While considering the ELSYE project structures illustrated in the preceding figures, it is important to note that there are a variety of feedback paths which are not shown on these diagrams. These feedback paths are presented and discussed in detail in the relevant chapters. Figure 3.8 shows in detail the forward paths between the ELSYE steps of project development.

It is also important to note that whether any particular stage of an ELSYE project is instantiated in any e-learning project will generally depend upon the nature and scale of the project. For example, a small e-learning project involving ten minutes' study time, developed by a single lecturer, would not require a feasibility report or a project plan, whereas a set of learning objects covering 50 hours of study time, intended for commercial distribution and developed by a team of consultant designers, graphic artists and courseware programmers, would probably require

Figure 3.7 ELSYE project steps

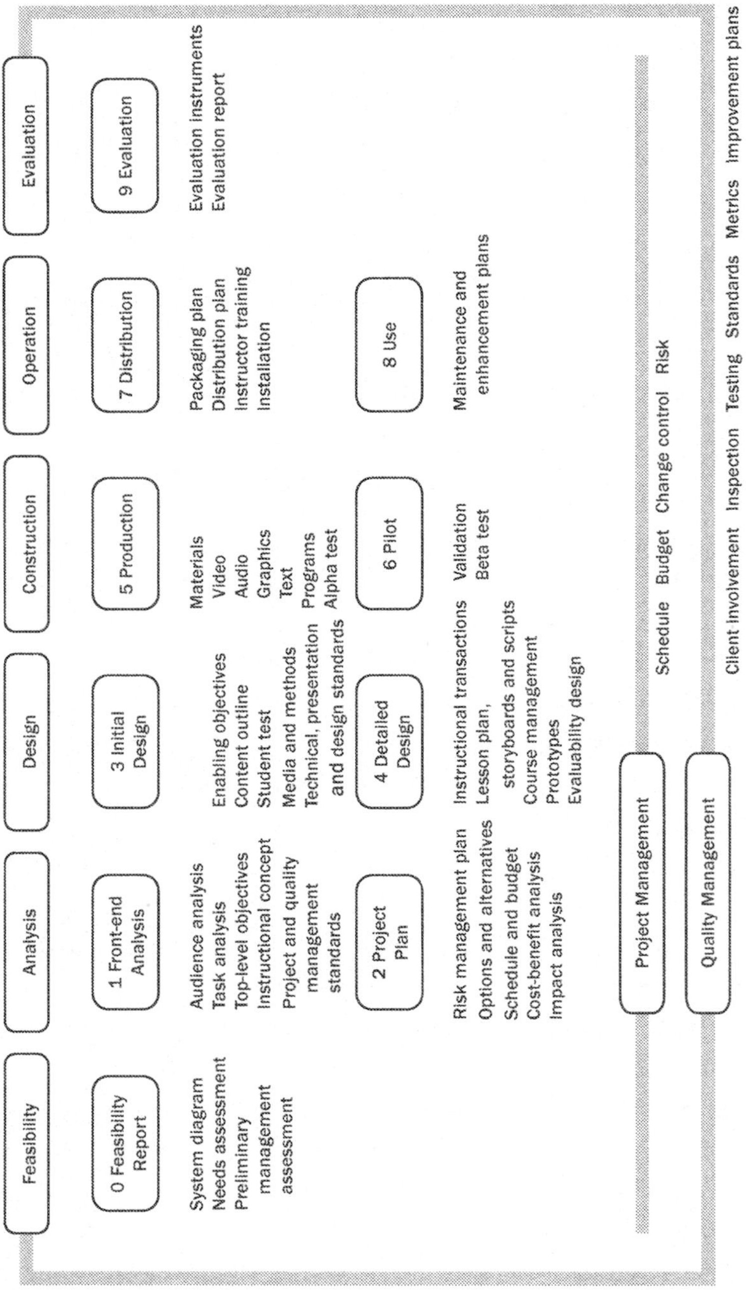

extensive documentation of all stages within the project. This point is discussed in more detail below.

To bring the discussion fully within current terminology, the ELSYE project structure discussed so far will now be called the ELSYE project life cycle, as shown in Figure 3.9.

The ELSYE project life cycle provides for six technical phases. Within these phases there are ten technical stages, and each of the stages comprises a number of steps. When each step is discussed in subsequent chapters, it will be made up of tasks. This terminology follows that of Business Systems Development (the latest version of SSADM4+ developed by its author, the UK Central Computer & Telecommunications Agency).

Table 3.1 shows the breakdown of the ELSYE technical stages into their corresponding steps. The steps are described and characterised as 'deliverables' or 'products'. While the ELSYE phases and stages represent the processes of development, the steps represent the products of development, those physical documents or materials that result from the tasks carried out in each step. In particular, the detailed discussions in the remainder of this text will focus on the tasks required in each step to construct the step's product (also called its deliverable, short for deliverable product), and on the techniques that are used in these tasks to achieve the step's purpose. ELSYE involves a number of e-learning design and development techniques, most of which are used in more than one task. These techniques, such as interactivity design, are discussed with the tasks where they first occur.

Throughout the text the ELSYE stage diagrams illustrate the linkages between the steps within each stage, and the linkages with previous stages and steps. Figure 3.10 shows the general structure of these stage diagrams, using the detailed design stage as an example. Each task is shown in the probable sequence it will be undertaken within the stage by reading from left to right, and from top to bottom. Most tasks

Figure 3.8 The full ELSYE life cycle: stages, steps and forward paths

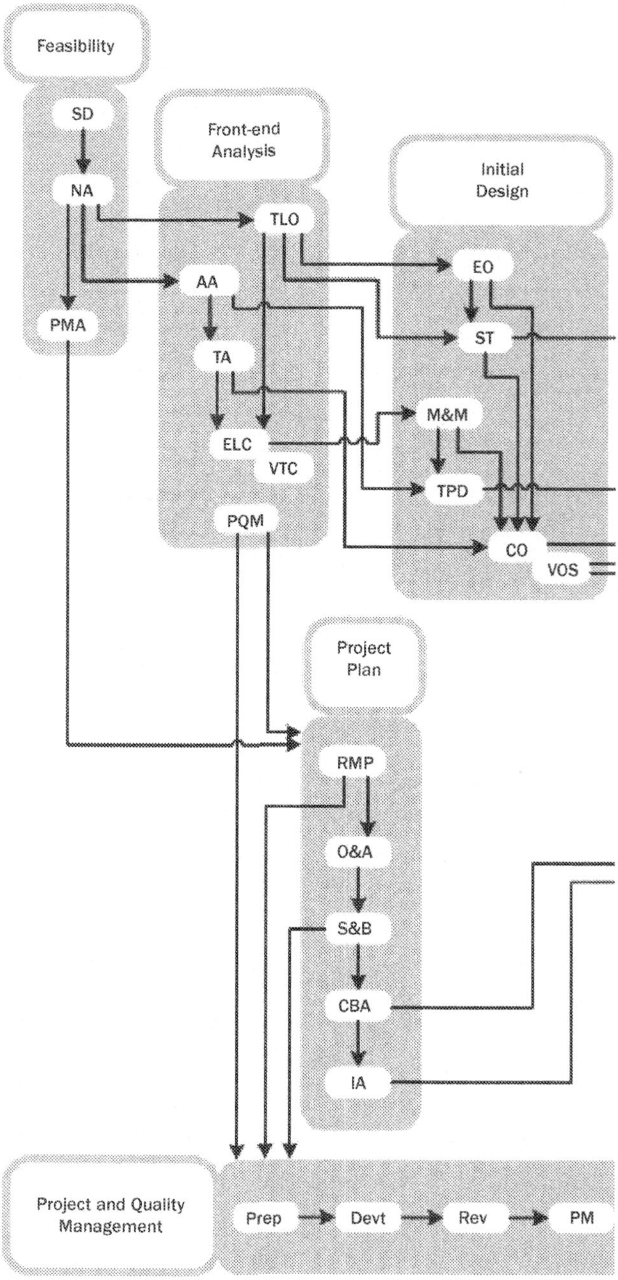

SD System diagram
NA Needs analysis
PMA Preliminary management assessment
TLO Top-level objectives
AA Audience analysis
TA Task analysis
ELC E-learning concept
VTC AV treatment concept
PQM Project and quality management standards

EO Enabling objectives
ST Student test
M&M Media and methods
TPD Technical, presentation and design standards
CO Content outline
VOS AV outline script

LT Learning transactions
LP Lesson plan
VFS AV final script
CMD Course management design
PT Prototypes
ED Evaluability design

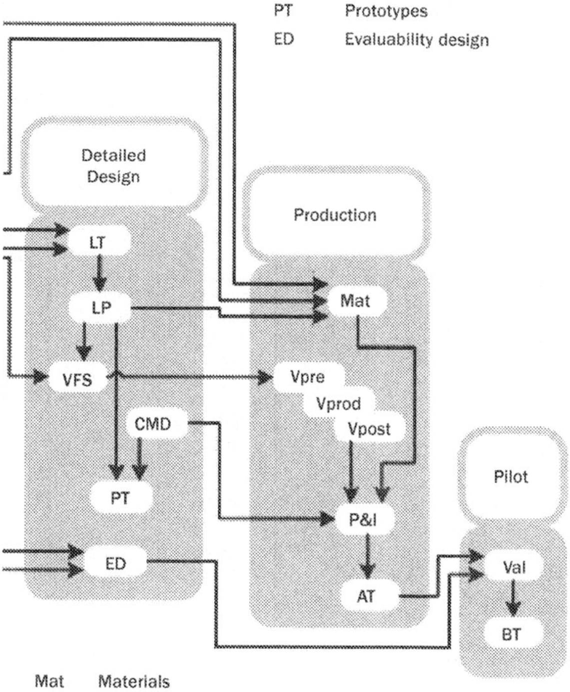

Mat Materials
Vpre AV pre-production
Vprod AV production
Vpost AV post-production
P&I Programs and integration
AT Alpha test

Val Validation
BT Beta test

Prep Preparation
Devt Development
Rev Review
PM Post-mortem

RMP Risk management plan
O&A Options and alternatives
S&B Schedule and budget
CBA Cost-benefit analysis
IA Impact analysis

Figure 3.9 ELSYE project terminology

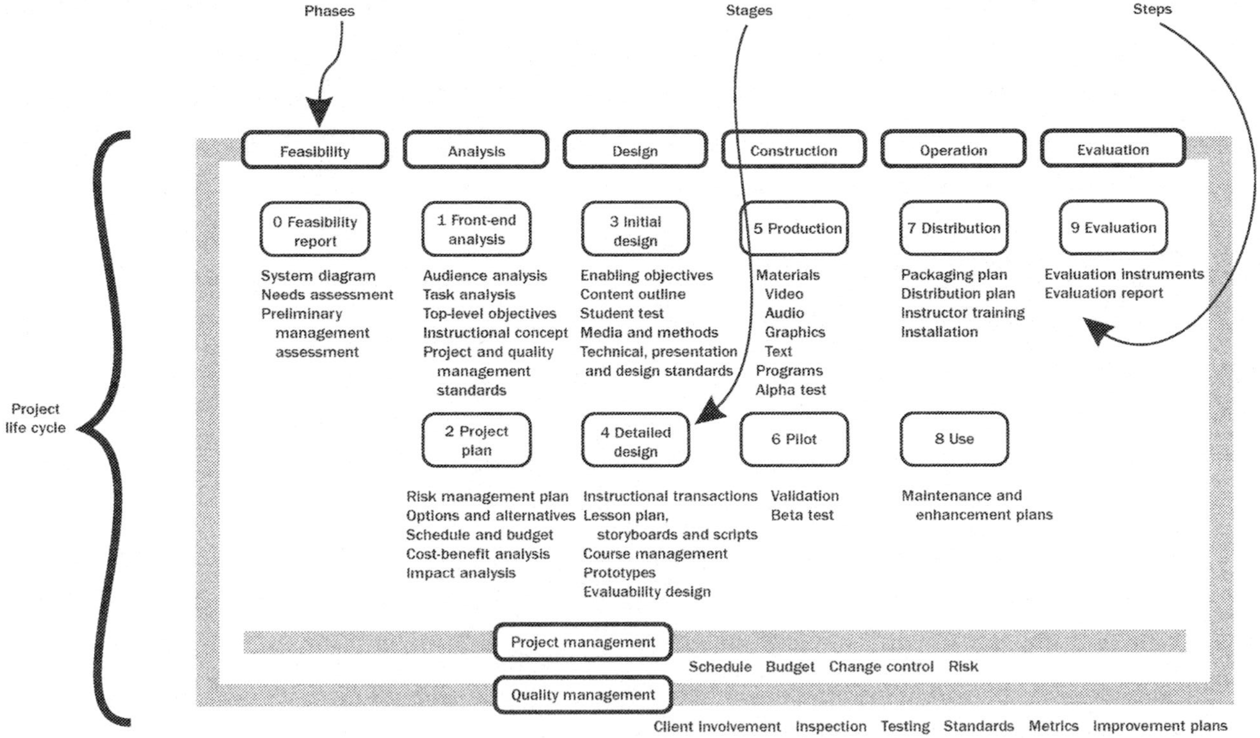

Table 3.1 **ELSYE stages and steps**

Stage	Steps				
FR **Feasibility report**	SD System diagram	NA Needs analysis	PMA Preliminary management assessment		
FEA **Front-end analysis**	AA Audience analysis	PQM Project and quality management standards	TA Task/content analysis	TLO Top-level objectives	ELC/VTC E-learning concept/AV treatment concept
PP **Project plan**	S&B Schedule and budget	CBA Cost-benefit analysis	O&A Options and alternatives	IA Impact analysis	RMP Risk management plan
ID **Initial design**	EO Enabling objectives	CO/VOS Content outline/AV outline script	ST Student test	TPD Technical, presentation and design standards	M&M Media and methods
DD **Detailed design**	LT E-learning transactions	LP/VFS Lesson plans, storyboards and scripts/AV final script	CMD Course management design	PT Prototypes	ED Evaluability design

Table 3.1 ELSYE stages and steps (*Cont'd*)

Stage	Steps				
Production	AV pre-production, production, post-production	Materials (graphics, text)	P&I Programs and integration	AT Alpha test	
Pilot	Val Validation	BT Beta test			
Distribution	Packaging plan	Distribution plan	User training plan	Installation plan	
Use	User support plan	Enhancement plan	Maintenance plan		
Evaluation	Evaluation materials	Evaluation plan	Evaluation results	Evaluation report	

Figure 3.10 ELSYE stage diagrams

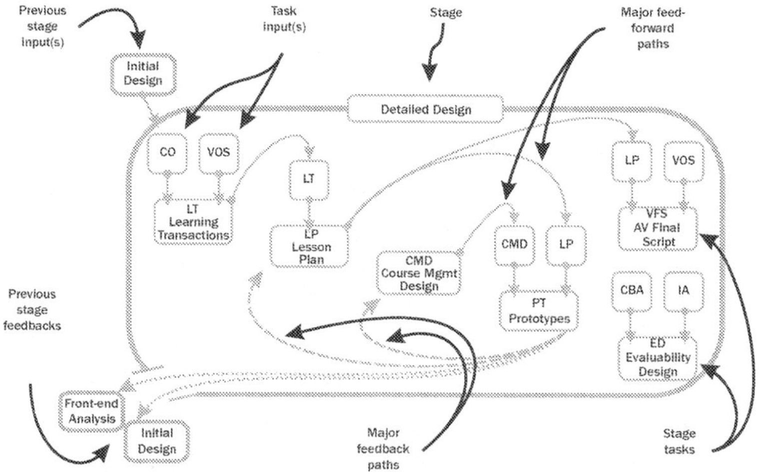

have feed-forward paths – identifying those tasks that follow on – and feedback paths – identifying those earlier tasks that might require review and revisiting following the work of the current task. Only the expected major feed-forward and feedback paths are shown, rather than every possible path. The point of showing these paths is to indicate explicitly that ELSYE project development is an inherently iterative activity rather than a perfectly linear one.

Some tasks are not explicitly linked, indicating that work can probably be undertaken in parallel on these tasks. Most tasks have their input illustrated, coming either from earlier tasks in the current stage or previous tasks in earlier stages.

The ELSYE life cycle as risk management

The ELSYE life cycle is 'nothing but' sound management theory. In general, the ELSYE life-cycle processes should be seen as tools of risk management rather than as prescriptive approaches to e-learning systems development. From this perspective, the question of whether and how to undertake and document front-end analysis, for example, is a question of balancing the risks of inadequate analysis and its documentation versus the possibly excessive costs of such analysis and documentation within a given project, rather than any question of what ought to be done according to some abstract principle of 'quality' or 'best practice' in project development.

There are other models of an e-learning development life cycle that may suit particular circumstances, in the same way as there are other models of software engineering. A useful survey of software engineering models is provided by Avison and Fitzgerald (2006); very little extrapolation is needed to apply any of these alternatives to e-learning systems development.

One particularly interesting alternative is called the 'handcuff' model, and is illustrated in Figure 3.11. In this model there is no attempt to specify separate analysis or design stages, and no requirement for independent documentation or formal quality assurance. The model describes an iteration through the activities of the customer stating what is required, the technician building something to meet the customer's requirements and the two jointly using the results to develop the required product further. What this model captures is that the technical designer is 'handcuffed' to the customer until such time as a satisfactory end product emerges from their collaboration. At first sight the handcuff model may seem laughably trivial, but for smaller e-learning projects it may be particularly effective. The project management skills demanded of all parties by operating such a model are, however, considerable.

Figure 3.11 'Handcuff' model for e-learning development

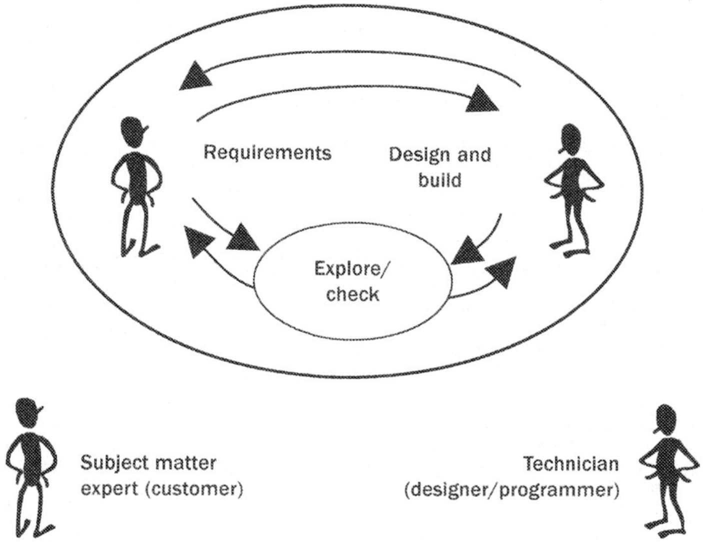

ELSYE stages relevant to various kinds of materials

The engineering of e-learning systems as presented in the text is focused on the design and production of e-learning for education and training. It is also useful for the design and production of other kinds of material where there is some information that needs to be provided for specified purposes, and in these cases there are some aspects of ELSYE design that are not necessary.

For example, the difference between informational materials and e-learning materials might be due to the fact that e-learning materials are characteristically designed to require the student to demonstrate their knowledge and skills, to give feedback to the student on their performance and to test or examine the student on their understanding.

None of these three pedagogical components typically applies to informational materials, and hence no design effort is needed on these components when developing such materials.

For the purposes of the following discussion, materials can be considered as lying along a dimension that could be called 'intentional instruction', which is the degree to which the materials are intended to have pedagogical purposes. Starting with negligible or insignificant overt pedagogical purposes, the dimension begins with 'entertainment', such as a historical novel or a film dramatisation. The next category is 'edutainment', an awkward term sometimes applied to computer games which have some educational component; followed by 'information presentation', where there is a strong intention to convey information which the audience presumably needs to know. Finally, there are 'education' and 'training', both of which have the strongest pedagogical intent of all the materials considered.

Table 3.2 cross-references the various kinds of materials against the ELSYE phases and stages which would be involved in their development. The table shows, considered broadly, that the ELSYE phases of feasibility, analysis, construction and operation are relevant to all forms of materials, and only the design phase may vary. Within the design phase, the stages of initial design and detailed design may vary according to the steps of these stages shown to be relevant. For example, entertainment materials do not characteristically require enabling objectives, and entertainment, 'edutainment' and informational materials do not characteristically require student test items. Readers with a particular interest in business presentations or website design may note that, with the exception of student test items, the whole of ELSYE is usually relevant to their enterprise. Within the details of the steps there may be

Table 3.2 ELSYE stages relevant to various materials' development

	Degree of intentional instruction				
	Entertainment	Edutainment	Information presentation	Education	Training
Examples of materials	Historical novel, film dramatisation	Computer game, simulation	Documentary film, CD-ROM encyclopaedia, website, business presentation	Course on 'European history 1919–1939'	Course on 'Learning to drive'
ELSYE stages Feasibility report, front-end analysis, project plan, production, pilot, distribution, use, evaluation	✓	✓	✓	✓	✓
Initial design Enabling objectives	–	✓	✓	✓	✓
Content outline	– / ✓	✓	✓	✓	✓
Media and methods	✓	✓	✓	✓	✓
Student test	–	–	–	✓	✓
Technical standards	✓	✓	✓	✓	✓
Detailed design E-learning transactions	– / ✓	– / ✓	✓	✓	✓
Lesson plans, storyboards and scripts	✓	✓	✓	✓	✓

Table 3.2 **ELSYE stages relevant to various materials' development (*Cont'd*)**

	Degree of intentional instruction				
	Entertainment	Edutainment	Information presentation	Education	Training
Course management	–	–	– / ✓	– / ✓	– / ✓
Prototypes/ samples	✓	✓	✓	✓	✓
Evaluability design	– / ✓	– / ✓	– / ✓	✓	✓

Key

✓ ELSYE stage usually required for these materials

– ELSYE stage not usually required for these materials

– / ✓ ELSYE stage sometimes required for these materials

further differences according to the kinds of materials under development, and these are discussed in the chapters relevant to each step. For example, the form of the lesson storyboard that is appropriate to website materials is somewhat different from that appropriate to e-learning materials, though in both cases some form of storyboarding is normally required.

4

E-learning systems structure and content

Pask's model of a learning system

An early application of systems theory was to the question of the constitution of a system that learns. The question is interesting because, if the nature of a system that learns can be established, the nature of effective and relevant learning and teaching can be deduced, and hence the enterprise of e-learning systems engineering can clearly target the design and construction of such materials and environments. The general system that was illustrated in Chapter 2, and whose control subsystem was considered there, is shown with minor modifications in Figure 4.1, where it is called a first-order system. In this figure the system of interest, or 'device', is shown separate from, rather than embedded in, its environment, making it easier to show the exchanges of materials and information between the environment and the system.

The simple first-order system of Figure 4.1 can achieve a specified goal, but cannot learn to achieve other goals. Its abilities are fixed and its behaviour is determined. The archetypal example of a first-order system is a central-heating system, whose boiler is controlled by a thermostat, its control subsystem. Such a system is excellent at achieving its

Figure 4.1 A first-order system incapable of learning

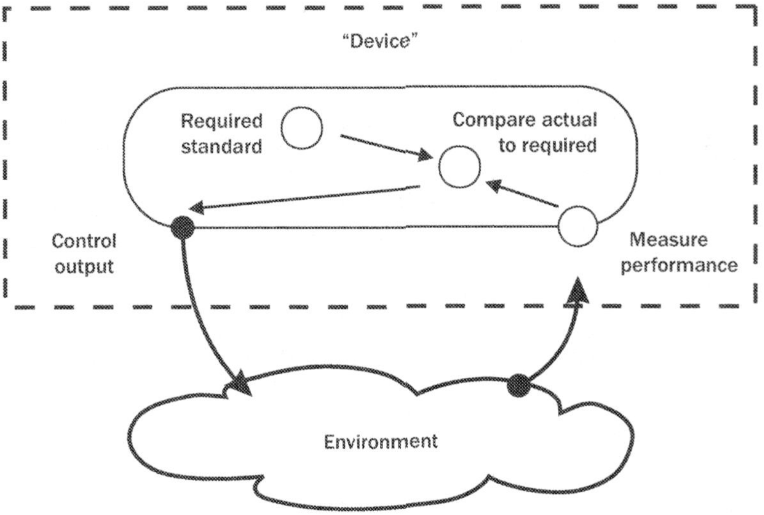

specified goal – keeping the room at a constant temperature – but cannot learn to achieve other goals, such as detecting intruders.

A system which can learn, on the other hand, is a system whose goals, and hence behaviours, change as a result of its experiences of operating in an environment. Pask has described a second-order system that is deemed able to learn and hence behave adaptively (Laurillard, 2001). Such a 'learning system' is illustrated in Figure 4.2. The structure of this system that can learn incorporates a higher, second-order control subsystem that has as its domain of control the first-order, lower control subsystem of the 'learning system' of which both are a part. The higher control subsystem has the task of modifying the lower control subsystem in ways which render the whole 'learning system' adaptive.

In practice, the Pask model of a system which can learn means that such a system must be able to change or adapt the components of its first-level control subsystem – its

Figure 4.2 A second-order system capable of learning

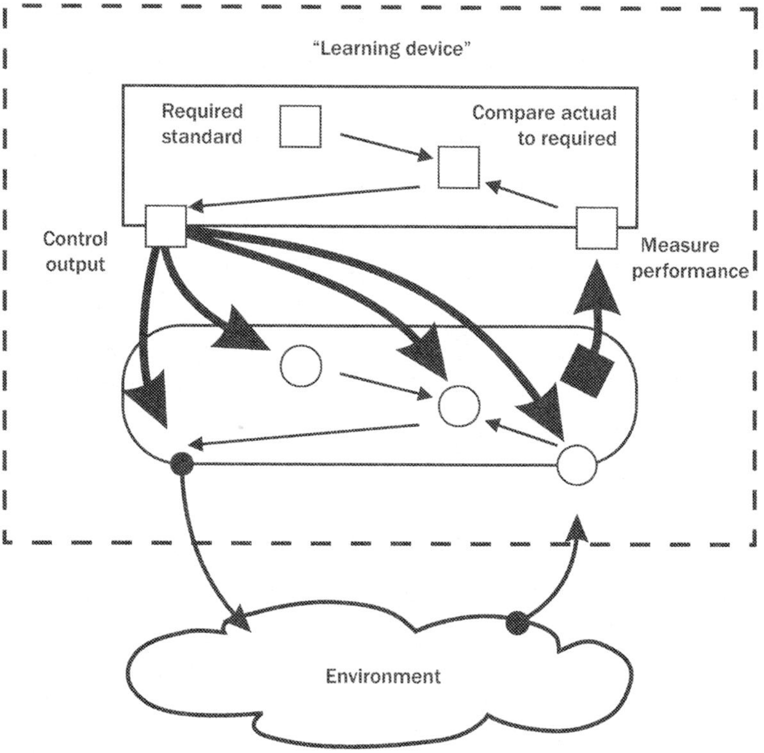

standards of performance, its methods of measuring its performance, its methods of comparing its performance against its standards and its methods of feeding control output into the rest of the system.

Laurillard's model of the learning and teaching environment

Pask's model of a learning system, which he calls a 'conversational' system, has been used by Laurillard (2001) to yield a model of the ideal learning and teaching environment. In analysing the components of this environment, the first step is to couple a model of the learner with a model of the teacher. Since both are learning systems, both are modelled as second-order Pask systems, and the coupled pair are shown in Figure 4.3. In considering the normal activities of the learning and teaching environment, Laurillard holds that the teacher and student interact at two levels. One level is termed 'discursive', where the teacher and student engage in a dialogue – verbal, intellectual – about what is being learned. At another level, the teacher and student engage in physical activities, called 'interactive' activities, where they manipulate objects, arrange experiments, demonstrate skills and so on.

The 'interactive' activities are those that couple the two 'worlds' or physical environments of the teacher and student. Typically, the teacher arranges a physical environment where learning is facilitated. The student explores and operates in this environment, demonstrating learning and understanding at a behavioural level. Student operations at this level tend to start as trial-and-error activities that are then shaped and selectively reinforced by the teacher. The physical environment and the effectiveness

Figure 4.3 The teacher and student modelled as second-order systems

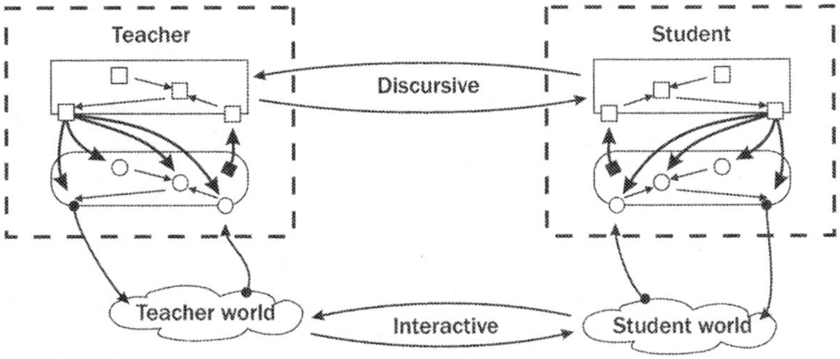

of the teacher's arrangement of this environment mediate the student's learning.

The 'discursive' activities are those that directly couple the second-order, higher control subsystems of teacher and student. Typically, the teacher talks about the learning that is required and the student talks about their understanding. At this level, these discursive activities can lead rather more directly to student learning and understanding, particularly of a cognitive kind. Given this characterisation of the 'discursive' activities, the second-order control systems may be thought of as 'cognitive descriptions', and the object of the teacher is to facilitate the student's learning of effective 'descriptions'.

Within the 'teacher' learning system, the coupling between the teacher and the environment involves the teacher operating upon the environment and receiving feedback as a result of these operations. Similarly, the student operates upon the environment and receives feedback as a result. These operating and feedback components may be labelled 'reflective' and 'adaptive'. The interaction of the two learning systems shown in Figure 4.3 may thus be translated into the description of the learning and teaching situation shown in Figure 4.4.

Four activities are identified in the discursive and interactive components: first, the teacher provides guidance to the learner; second, the learner responds; third, the teacher provides feedback to the learner; and fourth, the learner responds again using the feedback of the teacher. The cycle then repeats as the teacher provides further guidance. The fully elaborated model, Laurillard's 'conversational framework', is shown in Figure 4.5.

The framework represented in Figures 4.4 and 4.5 is used during all of the analysis, design and operation phases of ELSYE. It specifies a set of 12 activities which provide for a

Figure 4.4 **The basic learning and teaching situation**

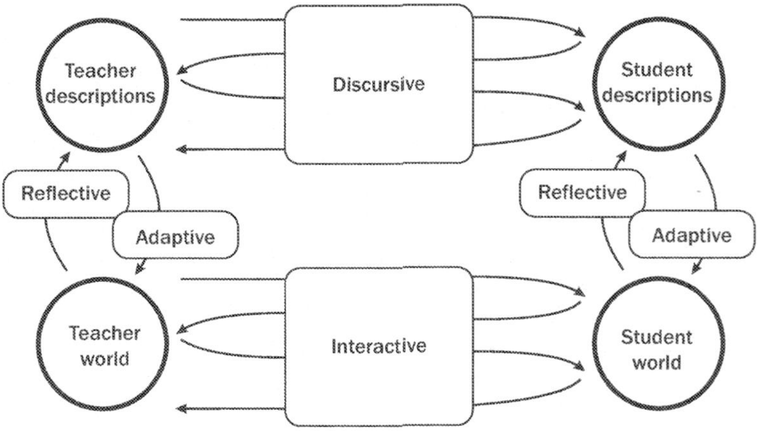

Figure 4.5 Laurillard's 'conversational framework'

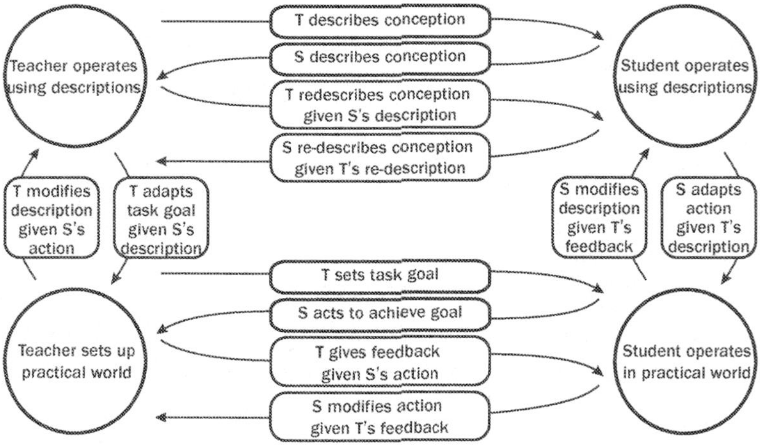

fully effective learning and teaching situation. The extent to which the specified activities are present in any learning and teaching situation is the extent to which that situation may be judged as more or less effective. What is important about Laurillard's conversational framework is the complete description it gives to the learning and teaching situation, based upon a very careful characterisation of what is involved in a learning system, and the consequent importance of feedback activities in effective teaching.

Pedagogic designs which are 'presentations'

The conversational framework may be used to distinguish, loosely at this introductory point, between the various kinds of pedagogic materials considered in Chapter 3. Materials which are designed simply for presentation involve the situation illustrated in Figure 4.6, where only one of the 12 conversational framework components is present: the teacher or instructor describes some conception to the student or audience.

The diagram in Figure 4.6 makes it clear that the pedagogical design for the 'system' which supports informational presentation is simple and unsophisticated, requiring none of the components of e-learning design that are discussed at some length in later chapters (particularly Chapter 9).

Figure 4.6 Simple presentation in the conversational framework

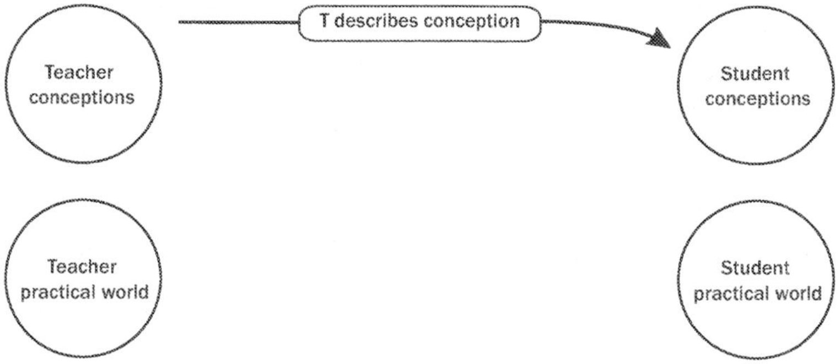

Pedagogic designs which are 'tutorials'

Materials which are used in an educational context, such as a small group tutorial on 'European history 1919–1939', may be characterised as illustrated in Figure 4.7. Here there is more interactivity at the level of verbal descriptions as the teacher and students discuss the ideas and conceptions of the tutorial topic.

The diagram of the tutorial situation, Figure 4.7, shows clearly that, in order to support such a pedagogical design, an e-learning tutorial needs to provide for exchanges and feedback – interactivity – at the verbal level between teacher and student, but not at the 'practical world' level.

Pedagogic designs which are 'training'

As a final illustration, Figure 4.8 shows a training situation where the student is being taught a skill, such as how to drive a car.

The conversational framework diagram of the training situation shows that the pedagogical design intended to support such a situation must involve mechanisms which

Figure 4.7 **Simple tutorial in the conversational framework**

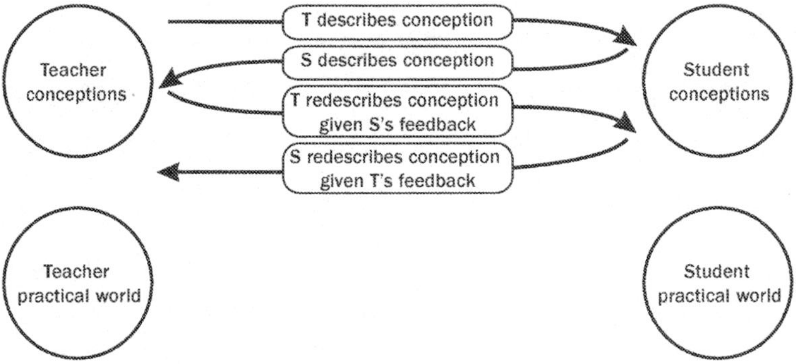

Figure 4.8 **Simple practical training in the conversational framework**

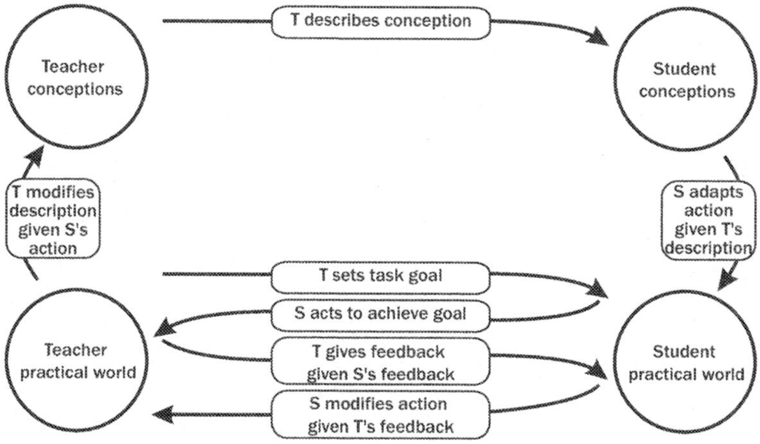

allow the teacher to convey a conception, to set up and modify equipment, and also allow the student to use and then modify their use of the equipment. The interactivity involved here is at a practical level rather than at the verbal level of the educational tutorial.

The structure of learning and teaching

The following discussion takes as given the idea that all learning and teaching has a point or purpose, and that this purpose is best contextualised and expressed by having the teaching explicitly address a problem or series of problems of interest to the student. The purpose of some e-learning is closely tied to its objectives and its content, and is represented in the following figures by a shaded oval.

The general features of the diagrammatic or iconic representation of e-learning are illustrated in Figure 4.9. Besides purpose and content, e-learning systems also involve

Figure 4.9 General features of an 'ELSYE icon'

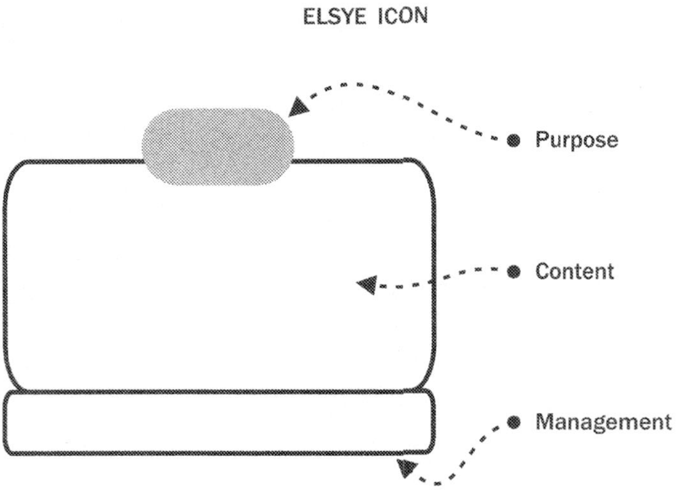

management issues such as registering students and reviewing the e-learning system with a view to improving it.

The content of e-learning may be analysed at a variety of levels. The following discussion identifies four levels, 'e-learning transactions', 'e-learning sessions' (or lessons), 'units' and 'programmes' (as in a programme of study), in ascending order of size and length of study.

The e-learning transaction

The smallest element of e-learning, the unit of analysis for the following discussion of the structure of learning and teaching, might be called the 'e-learning transaction'. This is illustrated in Figure 4.10, where five key exchanges are shown between the teacher and the student. An e-learning transaction is a simplified abstraction of a Laurillardian conversation, and the diagram is a correspondingly simplified abstraction of the full Laurillardian conversational framework.

Figure 4.10 **Structure of an e-learning transaction**

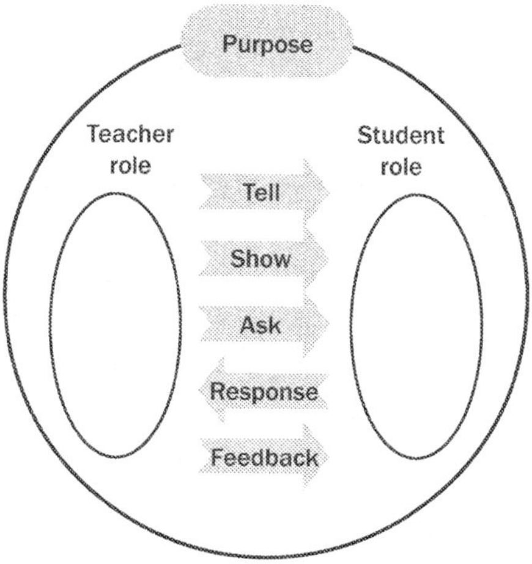

Like almost all of the diagrams in the book, Figure 4.10 is a model. As such, it attempts to capture just those features of a situation which are relevant and useful to a particular view of or approach to that situation. The model should not be confused with the situation it seeks to represent. A learning and teaching situation is far richer than that suggested by Figure 4.10, and it might be useful to discuss what the diagram is seeking to emphasise.

The first element of the diagram is 'purpose', and its inclusion is intended to emphasise the point that the development and use of any learning materials or teaching assets should be aligned with the overall purpose of the transaction. Far too many materials, assets and environments are decorated with components which are at best tangential and at worst completely extraneous to the learning and teaching situation they supposedly support.

The 'purpose' of a Laurillardian conversational framework is not particularly well drawn out in its diagrammatic presentation (in, for example, Figure 4.5), and this is rectified in the diagram of an e-learning transaction by explicitly identifying it.

The second elements of the diagram identify the two *roles* which exist in any learning and teaching situation. The diagram does not seek to assert which of these two roles is superior or more fundamental, and could equally have been drawn as illustrated in Figure 4.11 for those readers who might assume that what is on the left comes before what is on the right. The emphasis on *role* intends to establish the idea that any particular person could undertake either or both roles at different times in such a transaction, as might be imagined in learning which is self-directed or in group or peer learning. The exchanges labelled as 'tell' or 'show', for example, are exchanges which someone in the teacher role

Figure 4.11 **Alternative representation of the learning transaction**

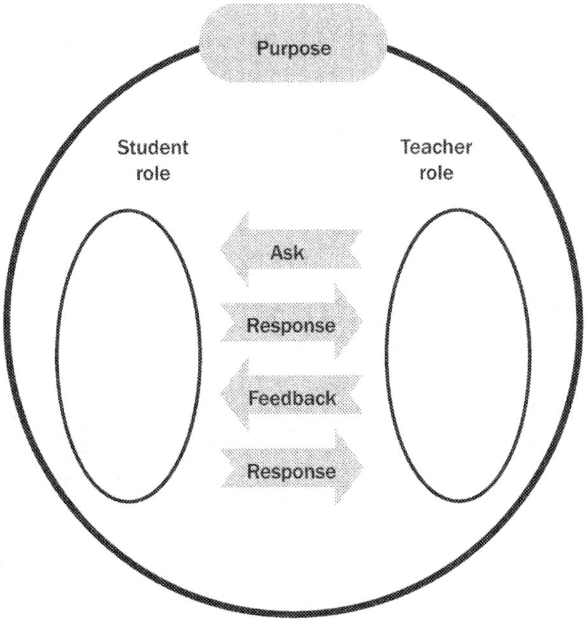

would undertake. This does not mean that they are necessarily undertaken by the person carrying the job title of teacher; they could as well be undertaken by a student peer in a group learning situation.

The five key exchanges in an e-learning transaction are:

- tell;
- show;
- ask student to use and apply;
- student responds;
- give feedback.

These five key exchanges between the two roles could be ordered differently, again as illustrated in the alternative representation of Figure 4.11. That is, listing the exchanges from top to bottom as 'tell', 'show', 'ask', 'response' and 'feedback' (Figure 4.10) is intended simply to emphasise the key point that all these exchanges ideally take place at some point in any learning and teaching situation, but this does not necessarily imply they must take place in this order, nor must all five take place in any particular transaction. The alternative representation of Figure 4.11 shows a Socratic dialogue, where learning and teaching proceeds first by the asking of a question and then by the discussion of the response, involving further questions, responses and commentaries. To continue to emphasise the significance of the *roles* involved, if Figure 4.11 is taken to model a Socratic dialogue, it is clear that the labels 'student role' and 'teacher role' could be exchanged without affecting the validity of the diagram.

It is also useful to note that the 'response' and 'feedback' exchanges are generalised characterisations, and would themselves involve exchanges of one or more components which could be labelled 'tell', 'show' and 'ask'.

Finally, a learning transaction is intended to be atomic, in the sense of a set of exchanges which is the smallest possible unit of learning that can stand by itself. A learning transaction thus defines a level of granularity in the analysis and design of learning and teaching situations, and suggests that the key defining characteristic of an atomic unit of learning is the 'ask' exchange: each 'ask' exchange is likely to include a minimum number of the other exchanges such that the resulting transaction could be said to be self-contained.

These key exchanges are elaborated in the 'design' chapters of this book (Chapters 8–11, and particularly Chapter 9), where detailed attention is given to the design of appropriate 'telling', 'showing', 'asking' and 'giving feedback' exchanges.

A learning and teaching session

In the course of teaching a particular topic, a number of e-learning transactions are assembled into what might be called a 'session'. Other names include 'lesson'. This is illustrated in Figure 4.12.

A session or lesson has a purpose, implied by locating the various transactions of the session within an environment labelled 'problem A.x.y'. The session is to be understood as being focused upon addressing problem 'A.x.y'. As mentioned earlier, the various e-learning transactions of the session refer to various small aspects, 'z', of the particular problem of interest to the session, 'A.x.y', itself part of a larger problem, 'A.x'.

The set of e-learning transactions, the content of a session, may be sequenced in a variety of ways, as illustrated in Figure 4.12. Certain transactions may be selectively undertaken in addition to the main sequence, and other transactions might be undertaken repeatedly. These different routes might be designed according to the outcome of an

Figure 4.12 Structure of a learning and teaching session or lesson

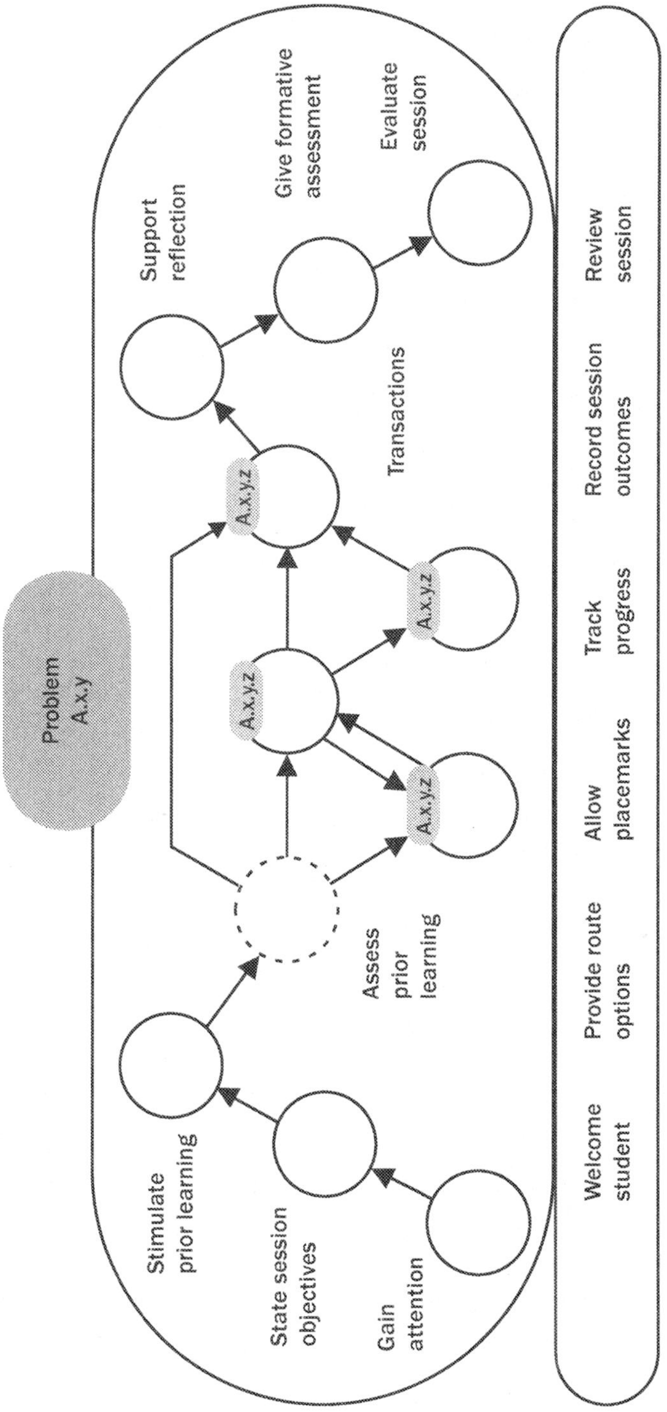

assessment of the student's prior learning. More usually, different transactions might be undertaken following the student responses to previous transactions. In this case, the session or lesson adapts to the student.

Underlying the content of a session or lesson are management and quality concerns, such as tracking student progress and reviewing the session.

The key e-learning transactions are elaborated in the 'design' chapters of this book (Chapters 8–11, and particularly Chapter 9), where detailed attention is given to the structuring of a session. Issues surrounding lesson objectives and assessment are considered in Chapters 6 and 8, while evaluation issues are considered in Chapters 11 and 13.

A learning and teaching unit

Teaching a substantial course usually involves a number of sessions. Such a collection of sessions might be called a 'unit'. Other suitable labels might be 'course' or 'module'. This is illustrated in Figure 4.13.

Again, a unit has a purpose, implied in the diagram by locating the various unit sessions within an environment labelled 'challenge A.x'. The sessions deal with various problems, 'y', of the particular challenge of interest to the unit, 'A.x'. This 'challenge' is itself part of a larger problem, 'A'.

The sessions may be sequenced in a variety of ways, as illustrated in the diagram. Certain sessions may be selectively undertaken in addition to the main sequence, and others might be undertaken repeatedly. Typically, the routing seen in a unit is not as flexible as that provided in a session, and the diagram illustrates this.

Management issues in a unit are as indicated, typically concerned with tracking student progress and recording marks from coursework and assignments.

Figure 4.13 **Structure of a unit, course or module**

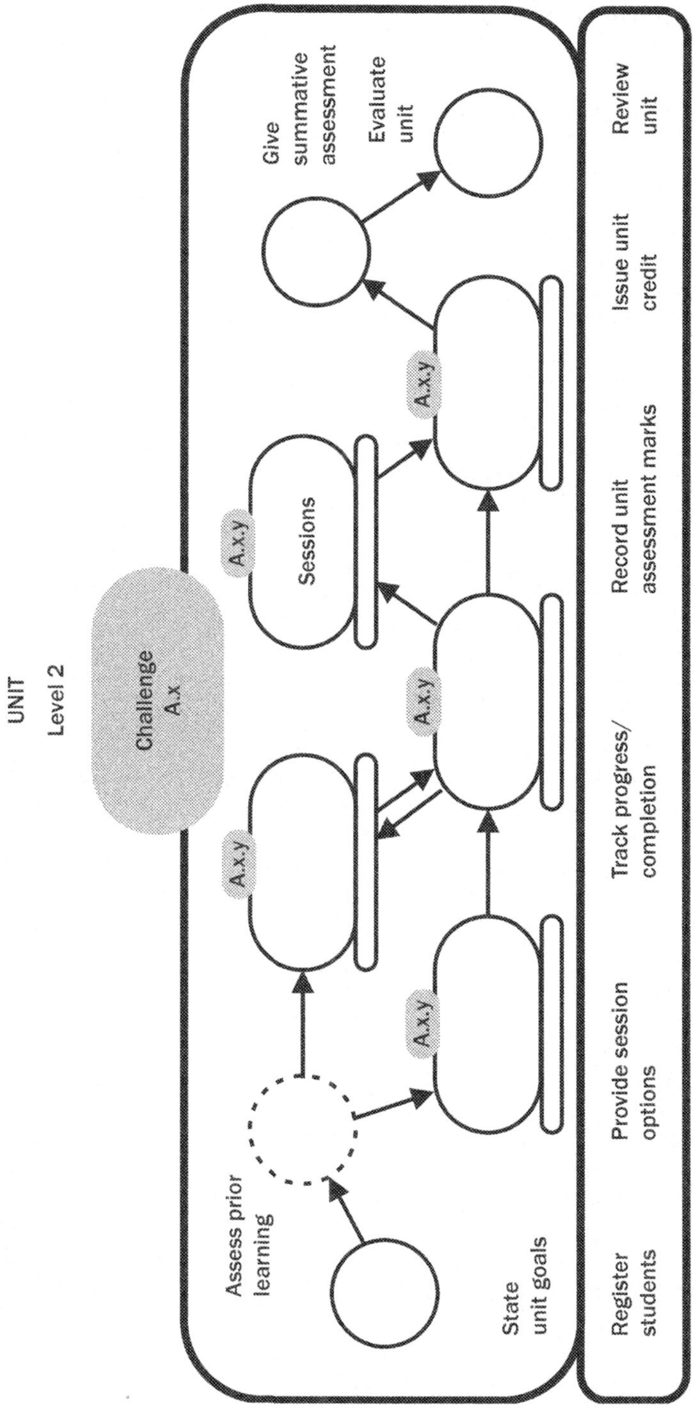

Figure 4.14 **Structure of a programme of study**

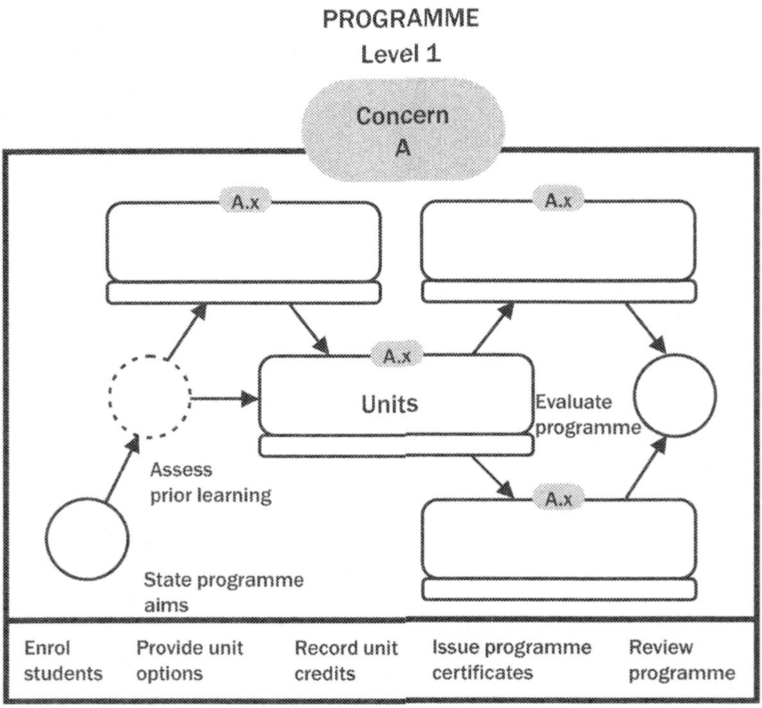

A programme of study

Finally, the largest block of learning and teaching explicitly considered here is what might be called a programme of study, a collection of units which address a broad concern or set of concerns, 'concern A'. Each unit in the programme considers a particular challenge, 'challenge x', of this greater concern. A programme is illustrated in Figure 14.4. In other contexts, a programme of study might also be called a 'course' or a 'curriculum'.

Figure 4.15 **Four-level structure of learning and teaching**

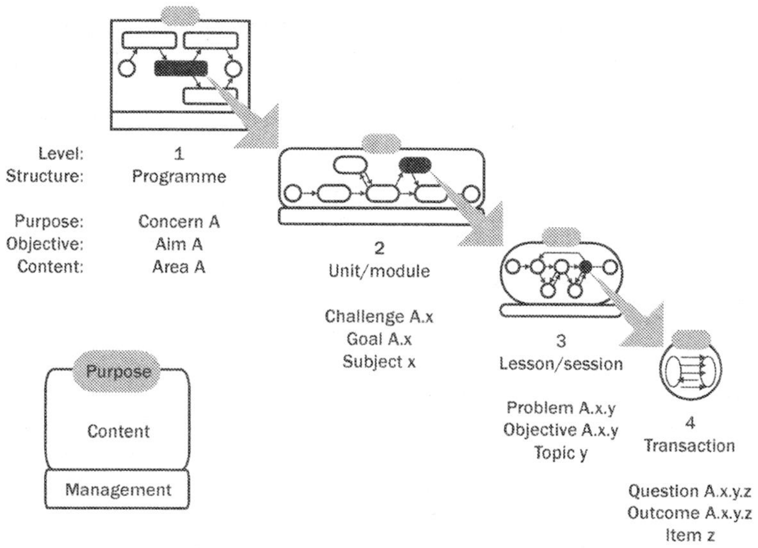

Decomposition of learning and teaching

The four levels of assembly represent successive decomposition of learning and teaching into ever-finer detail. This is illustrated in Figure 4.15.

In the design of learning and teaching, it is clear that the higher levels 1, 2 and 3 – the programmes, units and sessions – have broadly similar characteristics, in that they involve e-learning transactions and management concerns. Learning at level 4, the level of the e-learning transaction itself, however, has somewhat different characteristics, involving the fundamental exchanges or conversations between student and teacher.

Finally, programmes of study are typically embedded within educational or training systems, as illustrated in Figure 4.16, which shows the typical academic structure of a higher educational institution in the UK.

Figure 4.16 **Programme within a higher education institution**

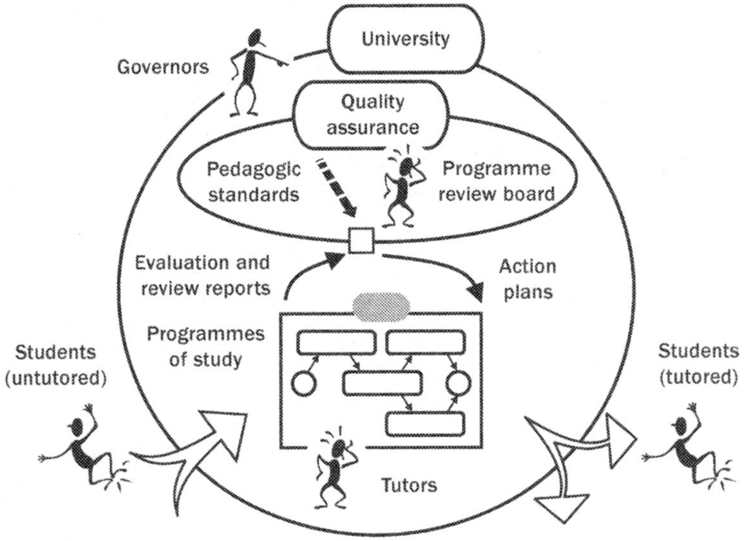

The e-learning transactions relevant to various kinds of materials

The e-learning transactions identified earlier are embodied in materials intended for education and training. They are also relevant to other kinds of material where information needs to be provided for specified purposes, but in these cases there are some e-learning transactions that are not necessary.

The differences between the e-learning transactions that might be thought necessary for e-learning materials and those needed for other kinds of materials may be illustrated by reference to Gagné's events of instruction (Gagné et al., 2004). The full list of Gagné's events of instruction comprises nine steps. According to Gagné et al., these nine events are necessary for a proper lesson on some topic of interest. The illustration earlier of a session or lesson identified two more events that might be usefully added to the list: assessing prior learning in order to route the student or help them decide on their own route through the session, and evaluating the session.

Table 4.1 cross-references these 11 e-learning transactions against the various kinds of e-learning materials, indicating

Table 4.1 The e-learning transactions relevant for various materials

	Degree of instructional intent				
	Entertainment	**Edutainment**	**Information presentation**	**Education**	**Training**
Examples of materials	Historical novel, film dramatisation	Computer game, simulation	Documentary film, CD-ROM encyclopaedia, website, business presentation	Course on 'European history 1919–1939'	Course on 'Learning to drive'
Supporting transaction					
Gaining attention	✓	✓	✓	✓	✓
Informing learner of objectives/goals/aims	–	– / ✓	✓	✓	✓
Stimulating recall of prior learning	–	–	– / ✓	✓	✓
Assessing prior learning	–	–	–	– / ✓	✓
Testing or examining performance (formative or summative assessment)	–	–	–	✓	✓

Table 4.1 The e-learning transactions relevant for various materials (*Cont'd*)

	Degree of instructional intent				
	Entertainment	Edutainment	Information presentation	Education	Training
Enhancing retention and learning transfer (supporting reflection)	–	–	– / ✓	✓	✓
Evaluating instruction	– / ✓	– / ✓	– / ✓	– / ✓	– / ✓
E-learning transaction for					
Presenting information (telling)	✓	✓	✓	✓	✓
Guiding learning (showing)	–	– / ✓	– / ✓	✓	✓
Eliciting performance (asking to use or apply)	–	✓	–	– / ✓	✓
Providing informative feedback	–	✓	–	– / ✓	✓

Key

✓ Transaction usually required for this form

– Transaction not usually required for this form

– / ✓ Sometimes required

which materials involve which transactions. The events of instruction are considered here to indicate those e-learning transactions that are applicable to the various kinds of materials that can be developed. The events of instruction themselves are discussed in greater detail in Chapters 9–11, particularly Chapter 10.

For example, some of the difference between informational materials and e-learning materials may be found, according to the table, by noting that e-learning materials characteristically involve transactions which require the student to demonstrate their knowledge and skills, which give feedback to the student on their performance and which test or examine the student on their understanding. None of these three e-learning transactions characteristically applies to informational materials, and hence no effort is needed to provide such transactions in these materials.

As before, materials can be considered as lying along a dimension that could be called 'intentional instruction': the degree to which the materials are intended to have instructional purposes.

5

Feasibility

Feasibility is the first phase in the ELSYE development life cycle, with the feasibility report as its single stage. It precedes the 'analyse-design-do-evaluate' technical phases with the question 'Is this the right thing to do?' The purpose of a feasibility study is to answer that question; if answered affirmatively, then the technical work can begin. In this sense, feasibility is a combination of technical and managerial tasks; in both areas, sufficient detail needs to be covered so that the question can be adequately addressed.

It may be worth noting that the 'feasibility' of a project is, in this sense, not so much a question of whether it can be done – it almost always can – but whether it is the right thing to do and whether it is viable, usually in a commercial sense. Using appropriate measures, the question is 'Does the project make sense?' or 'Is there a sound business case for the project?' At the point where the project enters the feasibility phase, it is likely that there exists a problem situation to which an e-learning system is presumed to be an appropriate solution. It is the purpose of the feasibility report stage to clarify the problem situation and test the presumption that e-learning is what is really required.

The feasibility report is the first of the ten stages of the ELSYE life cycle; an overview of the ELSYE life-cycle stages is provided in Figure 5.1.

Figure 5.1 Feasibility stage in the ELSYE life cycle

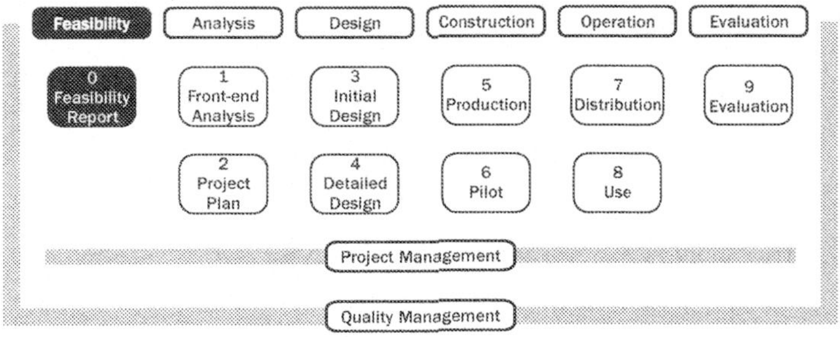

The feasibility report stage comprises three steps, enclosed in the relevant components of quality management, and with the relevant components of project management running in parallel with the technical tasks. The result of this stage is a feasibility report that is submitted for senior management's approval. The three technical steps of the feasibility report are shown in Figure 5.2, and they result in

Figure 5.2 Feasibility report technical steps

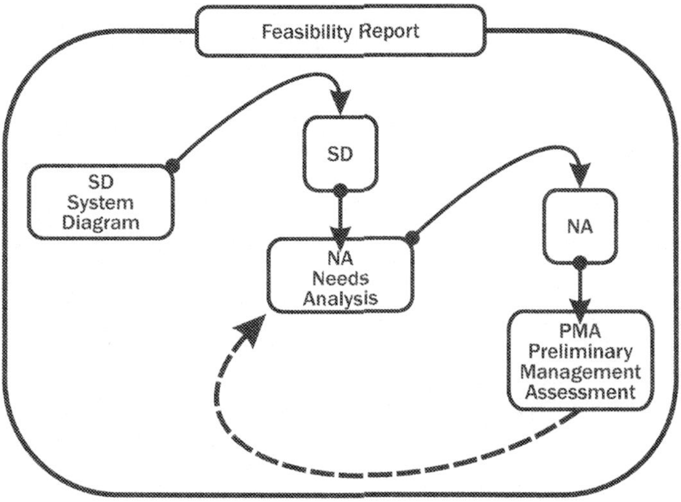

the deliverable products of the stage: a system diagram, a needs analysis and a preliminary management assessment.

The system diagram is concerned with describing and clarifying the problem situation, and the needs analysis is concerned with testing the presumed needs embedded within that situation, informed by issues of organisational power and politics. The system diagram is discussed in the first part of this chapter, while the needs analysis is considered in the second part. When the presumed solution to the problem situation is training, the needs analysis is more commonly called a 'training needs analysis', or TNA.

The needs analysis then feeds into the preliminary management assessment step, which is a 'mini' version of the project plan stage undertaken in the ELSYE analysis phase (Chapter 7). The third part of the chapter identifies the major components of a preliminary management assessment. As a result of this assessment, the needs analysis may need revision. Thereafter, the feasibility report is submitted for review and consideration before commitment to the next stage of front-end analysis (Chapter 6).

The feasibility report stage may seem to be optional within the ELSYE life cycle; after all, if you have been asked to provide e-learning, it is surely 'obvious' that the problem has an e-learning solution, and the job is simply to get on and do it. This should not be true for two main reasons. First, we should not assume that a particular problem requires an e-learning solution before looking at the problem in more detail. Secondly, the discipline of undertaking the feasibility report stage reveals much more about the project, particularly its politics, than is usually apparent without undertaking this analysis. The resulting feasibility report informs senior management, yielding a fully considered and properly authorised e-learning project.

System diagram

Most projects fail because of managerial rather than technical problems; and most managerial problems are problems of organisational power and politics. This section is concerned with some practical methods to characterise a problem situation properly by combining the earlier consideration of a 'system' with a modified soft systems methodology (SSM) approach. Identifying and discussing some practical techniques of organisational politics are taken up in Chapter 15 on project management.

Characterising the problem situation

The starting point of the feasibility report stage is to describe properly the problem situation for which some e-learning materials are the presumed solution. The approach taken here is to consider the problem situation as one that is embedded within a system and its environment, and to sketch the situation and the system in which it occurs by using a system diagram, based upon a 'rich picture' (Checkland, 1999; Checkland and Scholes, 1999). The relevant features of a system diagram are illustrated in Figure 5.3, and these are used to provide a checklist for a proper description of a problem situation.

The necessary features of a system diagram are derived from the earlier discussion of the component parts of any 'system' (Chapter 2), and from the work of Checkland and others on SSM (Checkland and Scholes, 1999). Specifically, characterising any problem situation involves identifying and describing the following system components.

- *The system and its boundary.* It may be stating the obvious, but it is important to distinguish carefully the system that is having the problem from its operating

Figure 5.3 **System diagram components of a problem situation**

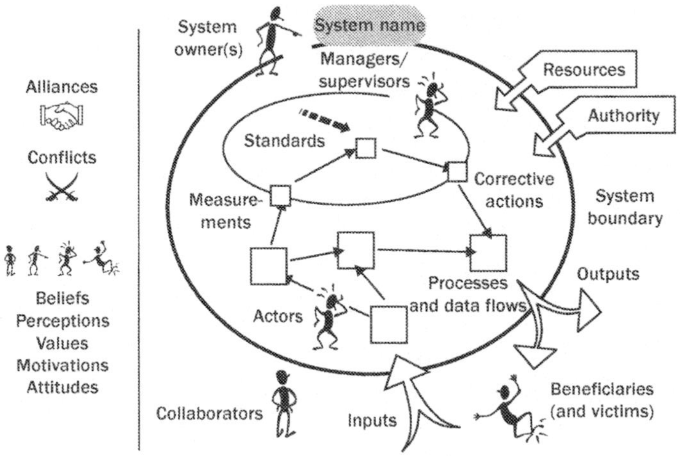

environment, draw a boundary between the two and thoughtfully name the system under study.

- *System owner(s)*. This is the person or persons who own the system under study. Ownership implies that the owner has authority for the system's activities and outputs and has the power, for example, to shut down and dismantle the system. The point of identifying the owner, who could well be different from the system's manager, is to establish the person who 'really' owns both the problem situation and its proposed solution; that is, who has the necessary power and authority to order the implementation of the solution.
- *Resources and authority*. In order to operate, a system requires some form of resources and authorisation. The resources are almost always the financial resources which the owner possesses or manages, and have nothing to do with the inputs to the system which define its essential purpose. The authority is usually delegated in some way to the owner or managers, and is ultimately derived from

the law or government of the environment in which the system operates.

- *Inputs and outputs*. The system under study takes inputs and produces outputs that define its unique character and essential purpose. The inputs into the system come from its operating environment, and are different from the two special 'inputs' of its resources and its authority.
- *Customers*. These are the people who benefit from the outputs of the system. For defective systems, people who receive negative benefits are victims.
- *Processes and transformations*. These are the key activities of the system. These key processes or transformations are those activities that take the system's inputs and produce the system's outputs.
- *Actors*. These are the people involved in the activities of the system; they are also stakeholders in the system not otherwise identified or described.
- *Standards*. This is the first of the four components of the control subsystem. The standards represent the desired or required system outputs, and may not always be readily or easily identifiable. The attempt to describe the standards during 'feasibility' often brings the realisation that they are not explicit and may even be unavailable.
- *Measurements*. This is the second of the control subsystem components. Processes or procedures should be present which monitor and measure the activities of the system. Again, the attempt to describe these processes may reveal their absence or incomplete implementation.
- *Manager/supervisor*. The third component of the control subsystem is usually human, but some aspects may be computerised. The system should have a manager or managers, different from the system owner, whose function is to compare the standards against the actual measurements.

- *Corrective actions.* This is the final component of the control subsystem. Processes or procedures should be present which allow the manager to implement required changes to the system's activities.
- *Values and beliefs.* The final component of a systems diagram, the part that makes it 'soft', comprises the beliefs, values, perceptions, attitudes and motivations of the persons involved in the system: owners, managers, actors, customers and any other stakeholders. These values and beliefs usually contribute more to the problem situation than any technical faults in system products or procedures. A clash of values or beliefs involves a conflict, and these are noted on the diagram. Equally, actors and agents may operate as an alliance, and this is also noted on the system diagram. When considering the problem situation, it is also useful to add a particular category of stakeholder, the supporter or prospective supporter of one or other of the proposed solutions to the problem.

Two examples of a simple system diagram are shown, one in Figure 5.4 for e-learning in HE and FE in the UK, and one in Figure 5.5 for a problem situation where training is being demanded for customer services staff.

In the example of Figure 5.5, constructing the system diagram has revealed a number of features of the problem situation that require further investigation. Most importantly, given the presumption that the customer services staff need some training, the diagram shows that all may not be well with the product itself, and that customer dissatisfaction may be due to product deficiencies rather than service deficiencies. The diagram also indicates that there appear to be no standards applicable to customer service, and that there is no clear owner of the customer services system. All of these features are significant for the design and implementation of any relevant training materials.

Figure 5.4 Illustrative system diagram for UK HE and FE

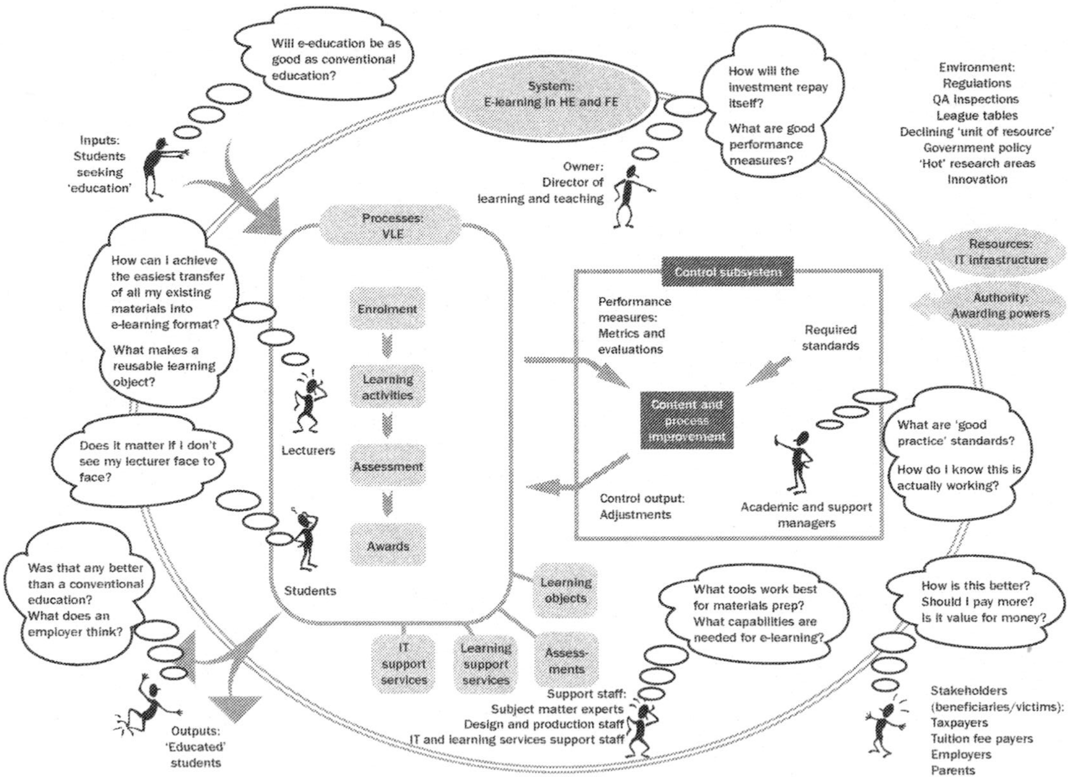

Figure 5.5 Example system diagram

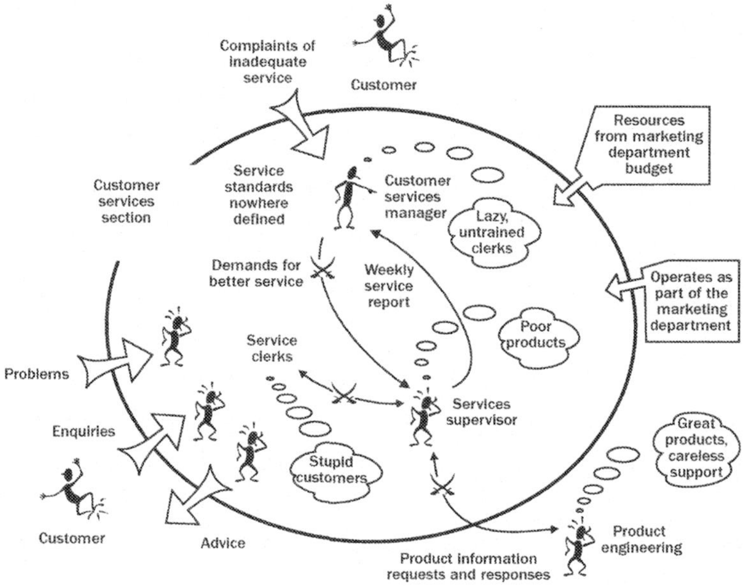

It is particularly important for the system diagram to show as many of the symptoms of the problem situation as possible, and to leave any analysis of causes or solutions to the needs analysis step.

A well-executed system diagram shows the conflicts and alliances between those involved, and hence where the exercise of power and political influence might be expected. It should also show where the project is located within its context, and hence the likely support or resistance it might expect. The issues surrounding the exercise of power and political influence are explored in Chapter 15 on project management.

Needs analysis

The needs analysis establishes the need for e-learning – for the presentation of information, for education or for training – by comparing what the target audience currently knows or does with what the target audience should know or be able to do, and then considering the reasons for the gap between what exists and what is desired. Having established a need for e-learning, the preliminary management assessment assesses whether the cost of e-learning provision is adequately paid back by the improvement in knowledge or skill. Given a management decision to go ahead with e-learning provision as a result of the feasibility report stage, the front-end analysis stage (Chapter 6) takes the needs analysis as input and develops a full analysis of the e-learning requirements for subsequent design and production.

An engineering problem-solving approach involves identification of the causes underlying the observed problems, specification of requirements for reducing or eliminating the causes and the design and implementation of a solution to the problems. This approach is illustrated in Figure 5.6. Identification of the problems and their causes and the specification of requirements to address the causes are undertaken in the ELSYE life-cycle phases of feasibility and analysis.

The system diagram describes the symptoms of a problem situation. The medical model for problem-solving, of symptom-diagnosis-treatment, may be more useful here than the engineering model, and is illustrated in Figure 5.7. Both the engineering approach and the medical approach are structurally similar, as the two figures show, but the medical model's terminology is more precise and more helpful in distinguishing the components of the problem situation. The ELSYE life-cycle phases of feasibility and analysis comprise, in the medical model, the identification and diagnosis of symptoms.

A needs analysis is concerned with the presumed performance gap between the existing and the desired performance of a learner or student. The idea of a performance gap is one way of looking at what might be needed in

Figure 5.6 Engineering problem-solving approach

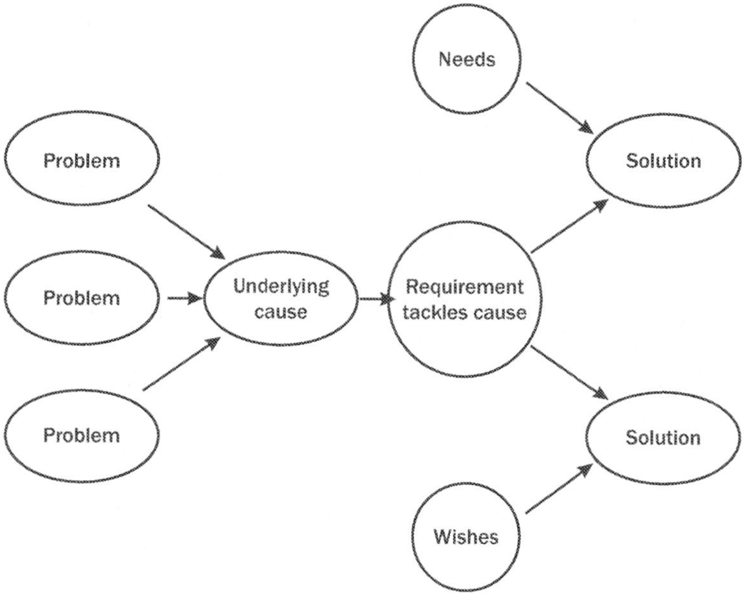

Figure 5.7 Medical problem-solving approach

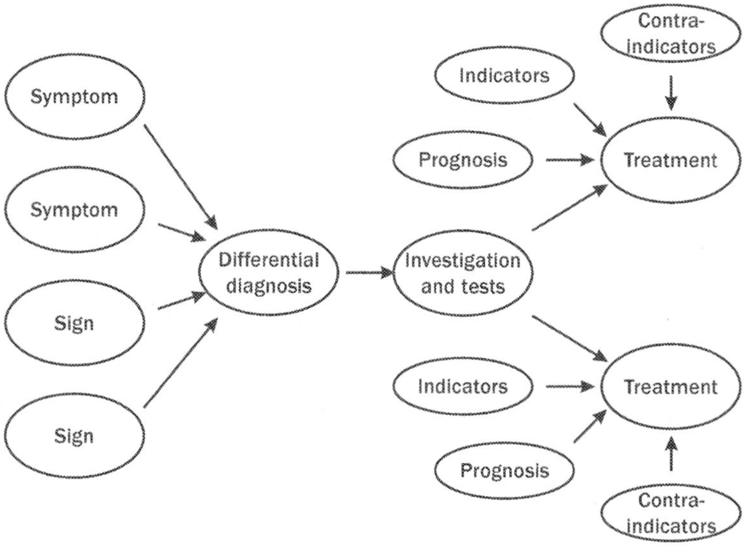

a learning and teaching situation. A demonstrated performance gap is a symptom that has a number of possible causes. The diagnosis of the cause of a symptom leads directly to an indication of possible treatments – solutions – and effectively sets the project on its course. Diagnosis is thus crucial to a successful ELSYE project, and is often a politically charged activity. During diagnosis, causes and effects are unclear and may well be contested by actors with differing points of view. As discussed in Chapter 15 on project management, a lack of agreement on causes and effects provides grounds for the exercise of organisational power and politics.

Table 5.1 lists some common causes of a performance gap, along with some possible solutions. It should be noted that a performance gap often has a number of causes, not just one, and a number of solutions may need to

Table 5.1 **Causes of and solutions to performance gaps**

Cause	Solution
Inadequate information provided	Provide better information
Unclear expectations set	Clarify the expectations
Deficient management or supervision	Improve management or supervision
Inadequate resources (equipment, facilities, time, etc.)	Provide better resources
Desired performance punished	Reduce or eliminate punishment
Desired performance inadequately rewarded	Improve incentives
Poor motivation	Address motivational issues
Lack of knowledge	Provide education or training Provide performance aids (checklists, flowcharts, etc.)
Inadequate skills	Provide practice, coaching or training
Required performance difficult	Reduce the job Restructure the job

be developed to address the gap in question. Also, of the ten or so causes identified in the table, only two – a lack of knowledge and inadequate skills – directly suggest an e-learning solution. This is illustrated in Figure 5.8.

The needs analysis is a relatively brief document that describes the current performance, specifies the desired performance and thus identifies the performance gap, then identifies causes for this gap and suggests possible solutions to address it (Figure 5.9). These components are summarised in Table 5.2.

Figure 5.8 Appropriateness of ELSYE to causes of performance gaps

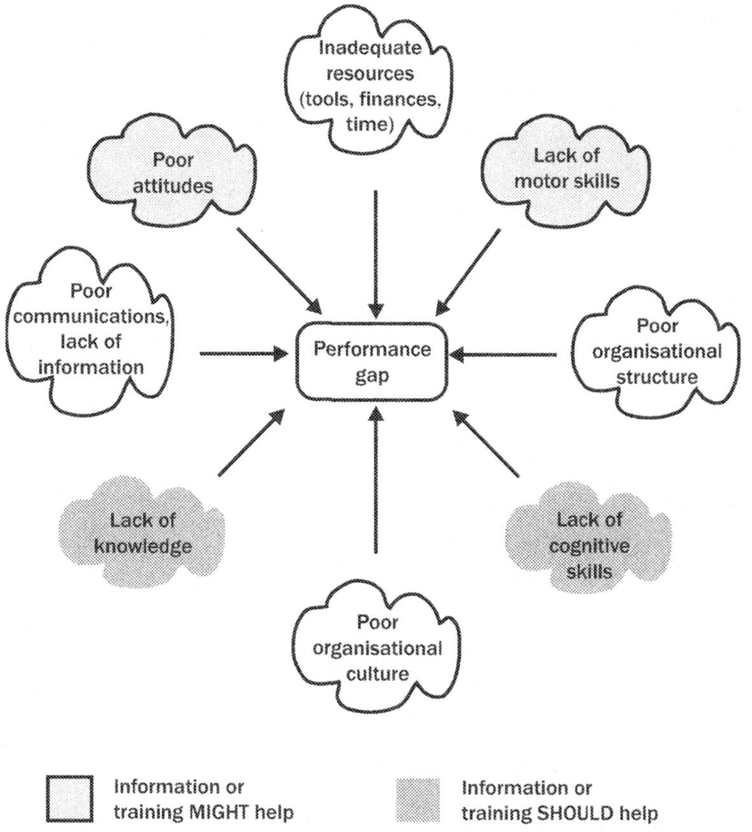

Figure 5.9 Needs analysis in the form of control subsystem

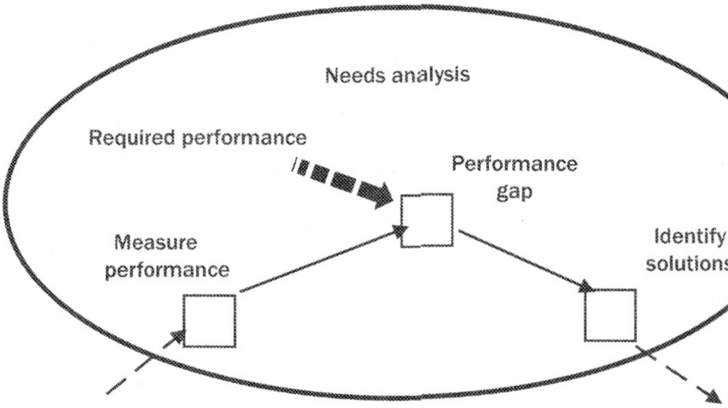

Table 5.2 Needs analysis

Describe current performance, ability, knowledge
Specify desired performance, ability, knowledge
Identify causes for gap between existing and desired performance, ability, knowledge
List possible solutions for each cause

Preliminary management assessment

The needs analysis lists a number of solutions to a problem situation, and it is likely that at least one solution is e-learning. The purpose of the preliminary management assessment is to assess the costs and benefits of each solution so that senior management can decide on whether formally to establish an e-learning project and authorise the next stage, a full front-end analysis.

The preliminary management assessment is a 'mini' version of the project plan stage (Chapter 7). For large or high-risk projects, there need be nothing 'mini' about it: it could be a full-blown project plan in its own right, undertaken on all the possible solutions to the problem situation, and not just on the e-learning solution which is the normal subject of the project plan stage following the front-end analysis.

The key component of the preliminary management assessment is a cost-benefit analysis (CBA) for each of the possible solutions, including the 'do nothing' solution. As necessary, other components from the full project plan could be included in the preliminary management assessment if desired.

A CBA begins by considering the cost of a proposed solution. Against this cost are set the benefits, and some formula is used to create a numerical expression, a figure of merit, of the cost-benefit value of the proposal.

Types of cost

Costs may be divided into tangible and intangible costs. Tangible costs are reckoned in money. Intangible costs can be reckoned in time, quality, expertise and social, political or personal rights, and indeed in anything considered valuable. Like intangible benefits, intangible costs can and need to be converted into tangible values for the purposes of a CBA.

Costs can be analysed into three areas: acquisition costs, ownership costs and opportunity costs. Acquisition costs for e-learning projects arise from feasibility, design, production and piloting costs, and launch, distribution, installation and initial training costs. Ownership costs arise from operating, evaluating, maintenance, support and enhancement costs. These costs are usually straightforward to identify and quantify. For example, a training programme on the handling of customer complaints might cost £20,000 to acquire and £5,000 per year to operate.

Opportunity cost, the cost of a lost opportunity, is often overlooked in ELSYE projects. It represents the cost of forgoing the most valuable alternative to the project under consideration. Obtaining a measure of the opportunity cost of a proposal is generally problematic, if only from the fact that numerous alternatives need to be considered and valued. The problem is significantly ameliorated by the approach suggested here: that a selection of alternatives are in fact formally considered as part of the preliminary management assessment and a CBA developed for each.

Types of benefit

Like costs, benefits can be divided into tangible and intangible. Operator training that reduces the cost of production by £20,000 is an example of a tangible benefit; improving customer confidence in the quality of the product is an example of an intangible benefit. From the point of view of management, however, every benefit must finally be expressed in monetary form one way or another, or else a rational decision is much more difficult to make.

The benefits of e-learning can be categorised into one or more of these general areas:

- *cost savings* due to reducing staff or other required resources;
- *productivity improvements* due to enabling higher levels of production or service without a commensurate increase in resources;
- *quality of information*, involving better decision-making, more accurate and more timely information, the reduction of unnecessary communications and the improvement of required communications;
- *organisational enhancement*, involving the ability to undertake new business ventures, penetrate new markets and develop new products.

It may be worth noting that benefits are outcomes of the proposed project, and that negatively valued outcomes are listed as negative benefits rather than costs. For example, it may be that, as a result of a training programme, a member of staff would be made redundant. The costs of redundancy would be shown as a negative benefit rather than as a cost of the programme.

Valuing 'intangible' benefits

Even if labelled 'intangible', such benefits must be valued in monetary terms, otherwise a number of risks will be run: financially driven management may only focus on the (tangible) valued benefits, and fail to approve the e-learning systems necessary to improve business competitiveness or viability in more general terms; users may deliberately and misleadingly inflate tangible benefits in order to 'sell' the proposed e-learning, while really wanting the intangible benefits; and e-learning may be approved on the basis of well-phrased intangibles and good intentions, without a realistic attempt at quantifying the actual 'cash value' of these intentions.

For example, the intangible benefit of being able to, say, handle customer complaints with greater sensitivity as a result of training could be valued by estimating that the current customer loss rate of 10 per cent per year could be reduced to 9 per cent. Other things being equal, if sales to the average customer average £20,000 per year and there are currently 500 customers, then five customers would be retained who would otherwise have left, adding £100,000 to annual turnover. Given a 30 per cent gross margin on sales, this values the benefit of training in complaints handling at £30,000 per year.

Options and scenarios

It is difficult to evaluate a single proposal without alternatives to consider and compare. For this reason, the preliminary management assessment stresses the need for a set of options or alternative proposals. At least three or four options can usually be found for any problem situation, and often more. Each option is subjected to a CBA.

- Do nothing; do not change the current system.
- Design and produce a 'best' e-learning solution.
- Design and produce a 'minimal' (smaller, easily afforded) e-learning solution.
- Design and execute a structural, procedural or managerial change (that is, something that is *not* an e-learning solution) to the system, as suggested in Table 5.1.

Evaluating costs and benefits

Payback

A simple method of evaluating a proposal is in terms of its payback period: in how many months will it pay back the investment to be made? For example, a proposed training course might cost £20,000 at first, and provide net savings of £24,000 per year thereafter. Payback will therefore be in ten months. Senior management may well be quite unwilling to consider paybacks over 36 months long, and frequently will demand payback within 12 months.

Net present value

A more sophisticated CBA involves calculating the net present value (NPV) of the cost and benefit cash flows of the proposal.

Table 5.3 Net present value of two options

	Year 1	Year 2	Year 3	Year 4	Year 5	NPV
Option A	0	–400	–400	–400	–400	–964.89
Option B	–4,000	1,000	1,000	1,000	1,000	–1,036.05

The key element of NPV is to discount future benefit income by some percentage or risk factor, such as the rate of inflation or the cost of borrowing money. NPV should be calculated using a spreadsheet, and is most useful where the investment decision depends upon projected benefits occurring well in the future. For example (Table 5.3), option A could be to do nothing and maintain an existing system, but to incur additional annual operating costs of £400 in subsequent years to cover current shortcomings. Option B could be to introduce a training programme at an initial cost of £4,000 and thereafter enjoy a yearly net saving of £1,000. Taking the cost of money (cost of a bank loan) at, say, 16 per cent per annum as the discount factor, and evaluating the benefit over five years, the NPV of option A is £–965 while that of B is £–1,036. Both options therefore have negative NPV (implying an effective overall loss of money), with option A marginally better than B.

Internal rate of return

Another sophisticated comparison of options involves the calculation of the internal rate of return (IRR), again using a spreadsheet. For example (Table 5.4), option C involves spending £3,000 in year 1 and obtaining net benefits of £1,000 for the next four years, while option D involves the same expenditure but obtains no benefits in year 2, with net benefits of £1,500 only materialising in each of years 3, 4 and 5. The IRR of C is 12.6 per cent and of D 14.7 per cent,

Figure 5.10 CBA layout

Option description

Description of the option in plain terms.

Option costs

Cost of each item or component identified, shown negative. Laid out per period, typically Year 1, 2, 3, ... etc.

Option benefits valued

Each benefit identified, valued, shown positive. Laid out per period, Year 1, 2, 3, ... etc.

Net present value

Overall option NPV shown, with discount rate. Other measures (e.g. IRR, pay-back) also shown as required.

CBA for option (b)

A network of 25 PCs will provide the required training using bought-in packages, ... An annual upgrade of facilities ... The expected benefits are as specified below ...

	Yr 1	...	Yr 5	NPV
COSTS				
Hardware	-25,000	...	0	
Software	-15,000		0	
Maintenance	-2,500		-1,500	
BENEFITS				
Productivity (a)	9,000	...	11,000	
Reduced error (b)	5,000		5,000	
Responsiveness (c)	3,500		3,500	
TOTALS	-24,000	...	18,000	19,455
		(Discount rate = 10%)		

NOTES

(a) Three existing clerks can ... no need to hire 4th clerk.
(b) Incorrectly invoiced stock ... reduced by 20%.
(c) Old customer loss (20 p.a.) reduced by 10%.

Table 5.4 Internal rate of return of two options

	Year 1	Year 2	Year 3	Year 4	Year 5	IRR (%)
Option C	–3,000	1,000	1,000	1,000	1,000	12.6
Option D	–3,000	0	1,500	1,500	1,500	14.7

indicating that D is a marginally better use of money (better return on investment), but neither option is as good as putting the £3,000 in, for example, an investment account which pays 15 per cent interest. Depending upon the prevailing economic climate, senior management would prefer to see an IRR that was well in excess of the best that could be earned by other forms of investment.

Cost-benefit analysis layout

The typical components and layout of a CBA are shown in Figure 5.10.

6

Front-end analysis

The technical development of e-learning materials starts with an analysis of the requirements of these materials; this stage is called front-end analysis. Within the ELSYE life cycle, the front-end analysis stage is part of the analysis phase, along with the project plan stage, as shown in Figure 6.1. After a successful analysis phase, the design phase takes the requirements specified in the front-end analysis and constructs the detailed blueprint for the e-learning materials to be produced.

The feasibility report stage has already addressed the question of whether the apparent learning and teaching needs can be effectively met by an e-learning project, and senior management has approved the preliminary management assessment. If the feasibility report stage has not been undertaken, then at the least the needs analysis step must be completed before proceeding with the front-end analysis stage, and completing the system diagram step would be helpful as well.

The front-end analysis stage is concerned with six issues, listed in Table 6.1, and these are addressed by the six steps of front-end analysis as shown in Figure 6.2.

As Figure 6.2 shows, there is considerable feedback within the front-end analysis stage between the technical steps of audience analysis, task analysis, top-level objectives and e-learning concept. As the investigations in each of these steps proceed, consequences for the other steps emerge and suggest changes to those steps.

Figure 6.1 Front-end analysis stage in the ELSYE life cycle

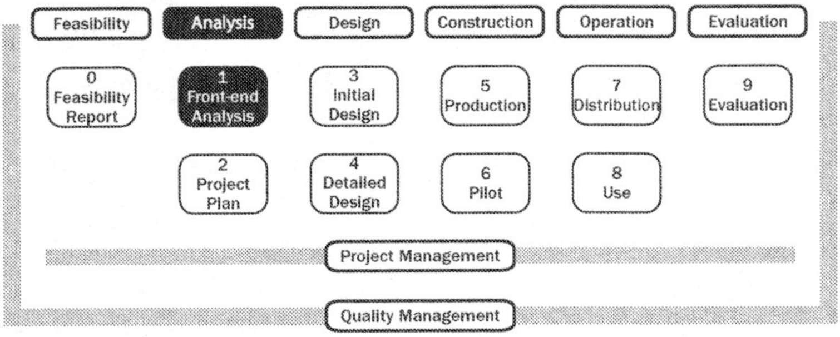

Table 6.1 Issues addressed in the steps of front-end analysis

Audience analysis	What are the characteristics of the intended or target audience, the learners or students?
Task analysis	What are the nature and structure of the subject matter content?
Top-level objectives	What are the intended e-learning outcomes, the objectives, of the e-learning? These will be linked to student assessment during the initial design stage
E-learning concept	What, in outline, are the learning and teaching treatment, the methods and media to be used?
Audio-visual treatment concept	If the e-learning concept is to use audio or video, what, in outline, is the treatment to be given to the AV materials?
Project and quality management standards	What project management and quality standards apply to the project?

Although it is common to start with the audience analysis step, given the needs analysis from the feasibility report stage, each of the four technical steps of the front-end analysis stage are closely tied together. Considerations and issues arising in one step affect other steps, and the front-end analysis stage is, in practice, carried out in an

Figure 6.2 Front-end analysis technical steps

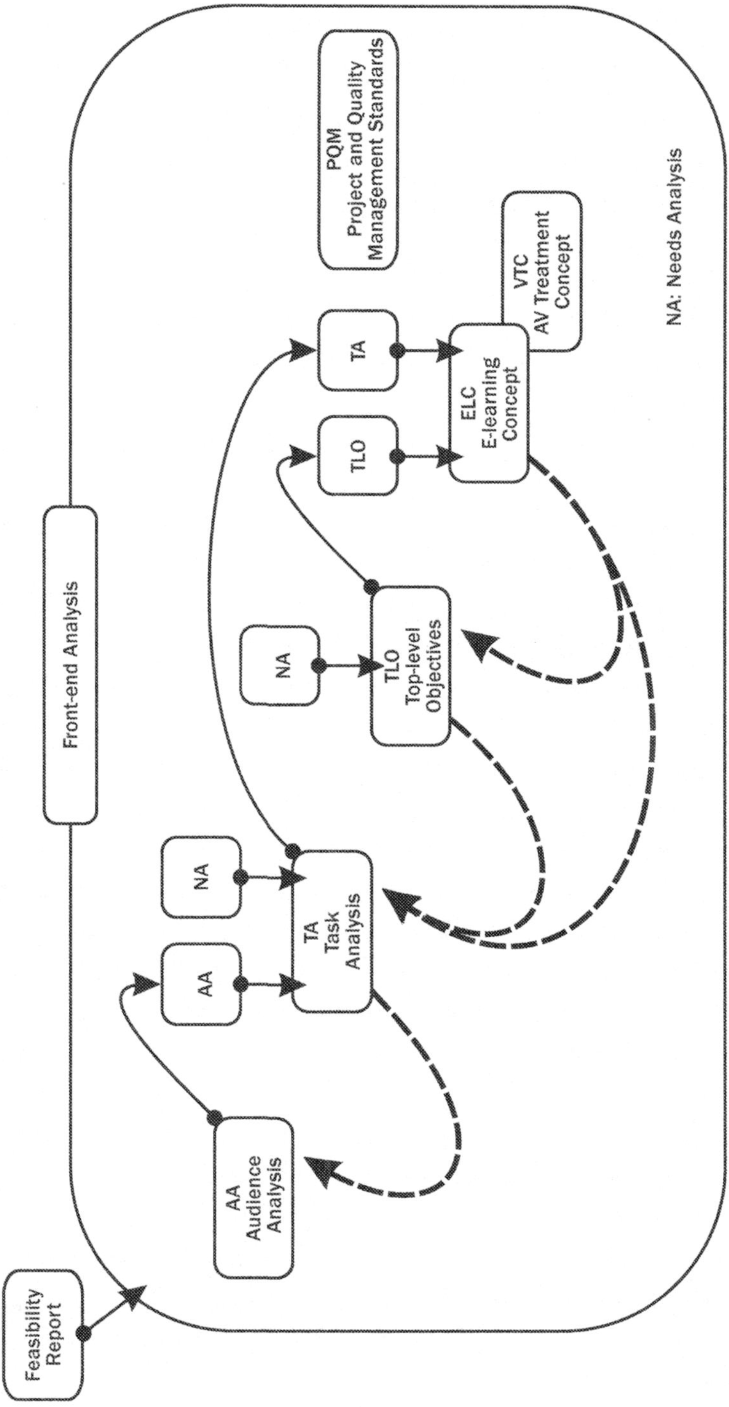

Figure 6.3 Inputs to ELSYE development

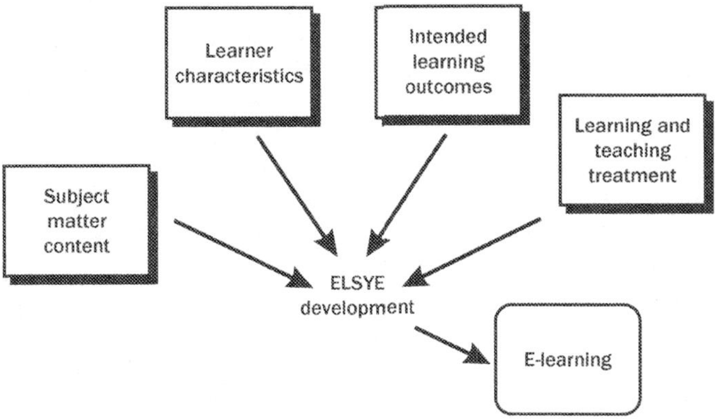

iterative, non-linear way. For example, the top-level objectives of the e-learning are cast in the light of the audience analysis, but it may turn out that detailed consideration of the first draft top-level objectives requires some changes to them, leading to adjustments to the initial audience analysis.

The inputs to front-end analysis, and hence to the engineering of e-learning, are illustrated in summary in Figure 6.3. The four inputs to the design and construction of e-learning are the learner characteristics (audience analysis), the subject matter (task analysis), the intended learning outcomes (top-level objectives) and the desired treatment of the learning and teaching situation, the media and methods (e-learning concept).

Audience analysis

An analysis of the characteristics of the intended or target audience is vital for the subsequent design of the e-learning. Issues such as reading age and geographical location, for example, will powerfully affect the initial design and detailed design stages. Table 6.2 provides a checklist of audience characteristics that require investigation and documentation. The audience analysis is also used in the later production and operation phases (Chapters 12 and 13) of the ELSYE project to ensure coherence and quality.

Table 6.2 **Audience characteristics checklist**

Category	Characteristic
Personal	Age profile Gender profile Special needs (e.g. colour blindness, dyslexia)
Education	Qualifications Achievements Language skill and level of literacy Numeracy Computer literacy
Experience	Previous relevant life experience Previous relevant job experience Current job
Interests	Social interests Hobbies Sports
Study factors	Amount of time available to study Times of day available for study Physical location and dispersion Travelling time involved Number of students
Contexts	Organisational attitude towards learning and training Peer-group attitudes towards learning and training
Attitudes	Learning associated with passive classroom-type teaching Value associated with training achievements Perceptions and preconceptions of learning situations Previous experience of learning and training Volunteers or conscripts?

Task analysis

The outline identification of the nature and structure of the e-learning's subject matter and content is the topic of the task analysis step. Further investigation in the initial design and detailed design stages will take the task analysis and refine it further and into greater detail. At this stage, carrying out the task analysis step provides a broad understanding of the knowledge and cognitive skills required by the student in order to achieve the aims or goals of the e-learning, and is most effectively undertaken using annotated diagrams rather than purely words.

It is useful to categorise the nature of the information or subject matter broadly into one of four types: facts, concepts, procedures and principles. For each of these types of content there is a diagrammatic approach that is particularly suited. (The definitions of 'fact', 'concept' and so on are provided in Chapter 9 on the detailed design of e-learning transactions.)

Facts

Facts are usefully analysed as a hierarchy, and subject matter that primarily involves factual information may be most usefully diagrammed using a tree-like structure. The form of this task hierarchy is provided in Figure 6.4.

Figure 6.4 Task analysis for facts

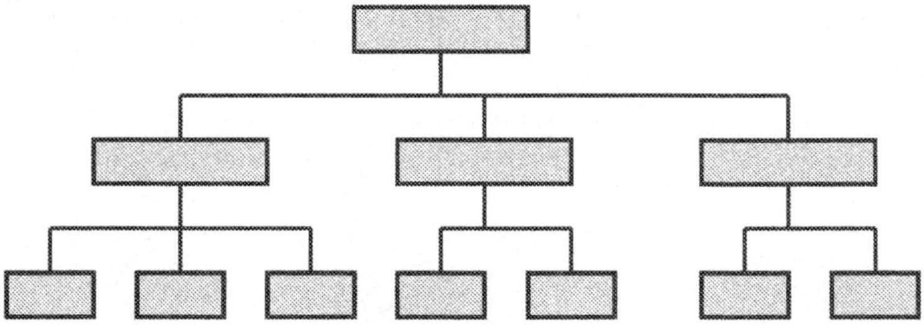

Figure 6.5 Task analysis for concepts

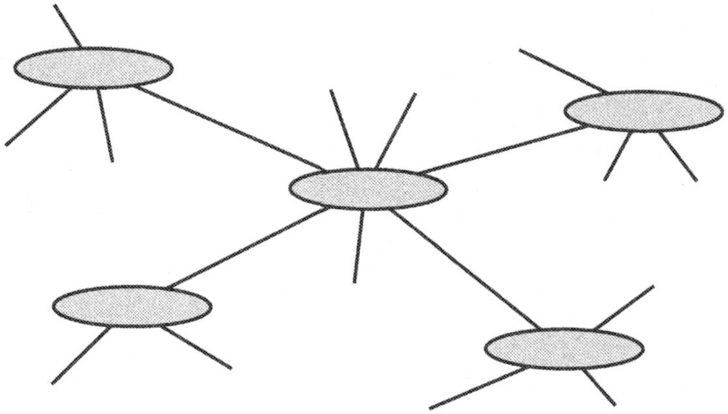

Concepts

Concepts are usefully analysed in a slightly less structured way than facts, using a bubble or spider chart. Figure 6.5 illustrates such a chart. The various lines provide linkages and connections between the 'bubbles' or concepts being analysed. Of course, if there are no multiple linkages between bubbles, the bubble chart becomes equivalent to a hierarchy chart.

Procedures

Procedures are most usefully diagrammed as a flowchart, illustrated in Figure 6.6. There are, of course, many ways of documenting a procedure, and a flowchart is simply one suggestion. The point here is that a rational and considered choice needs to be made between the various diagrammatic techniques available, and that the most appropriate technique should be matched to the nature and structure of the subject matter being analysed.

Figure 6.6 Task analysis for procedures

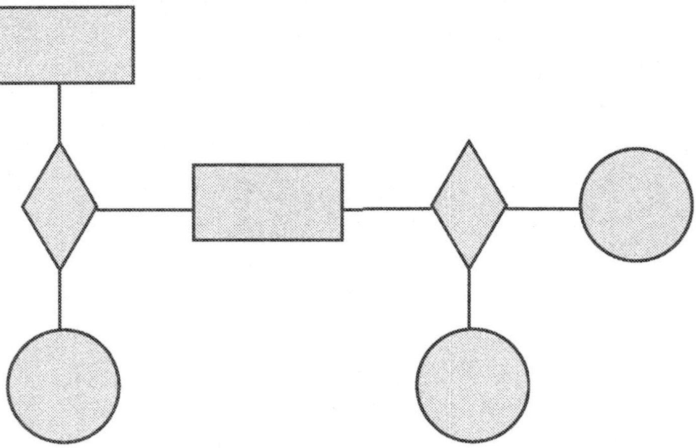

Principles

Finally, principles may be effectively analysed and diagrammed using a fishbone chart. Principles involve a cause-and-effect analysis, for which fishbone charts are most effectively used. Figure 6.7 illustrates the form of a fishbone chart. As can be seen, a fishbone chart is formally equivalent to a hierarchy chart.

Figure 6.7 Task analysis for principles

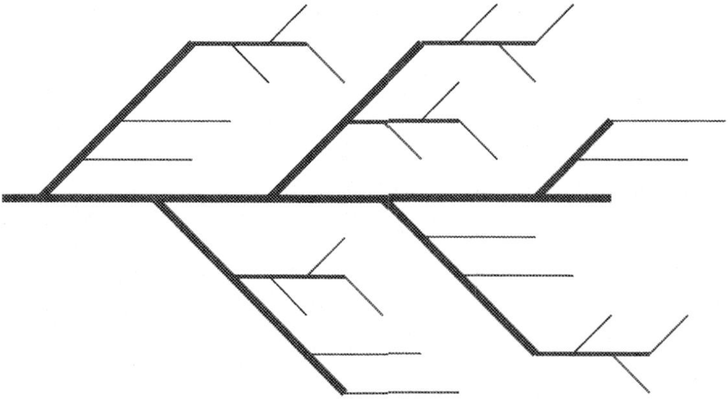

Top-level objectives

Given an understanding of the needs that the e-learning is to meet, of the nature of the e-learning content and of the intended student, it now remains to express the overall purpose of the teaching or training that is to be designed. This expression of purpose is specified as a set of top-level objectives.

The approach taken in ELSYE is that, unless the student's behaviour is actually changed as a result of e-learning, nothing of significance has occurred, the e-learning unit, module or programme is ineffective and the e-learning design defective. The aims or goals of the e-learning are therefore expressed in behavioural terms – what the student is expected to be able to do as a result of e-learning. This approach is part of the reason why ELSYE is largely indifferent to the distinctions that can be made between information presentation, education and training. In each of these forms of learning and teaching, ELSYE seeks behavioural change in the student as a result of the information presented, the education imparted or the training undertaken.

The point or purpose of e-learning is often loosely expressed as its aims, perhaps something like 'appreciate the role of systems theory in design' or 'develop an understanding of the methods of e-learning design'. A careful distinction is made here between such aims, which are a general communication of purpose and goals, and objectives, which are carefully crafted technical statements of teaching intent.

As will be seen in Chapter 8, objectives can be decomposed into greater and greater detail – called enabling objectives – and are matched against lesson content and student test items to ensure coherence and quality of the resulting materials and systems.

Bloom's taxonomy of educational objectives

The analysis and design of objectives are associated with Bloom (1956) and Mager (1997). Bloom identified a taxonomy of educational objectives, illustrated in Figure 6.8, involving three domains: cognitive, affective and psychomotor. Within the cognitive and affective domains were identified areas that were intended to form a hierarchy from lower to higher abilities.

There are theoretical and practical problems with Bloom's hierarchy within the cognitive domain, and it is currently more fashionable to identify three broad areas of ability within this domain: 'to be able to recall knowledge', 'to be able to use knowledge' and 'to be able to find new knowledge'.

There are additional domains of ability beyond those identified by Bloom: social and interpersonal skills, ethical and moral skills and possibly aesthetic skills suggest themselves. It is the case, however, that most e-learning is concerned with the cognitive domain, and this is where most attention will be focused.

Figure 6.8 Bloom's domains

COGNITIVE DOMAIN	AFFECTIVE DOMAIN	PSYCHOMOTOR DOMAIN
Knowledge	Receiving	
Comprehension	Responding	
Application	Valuing	
Analysis	Organisation	
Synthesis	Value complex	
Evaluation		

E-learning objectives

The basic form of an e-learning objective is specified thus: 'The student will be able to X', where X is a performance.

Whether explicitly stated or merely implied, an e-learning objective begins with a standard phrase, 'By the end of the course, the student will be able to...'. A statement of the performance that the student will be able to undertake completes the objective. The performance involves an ability that the student has learned, expressed in behavioural terms. This means it must be possible to observe and assess whether the student can actually exhibit the ability in question.

The statement of the performance begins with the ability and concludes with one or more measurable or assessable actions by which it can be observed that the student has learned the ability in question. The ability generally comprises a verb denoting the learned capability, followed by the object of the learned capability. Table 6.3 lists these basic components of an e-learning objective along with an example of each.

Table 6.3 **Components of a basic e-learning objective**

Component	Example
Objective	The student will be able to analyse target audience characteristics by listing those characteristics pertinent to the e-learning under consideration
Performance	...to analyse target audience characteristics by listing...
Ability	...analyse target audience characteristics...
Learned capability verb	...analyse...
Learned capability object	...target audience characteristics...
Assessable behaviour	...listing those characteristics pertinent to the e-learning under consideration

Table 6.4 Fully specified e-learning objective

Situation	Given a situation A
Constraints	and given constraints B
Basic objective	the student will be able to X
Standards	according to performance standards C
Tools	using tools D

The statement of a performance in terms of an ability and assessable behaviour provides the minimum form of an e-learning objective. It may be important, however, to define more closely what is intended as the learning outcome, and attention may then be given to the supplementary components of a fully specified objective: the situation or scenario within which the student needs to be able to perform; the standards of the performance; any constraints which may apply to the performance; and the use of any tools. Table 6.4 lists the components of a fully specified e-learning objective, and these are illustrated graphically in Figure 6.9.

Learned capability behavioural verbs for objectives

The essence of an e-learning objective is expressed in the performance 'X' which the student is expected to be able to do by the end of e-learning. In turn, the essence of the performance 'X' is expressed by the learned capability that it demonstrates. Accordingly, considerable attention needs to be given to appropriate choices of learned capability in order to formulate the well-specified objectives around which the e-learning is to be designed and produced.

Gagné et al. (2004) identify nine areas of skill and competence which learning and teaching could reasonably address, and suggest that a particular, specific ability verb,

Figure 6.9 **Components of a fully specified e-learning objective**

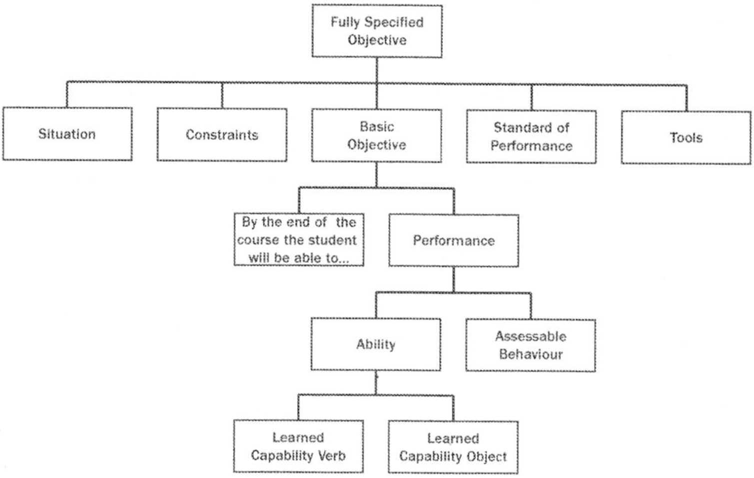

which they call a learned capability verb, or LCV, should be used in any objective which addresses one of these areas. Table 6.5 shows these skill areas and the verb associated with each.

Table 6.5 **Standard learned capability verbs, after Gagné et al.**

Skill or competence	Learned capability verb (LCV)
Knows facts	states
Discriminates	discriminates
Identifies concepts	identifies
Classifies information	classifies
Applies rules	demonstrates
Solves problems	generates
Applies procedures or strategies	adopts
Motor skills	executes
Attitudes	chooses

Table 6.6 **Observable ability verbs, after Merrill**

Capability	Standard LCV	Assessable behaviours
Knows facts	Recalls	Writing, drawing, indicating
Knows concepts	Defines	Writing, selecting
Knows procedures	States steps	Writing, drawing, flowcharting
Knows principles	States cause-effect relationships	Writing, drawing, graphing, specifying formula
Uses concepts	Classifies	Writing, selecting, sorting, arranging
Uses procedures	Demonstrates	Manipulating, calculating, measuring, constructing
Uses principles	Predicts	Calculating, drawing, graphing
Finds concepts	Invents	Sorting, specifying
Finds procedures	Devises	Experimenting, analysing
Finds principles	Discovers	Experimenting, analysing, observing, demonstrating

Merrill (1994) provides a similar list, shown in Table 6.6. The advantage of Merrill's list is that it also provides some suggestions for the assessable behaviour verbs, while requiring a more fine-grained analysis of the student's learned capability which underlies the objective being formulated. Merrill divides the cognitive domain into the three broad areas of 'know', 'use' and 'find', but combines these with the four kinds of subject matter (facts, concepts, procedures and principles) to identify ten specific verbs.

Reference to Bloom's work identifies a rich set of verbs that can be used as required for both the learned capability and the assessable behaviours by which that ability is demonstrated. These are shown in Table 6.7 for the cognitive domain and Table 6.8 for the affective domain.

Table 6.7 **Performance verbs for the cognitive domain, after Bloom**

	Cognitive ability	Assessable behaviour
Knowledge	Knows terms, specific facts, rules, trends, categories, criteria, methods, procedures, principles, concepts, theories	Name, label, define, state, recognise, list, recall, identify
Comprehension	Translates and paraphrases communications; interprets, summarises and explains relationships; extrapolates from given data	Explain, classify, summarise, extrapolate, interpret, convert
Application	Applies concepts, principles, rules, procedures	Calculate, solve, construct, use, prepare, predict, demonstrate
Analysis	Analyses elements, relationships or organisational principles; analyses connections, relationships or arrangements	Compare, contrast, infer, explain
Synthesis	Produces new arrangement or new result	Compose, originate, design, create
Evaluation	Judges on the basis of criteria and evidence	Appraise, argue, evaluate, criticise, assess, discriminate

Examples of top-level objectives

- 'Given a task analysis, by the end of the course the student will be able to identify appropriate wordings for a top-level objective by selecting them from a list with 95 per cent accuracy.'
- 'Given a description of a desired e-learning system, by the end of the course the student will be able to generate a

Table 6.8 **Performance verbs for the affective domain, after Bloom**

	Affective state	Assessable behaviour
Receiving	Indicates attention, shows willingness to receive, awareness of distinctive features	Describes, identifies, selects, demonstrates
Responding	Accepts need for regulations and responsibilities, chooses to respond in acceptable ways, shows satisfaction in responding	Demonstrates, tells, performs
Valuing	Endorses propositions, shows preference for values, expresses commitment to values	Explains, justifies, defends, demonstrates
Organisation	Understands relationship between values, develops a value system	Explains, defends, justifies
Value complex	Acts in ways consistent with values	Displays, practises, demonstrates

front-end analysis by first undertaking a needs analysis and then creating the task analysis, the target audience analysis and a set of top-level objectives.'

- 'When colleagues are implementing a talk-and-chalk lecture in a "traditional" way, by the end of the course the student will choose an e-learning systems engineering approach by preferring first to analyse and then design the lesson before constructing the lesson materials.'

Aims and goals

Detailed consideration has been given to identifying the objectives for e-learning. These objectives are intended to assist the e-learning designer during the subsequent stages and steps of materials design and production by giving explicit attention to the 'nuts and bolts' of what will need to be produced.

There is another level at which statements of e-learning intent may be usefully phrased in a more general way. Such general statements are usually called 'aims' or 'goals', and are often to be found prefacing a particular unit or programme of e-learning. There is an obvious and close relationship between programme aims and lesson objectives – the objectives instantiate and specify the intentions and purposes expressed in the aims – and so careful consideration needs to have been given to such aims and goals during the feasibility phase.

E-learning concept and AV treatment

The e-learning concept step in the front-end analysis stage is a little anomalous, since it is strictly a design activity rather than an analysis activity. That is, selecting the learning and teaching methods and media for e-learning should only occur once the e-learning requirements have been completely specified and signed off by the client and senior management; indeed, a full-blown media and methods step is part of the initial design stage (Chapter 8). The need for having a 'concept' media and methods component in the analysis phase of the ELSYE life cycle is to allow a fully developed project plan from this stage to lead to a properly informed sign-off of the analysis phase. The choice of e-learning methods and media has a profound impact upon the project's budget, schedule, risk factors, impact and cost-benefit calculations, so this choice needs to be made, in outline, as the last technical step in the front-end analysis before proceeding to the next stage, project plan.

The choice of e-learning methods and media is in fact far more of a business decision – what is affordable? – than a technical decision – what do the e-learning objectives require? – for two main reasons. The first, identified above, is the very large cost, schedule and other resource differentials between the cheapest and the most expensive methods and media. The second is that there is some evidence to show that, within broad parameters, the effectiveness of learning and teaching does not particularly depend upon the chosen media or even the chosen methods (Clark, 1983; Clark, 1994). There is considerable controversy about this, not least because it seems to contradict common sense. What seems much more important for the effectiveness of e-learning is its design and its adherence to the principles outlined in Chapters 8–11 on the initial design and detailed design stages, rather than the adoption of any particular medium or method.

Clark (Clark and Kwinn, 2007) recently introduced a classification of instructional architectures, listed in Table 6.9, which help to identify the overall e-learning concept. This concept, or instructional architecture, may inform the whole of the e-learning project, or, if a sufficiently large project, parts of it may have different and distinctive e-learning concepts or architectures.

A receptive architecture essentially regards the learner as a passive absorber of information, and the focus of the

Table 6.9 Instructional architectures

Receptive
Directive
Guided
Exploratory

e-learning is on the delivery of content. A directive architecture assumes that knowledge needs to be built up, and the focus tends to be based upon short sequences of tell, show and practise. A guided architecture assumes that learning by doing is more effective, and the e-learning focuses upon problem-based lessons. Finally, an exploratory architecture assumes that the students can make the best decisions about their learning, and focuses upon providing rich materials.

Resources, constraints, environment

The business decision on the choice of media and methods is based upon considerations of available resources, current constraints and the current training environment.

Resource issues include the size of the budget available to purchase or develop e-learning solutions, and the availability of the various kinds of expertise demanded by the development of ELSYE projects, particularly subject matter, e-learning design, graphic design and e-learning programming expertise. Constraints include the time available in which to specify and purchase or develop the required materials before they are needed. Environmental issues include the availability of teaching or training rooms, support equipment and expensive delivery hardware such as video players or multimedia computers.

Learning and teaching media

The media of learning and teaching should be distinguishable, in principle, from the learning and teaching methods that use those media. In practice, medium and method are difficult to disentangle, and it is usually unnecessary to do so.

Increasingly, attention is focused on learning and teaching environments, specifically technology-supported or technology-enhanced environments, where media and method remain tightly coupled. A list of most of the major learning and teaching media is provided in Table 6.10.

Certain of these media – simulators, interactive video, multimedia and computer-based teaching or training – may be designated 'technology-based' media. A technology-based project is characteristically more costly and more demanding to develop than a 'conventional' learning and teaching project, and some criteria to consider when evaluating the desirability and viability of e-learning projects are discussed below.

Only the smallest of e-learning projects involves a single medium. Almost all projects involve a variety of learning and teaching media, although it is true to say that a particular medium usually dominates or characterises the resulting e-learning.

Table 6.10 Some learning and teaching media

Stand-up instructor
Overhead projector
Simulator/training aid
Actual (live) equipment
Video/film
Audio
Printed materials
Interactive video (IV)
Multimedia
Computer-based teaching/training (CBT)
Slide/tape
35mm slide

The choice of media tends to focus on criteria such as whether they are flexible, economical, realistic and portable.

Learning and teaching methods

A list of most of the major learning and teaching methods is shown in Table 6.11. The selection of appropriate learning and teaching methods is considered in more detail in Chapter 8 on initial design. From the point of view of the e-learning concept step, the important issue is to identify the main methods which the proposed e-learning is likely to use, so that these can be reflected in the project plan (Chapter 7).

The selection of appropriate learning and teaching methods is more closely linked to the top-level objectives than the selection of media. Table 6.12 provides some

Table 6.11 **Some learning and teaching methods**

Lecture/exposition
Tutorial
Seminar
Self-study
Demonstration
Panel discussion
Role-play
Case history/case study
Practical/laboratory exercise
On-the-job (live) teaching
Project
In-basket exercise
Game
Simulation

Table 6.12 **Learning and teaching methods appropriate to objectives**

Domain	Merrill's category	Bloom's taxonomic category	Possible learning and teaching method
Cognitive	Know	Knowledge, comprehension	Lecture, seminar, demonstration, panel discussion
	Use	Application, analysis, evaluation	Tutorial, case study, practical exercise, in basket, on the job
	Find (create, discover)	Synthesis	Project, game, simulation, on the job
Affective			Role-play, practical exercise, on the job
Psychomotor			Demonstration, practical exercise, on the job
Social and interpersonal			Role-play, practical exercise, on the job, game, simulation
Ethical and moral			Role-play, practical exercise, on the job, game, simulation

suggestions for learning and teaching methods that are appropriate for various kinds of objectives.

Technology-based learning and teaching projects

Although costly and demanding, technology-based learning and teaching (TBLT) projects have particular relevance for certain kinds of e-learning requirements. Table 6.13 lists the criteria; if several of these apply, a TBLT project will certainly prove justifiable on technical grounds.

Table 6.13 Technical criteria for TBLT project viability

Technical criteria
There are large student numbers
Mastery of content is required and must be proved by test score
Statutory and possibly professional licensing needs test scores to obtain licence
An assured quality or consistency of achievement is required
Course content is stable
Course is repeatedly presented
Subject matter content or procedures involve hazard
Course involves expensive consumables
Course is irregularly scheduled and/or must run on demand
Course objectives are focused on lower cognitive skills
Course provides student refresher input or ensures prerequisite competence
Course must accommodate a specific set of student special needs
Students are dispersed, either geographically or over time
Course runs within a short time frame or is intensive

There are also commercial requirements for TBLT projects, outlined in Table 6.14. These are not so much requirements, but rather pleas to senior management about the degree of commitment and resourcing required for successful TBLT projects.

Project and quality management standards

The definition of project and quality management standards for an ELSYE project may not be necessary for smaller or single-person projects. For larger projects, or those that are

Table 6.14 **Business requirements for TBLT project viability**

Business criteria
Funding that recognises the high development costs of TBLT projects
Costings that separately identify development, delivery and maintenance costs
Development approach that is at least team-oriented if not team-reliant
Ready availability of and funding for the specialist roles in ELSYE
Management assessments or cost-benefit analyses that establish the cost-effective achievement of the project's goals

high risk, have high client involvement or external contractor involvement, certain standards need to be specified and implemented as soon as the project receives approval. The step of specifying project and quality management standards can be carried out in parallel with the other steps of the front-end analysis stage, and the resulting product can be implemented as soon as it is available.

Project management standards address the procedures and principles to be used for the various activities identified in Chapter 15 on project management: risk management, schedule construction and tracking, budget construction and tracking, change control, configuration management and metrics. These standards would include, for example, the specification of the timesheet format and contents to be used by staff.

Quality management standards address the three strands identified in Chapter 14 on quality management: procedures and principles to be used for inspections and reviews, testing and process improvement. These standards would include, for example, the explicit description of the quality assurance processes to be followed for all stage products, including rework and retesting procedures.

Chapters 14 and 15 expand upon the various issues in project and quality management which would require appropriate standards and their specification.

7

Project plan

Given the analysis of the requirements of the proposed e-learning materials in the front-end analysis stage, the project plan stage is concerned with establishing the commercial viability of the project. Within the ELSYE life cycle, illustrated in Figure 7.1, the project plan stage is part of the analysis phase along with the front-end analysis. After the project plan has been approved by senior management, the design phase takes the requirements specified in the front-end analysis and constructs the detailed blueprint for the e-learning materials and systems to be produced.

The steps of the project plan stage are shown in Figure 7.2. Earlier in the project, the feasibility report stage involved the construction of a preliminary management assessment which focused on a cost-benefit analysis for the project. Updated for the full project plan, the CBA joins a risk management plan, an impact analysis and a whole-project schedule and budget as a set of management products to be submitted to senior management for approval.

Like the front-end analysis, the project plan stage is constructed in an iterative process. In particular, the options and alternatives step takes the feasibility report and generates a number of potential solutions to the documented e-learning requirements. Each of these options and alternatives has an associated schedule and budget, CBA and impact analysis, and consideration of these feeds back to the risk management plan.

Figure 7.1 Project plan stage in the ELSYE life cycle

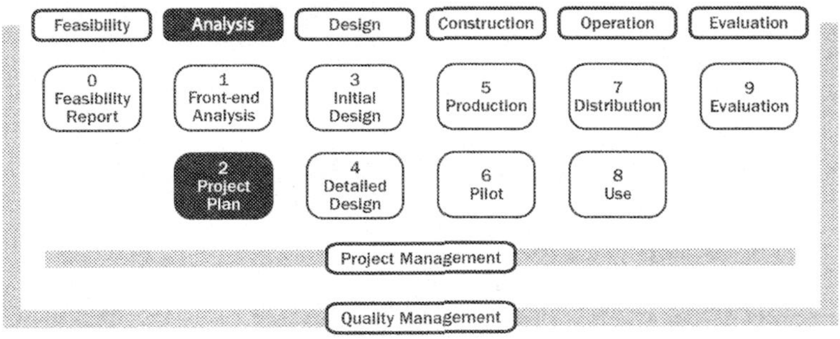

Figure 7.2 Project plan steps

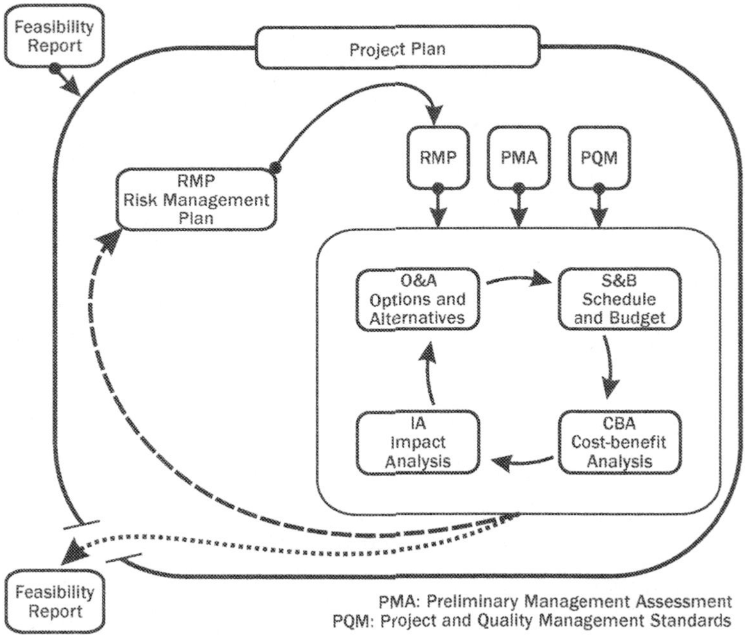

The project plan stage gains in importance as the ELSYE project gains in size. Small, one-person, low-risk projects do not require a full formal project plan, though they would of course always benefit from some attention being paid to the key issues of risk, options and alternatives, schedule, budget, impact and cost-benefit analysis.

Risk management plan

In one sense, the whole of ELSYE is an exercise in risk management, involving techniques, procedures, reports, reviews and all the project management and technical paraphernalia designed to ensure an effective e-learning product delivered on time and within budget. The risk management plan step of the project plan stage involves the formal consideration of all the risks to which the project is subject, an analysis of the potential losses and probabilities of these risks should they come to pass and the determination of strategies to ameliorate or avert the most serious of these risks.

Risk identification

The first task of risk management is the identification and quantification of the risks to which the project may be subjected. Some possible sources of risk for ELSYE projects are listed in Table 7.1; for each risk which may occur, a quantification of the risk needs to be made.

Risks are quantified by two factors: the probability or *likelihood* of the risk coming to pass, and the financial impact or *loss* sustained as a result of the risk occurring. From these two factors is derived the key measurement of the risk's importance, the risk *exposure*. The project's exposure to a particular risk is the product of the risk's likelihood and the risk's financial loss.

Risk likelihood

Some risks are more likely than others. In order to calculate the project's exposure to a particular risk, the likelihood of a risk needs to be expressed as a probability, a number between 0 and 1, which represents the chance of the risk

Table 7.1 Sources of project risk

Source	Possible risk
Personnel	Inexperience Incompetence Low morale and staff turnover
Estimates	Estimates of budget and schedule, expectations or constraints unrealistic No comparisons available with comparable projects
Subject matter provision	Imperfect client understanding Disagreement between subject matter experts Imperfect developer understanding
User interface	Inappropriate or unfriendly user interface
E-learning design	Inappropriate tone for target audience Incorrect assumptions for prerequisite skills Inadequate, insufficient or inappropriate interactivity Inadequate or inappropriate content
Graphic design	Unattractive product
Materials construction	Inappropriate topic and content sequencing Inadequate piloting
Gold plating	Inadvisable, unnecessary e-learning features
Management	Inadequate project plans Undefined development processes Inadequate technical or management standards Inadequate control, clout or commitment
Suppliers	Unsatisfactory purchased or contracted components Late or insufficient delivery Inadequate contracted skills or services Poor communication
Requirements volatility	Excessive changes in specified e-learning needs or e-learning design
Tools and equipment	Inadequate resources, equipment, tools
Technology	Reliance on new and untried technology Changes in technology during development Unachievable performance requirements
Market	Competitive products technically better or lower cost

actually occurring. Most people find it easier to estimate the likelihood of a risk using a word or phrase, such as 'unlikely', 'possible' and so on. Figure 7.3 provides a simple table for converting a linguistic expression of a risk's likelihood into a numerical probability.

For example, a risk classified as 'probable' would have a numerical probability of somewhere between 0.4 and 0.75; that is, as likely to occur somewhere between 40 per cent and 75 per cent of the time, or as having the chance of occurring somewhere between four times in every ten projects and three times in every four projects. The exact

Figure 7.3 Conversion table for risk likelihoods

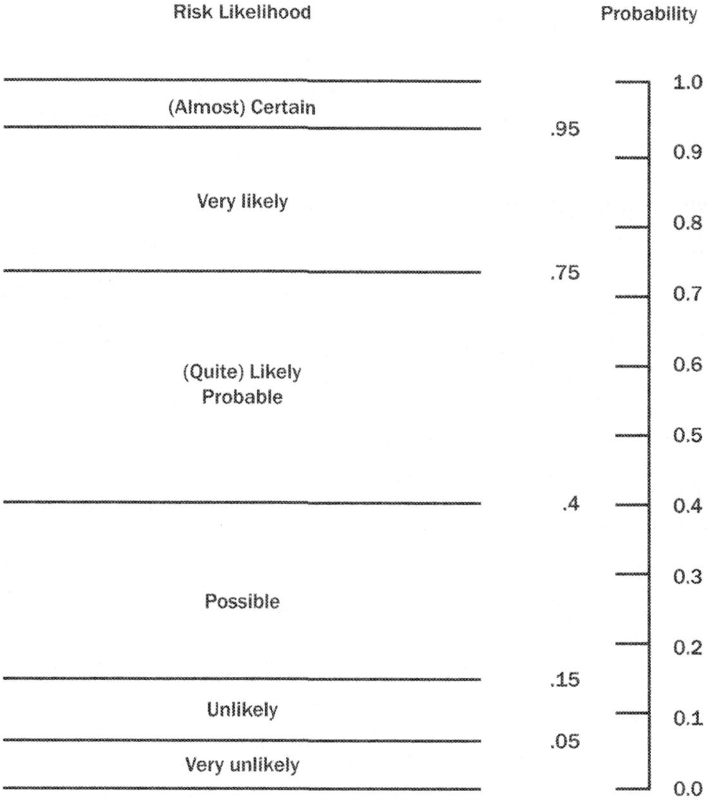

number chosen within this range depends upon the judgement of the developer.

Loss value

The impact if the risk comes to pass is expressed as a monetary value. Very generally, risk to the project focuses on three areas: schedule, budget and quality, as shown in Table 7.2. The result of impact in these areas is summarised in Table 7.3 with regard to the most serious outcomes. For each of the risks identified and likelihood estimated earlier, an assessment is made of the financial loss to the project if the risk comes to pass.

For example, a technology-based project would be subject to the risk that improvements in technology could overtake the project, requiring new equipment to be purchased and installed. As a starting point, the financial loss if such a risk came to pass could be calculated as the purchase and

Table 7.2 Primary areas of risk impact

Schedule	Not meeting target delivery date
Budget	Not meeting target budget
Quality	Excessive defects
Functionality	Materials not effective

Table 7.3 The most serious project risk outcomes

Termination	Premature termination
Rescoping	Radical cutting of project brief
Functional failure	Target audience fails to achieve e-learning objectives
Technical failure	Materials poorly implemented for technical reasons

installation costs of the equipment currently in use. If the project required four multimedia PCs, and if a suitable multimedia PC currently costs £2,500, then the loss value would be £10,000.

Risk exposure

The importance or significance of the risk to the project is expressed by the risk exposure. The risk exposure is a monetary value that can be thought of as the financial impact of the risk discounted by the likelihood of the risk occurring. For example, assuming that it was 'probable' (probability of 0.6 from Figure 7.3) that new equipment costing £10,000 would have to be purchased during the project, the formula shown in Table 7.4 calculates the exposure to this risk as £6,000.

The outcome of risk identification is a list of project risks and the calculated exposure for each. The list would be presented as shown in Table 7.5.

Table 7.4 **Formula for risk exposure**

Risk exposure = risk likelihood × risk impact

Table 7.5 **Risk exposures**

Risk source	Risk detail	Impact on	Probability	Impact cost £	Exposure £
...	...	...	...	...	...
Equipment	Obsolete before end of project	Budget	0.6	10,000	6,000
...	...	...	...	...	...

Risk analysis

The next task in the risk management plan is to list the risks in order of their exposures and consider ways of ameliorating or averting each risk, starting with those with the highest exposures. Table 7.6 provides some possible aversion strategies. The problem with any risk control measure is that it is not free of cost, so it is necessary to compare the cost of the risk control measure with the value of the reduction in risk exposure that is achieved.

A control measure that reduces the risk exposure by an amount equal to the cost of implementing it, for example, is probably not worth implementing. The comparison of the control measure cost with the reduction in exposure is called the risk leverage, and is calculated using the formula in Table 7.7.

For example, taking out an insurance policy for the duration of the project could ameliorate the risk of changes in technology overtaking the project. Such a policy might cost, say, £2,500 and would cover the cost of replacing the

Table 7.6 **Risk control measure examples**

Train project staff
Strengthen project management
Employ support staff
Increase quality inspections and reviews
Strengthen piloting and testing
Employ second (alternative) suppliers
Analyse competitive products
Prototype during analysis/design/production
Deliver in phases
Trade off learning and teaching methods and media

Table 7.7 **Risk leverage formula**

Risk leverage = Exposure reduction/Control measure cost
where
Exposure reduction = risk exposure before control measure – risk exposure after control measure

equipment, with an excess of £1,000 payable if a claim was made upon the policy. In this case the leverage of the control measure – taking out an insurance policy – would be calculated as follows. First, the exposure before the control measure is £6,000, as before. The exposure after the control measure is 0.6 times £1,000, being the probability of claiming on the policy times the new loss value, which is the policy excess of £1,000, giving £600. The exposure reduction is thus £5,400. With a control measure cost of £2,500 and an exposure reduction of £5,400, the risk leverage of this particular control measure, taking out the insurance policy, is 5,400/2,500 = 2.16.

The outcome of the risk analysis task is a list of all the project risks now ordered by the leverages offered by their control strategies, with the highest leverages first, as illustrated in Table 7.8.

Table 7.8 **Risk control measure leverages**

Control measure detail	Measure cost £	Revised exposure £	Exposure reduction £	Leverage
...	...	...	...	...
Insurance policy for replacement of obsolete equipment	2,500	600	5,400	2.16
...	...	...	...	...

Risk control

The final task of the risk management plan step is to select the risk control measures to implement. The risk leverage needs to be greater than unity for the proposed control measure to make sense, and usually a leverage needs to be greater than five or ten for management to feel the burden of its cost is justified, while leverages greater than 20 become rather attractive. The costs of the control measures feed into the project budget.

Options and alternatives

One of the key insights of recent work in software engineering and systems theory is the importance of having and deciding between a variety of options and alternatives, both for the project as a whole and within the project. Developing a good set of alternatives brings out hidden assumptions and clarifies criteria; selecting an alternative (or more usually, constructing a composite final alternative to select) allows a 'best choice' to be made, rather than a forced 'choice'; and evaluating the outcome of the chosen alternative provides comparative evidence for improving future criteria and choices.

Alternatives to the ELSYE project have already been identified and considered in the feasibility report (Chapter 5). It was suggested there that, besides an e-learning solution to the problem situation, at least two other solutions ('do nothing' and 'non-ELSYE solution') need to be outlined before the ELSYE solution is commissioned. If such alternatives to the project have not been yet developed, this needs to be done in this stage. Table 7.9 provides some suggestions for alternatives to an e-learning project.

Table 7.9 **Alternatives to an e-learning project**

Provide better information for staff to use
Make clear and explicit what is required
Improve management or supervision
Provide better equipment or facilities
Improve incentives
Provide performance aids
Provide on-the-job practice and coaching
Reduce the job
Restructure the job
Do nothing

Given that the project has been given the go-ahead (at least until the project plan review milestone), it is now necessary to develop options within the project. ELSYE project options characteristically centre on the learning and teaching media and methods to be used, and the work from the e-learning concept step of the front-end analysis stage (Chapter 6) is relevant here.

Most e-learning objectives can be achieved in a variety of ways. While the e-learning concept step will have identified what is presumed to be the 'best' way, some options need to be developed, quantified and considered in order to confirm the presumption. For example, the ELSYE project might involve a course whose aim is to improve customer service on the telephone, and the e-learning concept might have identified role-play, simulated exchanges with customers and the use of actual telephones as the 'best' learning and teaching methods and media for such a course. Such an approach would probably be highly successful, but would also involve considerable cost for course design and development as well as repeated course delivery.

One option to explore is an approach that is simpler and cheaper, such as the construction and distribution of a one-page job aid dealing with appropriate customer service manner, procedure and company policy. Another option is an approach that concentrates the life-cycle project costs into design and development, and reduces repeated delivery and operation costs. Such an option usually involves some form of technology-based learning and teaching, perhaps where the role-plays and simulated customer exchanges are provided by computer-based software. A third option to explore is to avoid design and development costs altogether, and hence their attendant risks, by purchasing a suitable training course off the shelf from an outside supplier. Table 7.10 shows some examples of options applicable to most e-learning projects.

Each of these options has radically different cost, benefit, schedule and impact implications. For each option, therefore, a schedule, budget, CBA and impact analysis must be developed and considered before the choice is made to commit to a particular approach to the project.

Table 7.10 Example options within an e-learning project

Option example	Service stance	Approach involved
Simple, cheap, cheerful	Provider	Text-based self-study
Reduce delivery and usage costs, incur design and development costs	Provider	Technology-based
Reduce design and development costs, incur delivery and usage costs	Provider	Instructor-based
Outsource the required e-learning	Purchaser	

Schedule and budget

The schedule and budget developed for a particular option involves the same components as any project schedule and budget. Each option is treated as a potential project in its own right, and documented accordingly. Schedule and budget components are discussed in Chapter 15 on project management.

Cost-benefit analysis

A cost-benefit analysis is developed for each option. The structure and content of a CBA were outlined in Chapter 5. The CBA of this stage identifies the value to the stakeholders of the e-learning, and will be used in the evaluation stage as guidance for the evidence to seek so that such value can indeed be demonstrated. The design of the measurements and instruments to obtain the relevant information is the subject of the evaluability design step of the detailed design stage (Chapter 11).

Impact analysis

The fourth, new, component of the project plan stage is the development of an impact analysis for each of the alternatives and options under consideration. An impact analysis addresses the likely non-technical outcomes and effects of implementing an e-learning project. Within an organisation, these are likely to be in terms of job security, job and organisational structure, pay, promotion and so on. An e-learning project or any of the other kinds of project illustrated in Table 7.9 is an intervention in the 'normal' functioning of a system with the intention of bringing about some change. The directly intended immediate changes are specified in the project's aims and objectives, but other changes also occur, sometimes quite unintended and sometimes far more important.

The impact analysis provides an opportunity to reflect on the system diagram, which is a view of the problem situation and the system in which it is embedded, and to consider systematically the changes to the people and the system that the project may bring about. Technicians who are focused upon technical issues staff most projects, and there is often a lack of focus upon social and organisational factors that also determine both the project's value and its long-term viability. Table 7.11 provides the topics that an impact analysis considers within an organisation, in approximate order of importance. The impact analysis is not restricted to an e-learning project, but is applicable to all options and alternatives, including the 'do nothing' alternative.

Impact will be assessed during the evaluation stage, and the design of the measurements and instruments to obtain the relevant impact information is the subject of the evaluability design step in Chapter 11.

Job security

The most important consideration in any intervention is whether anyone is likely to lose their job, whether a large component of their job is to be eliminated or transferred, or whether their career prospects are to be significantly reduced. The impact analysis must address this issue squarely, since it has the most profound impact upon the staff concerned and upon management actions and decisions that implement the intervention.

A distinction may be made between intended and unintended impacts, and it may be thought that the impact analysis focuses upon the intended outcomes of the project. This is not so: intended outcomes are usually explicit,

Table 7.11 **Impact analysis within an organisation**

Impact area	Detail
Job security	Job gains or losses Part-job gains or losses Career prospects
Job content	Task variety Physical and mental effort required to do tasks Personal autonomy and discretion New skills to be gained Old skills to be lost Work pace, deadlines, pressure to finish Workload and work quantity Performance monitoring and measurement
Organisational procedures and structures	Standardisation and formalisation Power, status and influence Upstream and downstream workflow Communication up, down and laterally
Personnel policies	Pay and other rewards for performance Promotion and other rewards for potential Appraisal criteria and processes

well articulated and carefully justified in a variety of other project documents. The impact analysis is the primary project document (along with the system diagram) that assesses unintended project consequences. For example, suppose an e-learning project aiming to reduce materials wastage in the machine shop has been conceived and implemented in order to reduce unit production materials costs. If successful, there may be a sharp drop in waste materials to be collected, consolidated and disposed of, leading to eventual redundancy of one of the two factory workers whose job is to process waste. Such a potential outcome requires careful study beforehand and formulation of management plans to deal with it properly, otherwise training plans may come to be seen as underhand trickery to achieve management targets.

Job content

The job content areas listed in Table 7.11 are those in which staff are usually rather sensitive to changes, particularly imposed changes. Some of these areas may seem unlikely to be impacted by an e-learning intervention, but all deserve consideration for unintended outcomes. For example, it is unlikely that some training on how to do a job better will have a negative impact on the performance of a trainee, but it is possible. Perhaps doing a 'better' job in the way taught on the training course causes the job to take longer; if the trainee's performance is measured according to some time-based criteria, they could be disadvantaged and would be unlikely to utilise the training provided.

It is also important to realise that no generalisations can be made as to whether, for example, a reduction in task variety is likely to be a good or a bad thing. It will depend upon the circumstances and the staff concerned, and there may need to be some enhancement of the audience analysis (Chapter 6) in order to clarify which of the two possibilities is more likely.

Organisational structures and procedures

The important issue here is the impact of the proposed intervention upon the rest of the system. An e-learning intervention has two usual intended outcomes: better job performance and better utilisation of information. Both of these outcomes may have quite unintended consequences for the organisation.

As illustrated earlier, improved job performance in one part of the organisation could cause upstream or downstream problems in another part: for example, better practice in the machine shop could cause problems in the cleaning and recycling department; or improved ability of the accounts department to extract management information from the computer system (as a result of training) could lead to a change in political power as the engineering department finds it can no longer 'hide' the real costs of botched prototypes.

Personnel policies

Finally, consideration needs to be given to the longer-term consequences of change, particularly to those of an e-learning intervention. Implicitly or explicitly, staff consider that training or education should eventually lead to improved benefits and prospects; if these expectations are incorrect, they must be addressed. In particular, the personnel policies of the organisation may need to be developed to make clear the difference between performance and potential, and to ensure clearly differentiated rewards for improved performance that, for example, do not necessarily include promotion.

Project plan stage review

The deliverable product of the project plan is a risk management plan and a set of options and alternatives for the project, where each option is supported by a schedule and budget, a CBA and an impact analysis. Together with the front-end analysis, these products are submitted to senior management. Management determines which of the options or combinations of options to approve before design begins.

8

Initial design

The initial design stage is concerned with outlining the e-learning content of the project, given that the project has been defined and agreed by the end of the analysis phase. Within the ELSYE life cycle, illustrated in Figure 8.1, the initial design stage is part of the design phase along with the detailed design stage. The design phase takes the e-learning and management objectives specified in the front-end analysis and project plan stages and assembles the detailed blueprints for the e-learning materials to be developed in the following construction phase.

The steps of the initial design stage are shown in Figure 8.2. This stage takes the requirements of the e-learning to be developed, as expressed in the task analysis and top-level objectives of the front-end analysis stage, and assembles a design outline called the content outline. This details the content of the e-learning and provides the student test items, expands upon the media and methods to be used and details the technical, presentation and design standards to be followed by the remainder of the project. The initial design stage is the heart of ELSYE, where the e-learning project is cast into its intended shape.

Figure 8.1 Initial design stage in the ELSYE life cycle

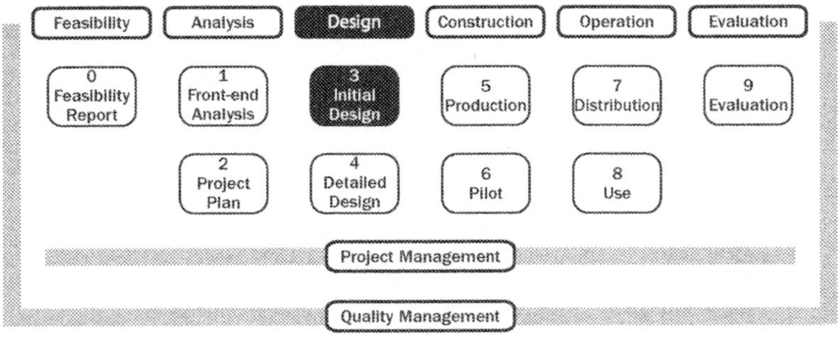

Enabling objectives

The first step of the initial design stage is to refine and expand the top-level objectives into a set of enabling objectives, also known as an objectives hierarchy. Given a top-level objective, the question being asked here is 'What must the student be able to do in order to achieve this?' The result is a set of lower-level objectives and prerequisite objectives called the enabling objectives. An example of a top-level objective being broken down into a set of enabling objectives is illustrated in Figure 8.3. The top-level objective in the example is 'By the end of the course the student will be able to construct a logicalised data flow diagram'. In order to achieve this, a number of enabling objectives are identified, for example, 'Construct a current physical DFD'. Then, to achieve this enabling objective, a lower-level enabling objective is required, such as 'Discriminates DFD symbols and notation'. Recall that the general form of an objective is 'By the end of the course the student will be able to X'. For ease of use, only the 'X' is usually specified for the enabling objective; the remainder is understood.

Specifying the enabling objectives has a number of purposes. By clarifying and detailing exactly what the student should be able to do, it:

Figure 8.2 Initial design steps

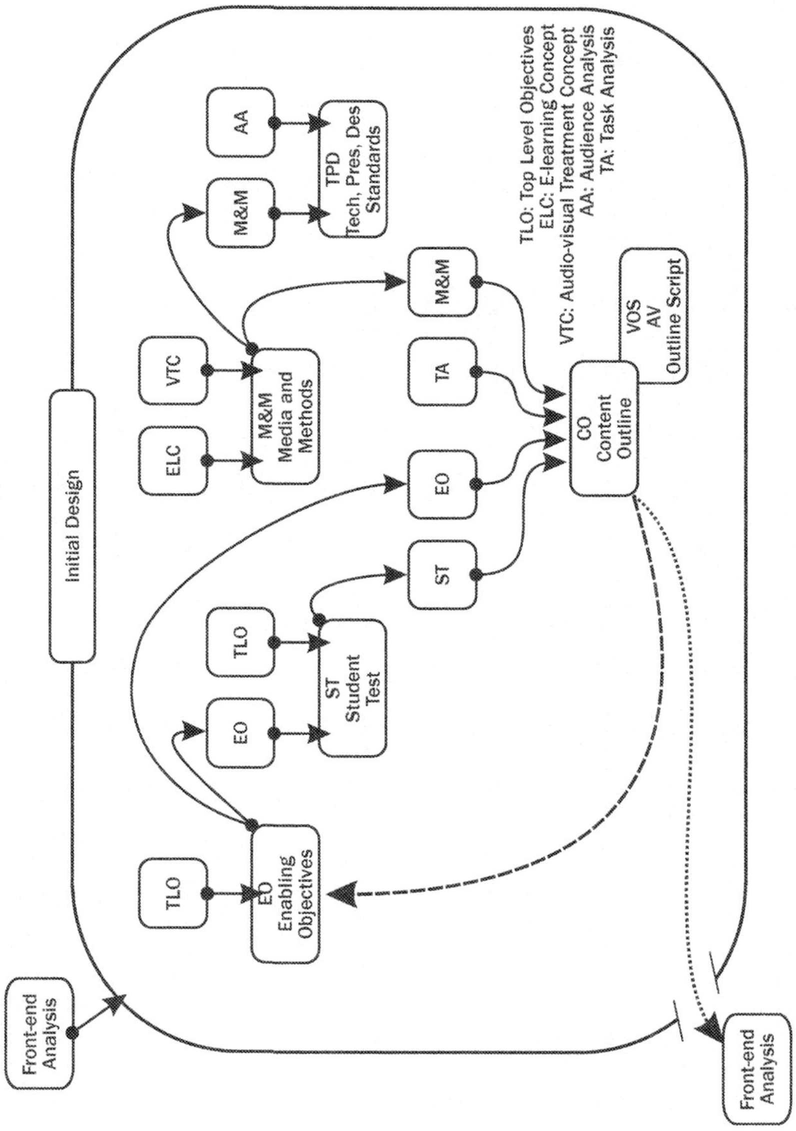

Figure 8.3 Enabling objectives hierarchy example

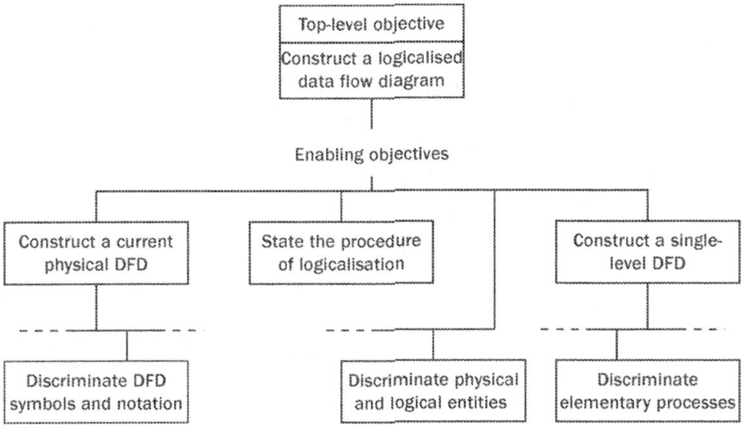

- provides a template against which the subject matter content is matched, ensuring that the e-learning contains all the subject matter that is needed by the student;
- explicitly identifies the prerequisite objectives, which are those enabling objectives that the e-learning does not attempt to teach;
- drives the design and content of the student assessment specified in the student test step;
- drives the selection of the e-learning methods and media step;
- drives the structure and content of the lessons to be developed in the detailed design stage.

An enabling objectives hierarchy is schematically illustrated in Figure 8.4.

Prerequisite objectives

As mentioned earlier, some of the enabling objectives may be identified as prerequisites, skills or abilities that the

Figure 8.4 Characteristics of an objectives hierarchy

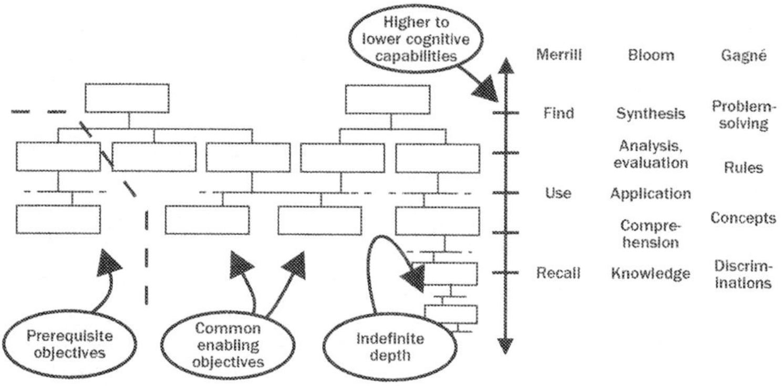

e-learning does not teach, and which it is expected that the target audience will possess when studying this particular material. For example, if the aims were to teach skills in the reading and understanding of company accounts, it may be taken as prerequisite that the student possesses an understanding of double-entry bookkeeping.

Common enabling objectives

As the set of enabling objectives is explored for each top-level objective, it is very likely that some of these enabling objectives will be common to a variety of top-level objectives. For example, if the aims were to teach skills in the understanding of a company balance sheet and profit-and-loss account, a number of common enabling objectives would involve skills in the presentation and standard description of company financial information.

Indefinite depth

The question 'What skills are needed to support skill X?' is capable of virtually infinite refinement; almost any skill is composed of further, lesser skills. The issue of where to stop in the development of enabling objectives rests on two considerations.

The most important consideration is the nature and purpose of documenting the enabling objectives in the first place. If the e-learning project is being developed by a small team who work together in a content area with which they are all familiar, if not expert, then an extensive set of enabling objectives would not be expected. On the other hand, if the project is structured such that several e-learning designers are teamed with a number of subject matter experts for just this (large) project, with the resulting design to be produced by an external company, then a very comprehensive set of enabling objectives would be required. The issue here is to ensure that the development team and their customer have a clear understanding of what is required from the project. Once this understanding is achieved, further documentation is a matter for risk management rather than technical design management, as insurance against changes to the development team, the customer's requirements and so on.

The second consideration is by reference to the audience analysis. For example, consider some e-learning which aims to provide an understanding of a company profit-and-loss account. If the target audience was the middle managers of the company, rather less in the way of enabling objectives would be required than if the target audience was, say, staff from the factory floor who were being considered for promotion into their first supervisory positions.

Higher to lower cognitive abilities

As the enabling objectives are developed and the question 'What skills are needed to support skill X?' is asked repeatedly, it turns out that the enabling objectives hierarchy becomes arranged in a rough taxonomy of 'higher' skills at the top and 'lower' skills at the bottom.

For Bloom (1956), 'higher' cognitive skills include evaluation, synthesis, analysis and application, while 'lower' skills include knowledge and comprehension. For Gagné (Gagné et al. 2004) the highest skill is problem-solving and the lowest discriminations. For Merrill (1994) there are three levels of skill: the highest is the ability to 'find' new knowledge, in the middle is the ability to 'use' or apply existing knowledge and at the bottom is the ability merely to 'recall' knowledge. These different arrangements of cognitive skill are illustrated in Figure 8.4.

Student test

In this step of the initial design stage, attention is given to constructing a set of test items which, when successfully answered by the student, demonstrate mastery of the subject matter and achievement of all of the objectives of the e-learning. In some contexts the student test is a natural part of the training or educational experience, particularly where some form of certification is required. In other contexts a student test might be thought a rather peculiar or unnecessary component of the e-learning, but its construction fulfils a primary principle of ELSYE – that the intended outcomes of the e-learning can be shown to be achieved. There are two issues here.

The first concern is that the aims of some e-learning can be known to be achieved. This is a general issue of evaluation in the 'plan-implement-evaluate-improve' systems approach to e-learning systems development, and successful student achievement on the student test is a common indicator of quality and effectiveness.

Table 8.1 Types of student test item

Computer-scorable	Yes/no Multiple choice Arrange, order or rank items in a list Match items in one list with those in another Fill-in-the-blank or provide one word or number
Instructor-scorable	Free response (short answer) Free response (essay) Observation of performance

The second concern is that the mere transmission of information to the student is of little interest. ELSYE is based upon the presumption that, for e-learning to be deemed effective, it must bring about a change in the student's behaviour. The student test is the observable and objective means of demonstrating that the student has indeed learned new behaviour.

Ideally, every objective (top-level and enabling) will have or can be matched with a student test item which, when passed by the student, indicates successful achievement of that objective. Table 8.1 provides a list of the various types of test item, and identifies those that can be easily administered and scored by computer.

MCQ testing

Multiple-choice question (MCQ) tests are the most popular method of computer-scorable assessment. If MCQ, or indeed any form of computer-scorable assessment, is a new method to either the developer, teacher or student, there are some guidelines which may help, outlined in Table 8.2.

Table 8.2 **Guidelines for the introduction of MCQ assessment**

Stage	Guideline
Preparation	Prepare, distribute and run mock assessments Provide coaching to students on how to answer MCQ tests
Review	Conduct wide inspections and reviews of MCQ items
Pilot	Restrict first use of new MCQ items to pilot tests

Table 8.3 **Effort required for MCQ assessment**

Effort distribution	Effort is front-loaded, put into setting of the assessment, not the marking Exact reverse of essay-type assessments Effort for MCQ tests is largely independent of class size
Total effort	Total effort is similar for MCQ and essay-type assessments in their first application, depending upon class size and number of items required Subsequent-use MCQs take up much less effort MCQ tests unlikely to be cost-effective for small classes

MCQ tests require a different distribution of effort in their development, delivery and marking from essay-type assessments. Table 8.3 summarises these differences, and Figure 8.5 illustrates the trade-off of effort against class size.

Constructing the MCQ assessment

Domain sampling

Each question item is modest in itself. Many items will be needed, so the domain of the assessment must be clearly

Figure 8.5 MCQ versus essay test effort against class size

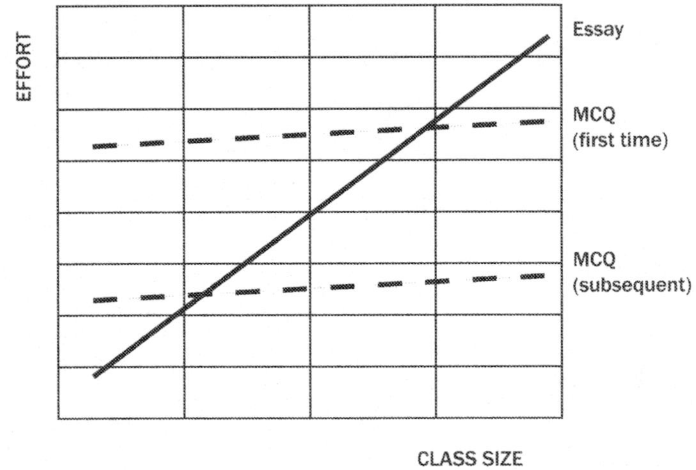

identified and then systematically sampled. The domain to be sampled might at first be thought to be subject matter content, but in fact it is the top-level and enabling objectives which are sampled. Of course, for well-designed e-learning every objective has corresponding content, and every item of content is in service of a corresponding objective, so the distinction is not

Table 8.4 Guidelines on MCQ item construction

Stem	Text (diagrams, etc.) specifies some facts, a theory, a scenario, possible events or outcomes, etc.; the stem may be quite lengthy, so that a number of questions can be asked about it
Correct answer	Keep free of extraneous clues
Distractors	Keep free of extraneous clues Incorrect options should be phrased so they are as attractive as the right answer to someone without the required understanding, but are not so esoteric as to confuse someone who has the required understanding As many as possible; three at the least, four preferable

important in practice. Usually, it is the cognitive domain which is most heavily sampled, but there may also be psychomotor items and items to do with affect (values and feelings).

Item structure

An MCQ test item consists of a stem, a correct answer and distractors. Table 8.4 provides some guidelines on MCQ item construction.

Evaluating item and test quality

Difficulty level

The difficulty level of an item is simply the proportion of students taking the test who answered the item correctly. Items with a range of difficulty levels are needed in an MCQ test. While most items (perhaps 70 per cent) should show difficulties between 0.4 and 0.6, the rest should show difficulties as low as 0.85 and as high as 0.15. This is to enhance discrimination between students in the upper and lower quartiles. A 'good' item is not judged on its difficulty alone.

Distractor attractiveness

Each of the distractors should be roughly equally attractive, and a histogram or count of the number of students choosing each distractor should show a uniform distribution. For example, it would be a poor MCQ item if it had a distractor which failed to be the choice of any student.

Item-test correlation

The most important measure of a 'good' item is its correlation with the student's overall mark. That is, a student who did well on the assessment as a whole should tend to get the item right, and a student who did poorly overall should tend to get the item wrong. The correlation is usually measured using the point-biserial coefficient r (identical to the Pearson product-moment r when one of the variables is dichotomous). An analogue of the item-test correlation can also be measured by the inter-quartile range, or a *t*-test, between the mean mark of those who pass and those who fail the item.

Test psychometrics

There are established criteria for evaluating the quality of a test of knowledge, traits, skills or competencies, the most important being test reliability and test validity. These are summarised in Table 8.5.

Table 8.5 Psychometric evaluation of tests

Psychometric consideration	Characteristic	Measure	Ideal value
Reliability	Internal consistency	Correlation between items	0.8
	Alternative forms	Correlation between alternates	0.75
	Test-retest	Correlation between instances	0.7
	Inter-rater	Correlation between scorers	1.0
Validity	Content	Inspection of declared aims and actual content	n/a
	Predictive	Correlation with outcome	0.7
	Construct	Correlation with other measures of the same skill or competence	0.6

Figure 8.6 KR-20 formula for internal consistency

$$\text{KR-20} = \frac{k}{k-1}\left(1 - \frac{\Sigma pq}{s^2}\right)$$

k = number of items making up the assessment

s = standard deviation of overall assessment raw scores

p = proportion of students answering an item correctly

q = 1 – p

Test reliability takes a number of forms. One of the most useful, and one of the easiest to measure, is the internal consistency of the test items. A popular formula for calculating internal consistency is known as Kuder-Richardson formula 20, shown in Figure 8.6. One of the strengths of computer-scorable tests is that their inter-rater reliability measure is 1.0, i.e. perfect.

Test validity takes three forms, known as content or face validity, predictive validity and construct validity. Establishing the specific validity of a student test is rarely undertaken, perhaps because the test is not usually stable over time, and the cost of demonstrating or achieving adequate validity could well be equal to the cost of the entire e-learning unit or programme of which it is a part. Nevertheless, where the indicators for technology-based learning and teaching are positive (discussed as part of the e-learning concept in Chapter 6 on front-end analysis: there are large student numbers, statutory licensing is involved, an assured quality or consistency of achievement is required, subject matter content or procedures involve hazard, etc.), some effort at establishing student test validity is indicated as well.

Factors affecting test psychometric statistics

In general, the more items, the higher the test reliability. Almost any test can be improved by increasing its length (i.e. the number of questions).

For 'power' assessments, ample time must be allowed for a student to complete every item. Interpretations of usual statistical quality indicators are valid. For 'speed' assessments, many trivially easy items are required, and the student score is based upon the quantity of items attempted. Interpretations of the 'usual' psychometric quality indicators are not valid for 'speed' tests.

Test re-marking

Another strength of computer-scorable tests is the facility to remove poor items from the test and re-mark it. The psychometric indicators mentioned earlier allow poor items to be identified, and the overall test internal consistency can be recomputed following their removal. The process is to remove the item with the lowest point-biserial, and re-mark the whole test, observing the increase in value of the KR-20 statistic. The process can be iterated prudently.

Guessing

Some developers are wary of computer-scorable assessments because of the perceived ease of guessing the right answers. The argument is that completely ignorant students can score 25 per cent (four distractors) or 20 per cent (five distractors) by chance.

A correction formula may be applied to allow for guessing or random responses. The formula is to subtract W / (Opt – 1) from the number of correct answers obtained by the student, where W is the number of wrong answers obtained by the student and Opt is the number of options or distractors per question.

But if a 'correction formula' is applied, i.e. students are penalised for incorrect answers, undesirable psychological factors are introduced into the assessment, since some students are more willing to take risks than others. 'Shyer' or risk-averse students who may well know the answer, or may have a good chance of selecting the right answer, may be put off.

There is in fact no need to penalise students for guessing, and no need to apply a correction, if students are simply instructed to attempt every question. The argument that monkeys, i.e. ignorant students, get 25 per cent on a MCQ test is a simplification which does not stand up to close scrutiny. One could as well argue that monkeys can write the works of Shakespeare. Students can get 25 per cent in an essay without understanding very much and dressing up what they do understand in attractive prose. We may imagine that students bring some desirable intelligence and knowledge to their answers in an MCQ test, even when unsure of the correct answer. The marks distribution will probably be adjusted later anyway, using a statistical technique such as scaling.

Scaling

There is no such thing as a student's 'real' mark. Essays, for example, may be marked leniently or strictly. An MCQ assessment could have predominantly easy or difficult items. A student's mark is relative to both other students, in this class or previous classes (norm-referenced), and some standard of achievement or performance specified by the course objectives (criterion-referenced).

Figure 8.7 Scaling formula

$M' = x + (M * z)$

M' = new mark

M = original mark

x = origin shift

z = dispersion adjustment

Scaling – that is, adjusting the marks distribution – is simply done by applying a formula to every score, as shown in Figure 8.7. The choice of the parameters 'x' and 'z' usually needs some justification.

Item banks

The cost-effectiveness of MCQ assessments is only secured by the construction and maintenance of item banks. This follows from the fact that the first deployment of an MCQ test is usually costly, and may well be more costly than a conventional essay-type assessment. Subsequently, a required assessment is constructed by sampling most of the desired items from the item bank.

Every assessment must also have a proportion of new items. The 'good' new items are placed into the bank, the 'bad' ones discarded or rewritten and piloted later.

An item bank must be periodically and systematically reviewed and maintained. Out-of-date items and ones with lower point-biserials are discarded. Every time a bank item is used, its performance in a particular assessment must be recorded (the item's difficulty level, its distractor histogram and its point-biserial) and a link established to the test in which it was used.

Separately, the characteristics of each test must be recorded: at the least, the number of students, the number of items used in the assessment, any correction for guessing, whether students were instructed to attempt every item and the assessment's KR-20.

Example MCQ items

Table 8.6 illustrates a selection of MCQ templates or fragments (sampled from Bloom and Hastings, 1971) designed to address one or other objective drawn from Bloom's cognitive domain. These are illustrated simply to provide ideas for developers who might otherwise wonder how MCQs can assess higher cognitive skills.

Formative and summative assessment

The test items identified may be used in one of two distinct ways. On the one hand, the student test items could be used to support the student during learning, and in this case one or more test items would be assembled into a formative assessment. On the other hand, the items could be used to check that the student has indeed achieved the e-learning objectives prior to being credited with the lesson, unit or programme concerned. In this case, one or more test items would be assembled into a summative assessment.

Another way of looking at the distinction between formative and summative assessment is to ask whether feedback to the student on their performance in the assessment is vital to their learning of the topics in question. An assessment may be deemed summative if feedback from that assessment is either never returned to the student, is delayed for such a period of time as to be of little use when it is eventually returned or is returned in such a reduced form that it cannot in fact directly assist in the learning and teaching process. An assessment may be considered

Table 8.6 **Example MCQ templates for Bloom's cognitive domain**

Domain	Scenario or case	Distractors	Possible questions
Comprehension	Show a diagram, picture, scenario, vignette or statements. For each of the following questions, use the above information to make a decision and indicate your answer using a single letter as follows:	A True B Probably true C Insufficient information D Probably false E False	Q1 The [X] shows [Y] Q2 There are N [F]s Q3 Most of the [Z]s are [W]s
Application	The following are some basic procedures for [X]ing:	A Procedure [1] B Procedure [2] C Procedure [3] D Procedure [4] E Procedure [5]	For each of the following questions or statements, indicate (by using a single letter) the procedure involved or the most useful procedure to involve. Q1 An [X] which includes a [Y] Q2 The [X] uses the tool [Z] Q3 Situation [W] applies while [X]ing Q4 The goal of the [X] is [G]
Analysis	Text, diagram etc. illustrates a situation or phenomenon [X]. For each question, indicate how the statement of the question illustrates:	A The fundamental purpose of [X] B Achievements incidental to the fundamental purpose of [X] C Evidence of how [X] is regarded by [Y] D Evidence of the involvement of [Z] in [X] E None of the above	Q1 [M] assured [N] Q2 [X] became associated with [U] Q3 [P] did much to improve [R] Q4 [T] was organised around [F] Q5 [J] demonstrated [K]

Table 8.6 Example MCQ templates for Bloom's cognitive domain (*Cont'd*)

Domain	Scenario or case	Distractors	Possible questions
Synthesis	The facts [X], [Y], [Z] etc. have been found to be the case. Some procedures to follow include:	A Procedure [R] B Action [S] C Procedure [T] D Action [U] E Procedure [V]	For each question, indicate the appropriate procedure or action: Q1 [G] is required Q2 Because of [H], [J] is to be avoided Q3 [K] is required as well as a good [L]
Evaluation	Text, diagram, etc. outlines a situation or scenario [X]. Views on [X] could be:	A It is thoroughly improper B Proper as regards [Q] but not as regards [W] C Proper as regards [W] but not as regards [Q] D It is thoroughly proper E None of these views clearly applies	In discussing [X], various speakers made the following statements. For each statement, indicate the view that the speaker is likely to hold. Q1 Hobbs said [V] Q2 Plato noted [H] Q3 Mill was right to say [G]

formative if feedback to the student on their performance is such as to assist their studies materially.

Of course, a particular assessment might well combine elements of both formative and summative assessment. In this case, the e-learning designer needs to take particular care during the detailed design stage to construct properly the feedback required for those aspects of the assessment which are considered to be formative.

Diagnostic or routing assessment

There is a third way in which test items might be developed and used in e-learning, and that is for the diagnosis of achievement of prerequisite objectives and the routing of the student to appropriate lessons or units of study. Such test items would have more of the character of summative rather than formative assessment.

Media and methods

The learning and teaching media and methods were considered earlier in the front-end analysis stage (Chapter 6). At that stage, the step of e-learning concept and AV treatment provided a broad conception of the media and methods appropriate to the top-level objectives that were then identified. In the initial design stage, given the decomposition of the top-level objectives into a larger number of enabling objectives, attention is paid to identifying the appropriate media and methods for each enabling objective. For most enabling objectives the media and methods will be the same as those specified in the e-learning concept, but for some different media and methods may now be deemed appropriate. These differences are noted in this step. In particular, if audio or video is to be recorded, a start is made on identifying where such specialist media are required.

Content outline

The real work of the initial design stage now begins. From the front-end analysis there is a broad understanding of the subject matter, specified in the task analysis. From the initial design stage there is a more detailed understanding of the objectives and intended learning outcomes, specified in the enabling objectives; provision for measuring whether the student has achieved the intended outcomes, specified by the student test items; and identification of the learning and teaching media and methods appropriate to each objective, specified in the media and methods.

The content outline step integrates these components into a single document, where the subject matter is developed, itemised in more detail and matched with the relevant enabling objectives. The format of the content outline is illustrated in Table 8.7. The content outline is then developed in the detailed design stage (Chapter 9) using Merrill's component display theory (Merrill, 1994).

The important point of the content outline is that it takes each enabling objective in turn and identifies the subject matter required to achieve that objective. Equally, it ensures that each item of subject matter supports the achievement of a specified enabling objective.

It is entirely possible that the e-learning designer has identified an enabling objective for which there is no corresponding subject matter as outlined in the task analysis. This circumstance provides the opportunity for the designer

Table 8.7 **Content outline format and example entries**

Enabling objective	Subject matter	Method	Media	Student test item
...	...	...	...	...
Identify DFD symbols	Symbols for data stores, data flows, document flows, external entities, processes and elementary processes	Self-study	CBT and handouts	Questions 6 to 11 in Test A
...	...	...	...	...

and the customer to consider whether the enabling objective is really needed, or whether the task analysis was inadequate.

Similarly, it is entirely possible that the customer has identified subject matter for which there are no corresponding e-learning objectives. This is a surprisingly common occurrence, particularly in education rather than in training, when it can be thought desirable that the student should know some item of content without being clear as to why that content should be learned. This circumstance provides the opportunity for the designer and the customer to consider whether the subject matter really needs to be taught, or whether the identification of the e-learning objectives was inadequate.

Having clarified the connections between the subject matter and the enabling objectives, the content outline is then expanded by assigning each item from the student test to one or other pairing of subject matter and enabling objective. Again, it is entirely possible that gaps appear. For example, there may significant areas of content that are not tested; far worse, there may be test items for which no content and no objectives have been identified.

Audio-visual outline script

Where the content outline identifies audio or video recordings, a separate script is now developed which documents the required audio or video sequences. The audio or video requirements will be extensively developed during detailed design, and so the AV outline script simply needs to list each specific sequence or clip, estimate its duration and describe its content in outline. If audio or video is required, its cost usually dominates the project, and its cost is usually a direct function of its duration. Firm estimates of duration are therefore particularly important for cross-reference against the project plan.

Technical, presentation and design standards

The final step of the initial design stage is to create the technical standards for the project stages to come: detailed design and production.

These technical standards provide instructions and guidance for the project designers, programmers and graphic artists in a wide variety of areas relevant to the look, feel, operation and architecture of the e-learning materials. If audio or video is required, attention is given to specifying the required formats and quality levels.

Note that the standards do not in general define or decide whether a design component is to be present in the e-learning. This is a design issue. Rather, standards generally define the look, feel and functionality of the component if it is included in the design. For example, there may be standards for keeping student records secure, but the design might not call for the collection of such data.

Learner options

The learner options specify the facilities available to the student as they browse or use the materials. During the initial design stage, the designer must specify where, how and whether the learner can, for example:

- go back to a previous screen or display;
- review topic so far but without interactions;
- skip ahead without interactions;

- bookmark their current place;
- change or retry a previous response;
- quit to topic or section menu;
- quit to course or main menu;
- quit the entire course;
- access any hint, help or glossary lists;
- obtain extra examples, practice or exercise;
- obtain more details;
- print the screen or particular graphics or text;
- copy and paste the screen or particular graphics or text;
- be granted other facilities, such as access to the operating system or other software.

Definitions

A particular customer may have terms or names for elements of the e-learning materials and course that are different from normal. These must be documented and specified. For example:

- What exactly is a course, module, unit, topic or section?
- What is a menu, main menu or sub-menu?
- What is a display, screen, frame, window or page?
- What are sequences, entry points, exit points, branches and inter- and intra-sequence branches?
- What are the formats and layouts for displays, screens, frames, windows?
- What are keywords?
- Form and structure of file names?

Displays

Standards need to be set for the presentation and display of information.

- Accessibility and disability discrimination.
- Screen and page display template(s).
- Standard components such as introduction, contents, conclusion.
- Margins, window sizes, positions of structural, text and graphic elements.
- Text fonts and styles for headings, body text, page numbers and special names.
- Capitalisation, abbreviation, punctuation.
- Colours for emphasis, colours for themes.
- Conventions for standard location of screen and page elements.

Graphics

Standards are required for the graphic elements of the materials.

- Graphic content and style – icons, symbols, representations.
- Animations.

Video

Standards are required for any video clips or sequences.

- Resolution or screen size.
- Lengths of lead-ins and lead-outs.

- Freeze-frame capabilities.
- AVI/MOV etc.
- NTSC/PAL/SECAM.

Sound and audio

Standards are required for the sound elements, if any, of the materials.

- Sounds associated with actions or keystrokes.
- Sounds drawing the student's attention to an error or completed event.
- Background music.
- Voice-overs.

Special keys

Standards are required for how the student uses the keyboard and how the editing and cursor movement keys operate.

- Function keys.
- ESC, Enter, Tab, space bar.

Student feedback

Standards are required for the way in which information is to be given to the student and the way the system responds to input.

- Acknowledgement.
- Confirmation.
- Prompt, hint.

- Judgement or reinforcement.
- Correction.
- Explanation.
- Consequence.
- Referral.
- Use of student's name.
- Retries.
- Handling unanticipated answers.

Management of e-learning

Standards are required for the way in which the lessons, units and programmes are to be managed. These standards centre on routing issues and evaluation issues.

- Presenting lesson, unit and programme route options.
- Tracking student progress through lessons, units and programmes.
- Keeping records of progress and marks.
- Security of student records, personal information and marks.
- Evaluation forms or questionnaires.
- Evaluation analyses.
- Security and handling of evaluation data.

9

Detailed design: e-learning transactions

The stage of detailed design is located within the design phase of the ELSYE life cycle, as illustrated in Figure 9.1, and its steps are illustrated in Figure 9.2. During the detailed design, the content outline from the initial design stage is refined into a set of e-learning transactions and then developed into lesson plans. Along with the course management components identified in the course management design step, the lesson plans are prototyped in the prototype step and the outcomes fed back within the stage, and to earlier stages and phases if necessary. Attention is also paid to designing the materials so they can be effectively evaluated in the evaluability design step.

CDT primary presentation forms

The content outline from the initial design stage provides a statement of what is to be taught, derived from the task analysis and the e-learning objectives. The question that now arises is how the required subject matter is to be taught.

One approach to systematically developing e-learning transactions is that of Merrill's component display theory, or CDT (Merrill, 1994). The following discussion presents a simplified version of CDT. Merrill (1999) later updated CDT

Figure 9.1 Detailed design in the ELSYE life cycle

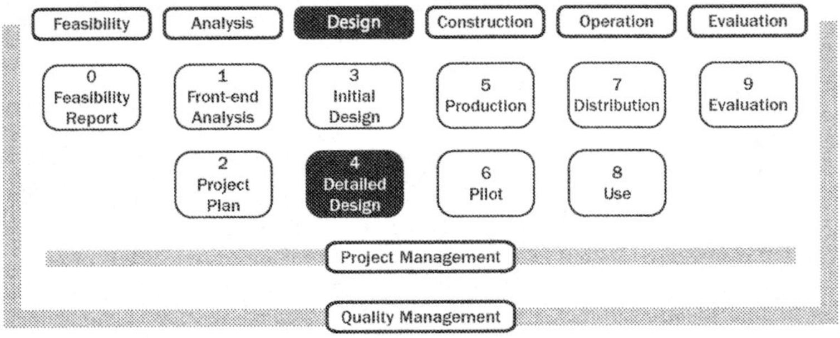

to a new formulation called instructional transaction theory (ITT), but this chapter uses the original CDT for two reasons. First, CDT retains a coherence among its components which is less clear in ITT. Second, the simplifications to CDT in this chapter serve to bring it closer to the newer ITT anyway.

For each item of subject matter, CDT suggests a teaching strategy appropriate to that subject matter and its e-learning objective. CDT considers that any item of subject matter or course content falls into one of four categories – fact, concept, procedure or principle. CDT also considers that any e-learning objective can be classified into one of three types – know, use or find – and that there are two fundamental teaching acts – tell and ask. Finally, CDT considers that an item of subject matter can be either a generality or something specific. From these considerations, CDT first identifies 23 teaching acts, and then derives prescriptions for appropriate combinations of teaching acts to yield an e-learning transaction.

Subject matter in CDT

CDT considers that any item of subject matter falls into one of four categories: fact, concept, procedure or principle.

Figure 9.2 Detailed design steps

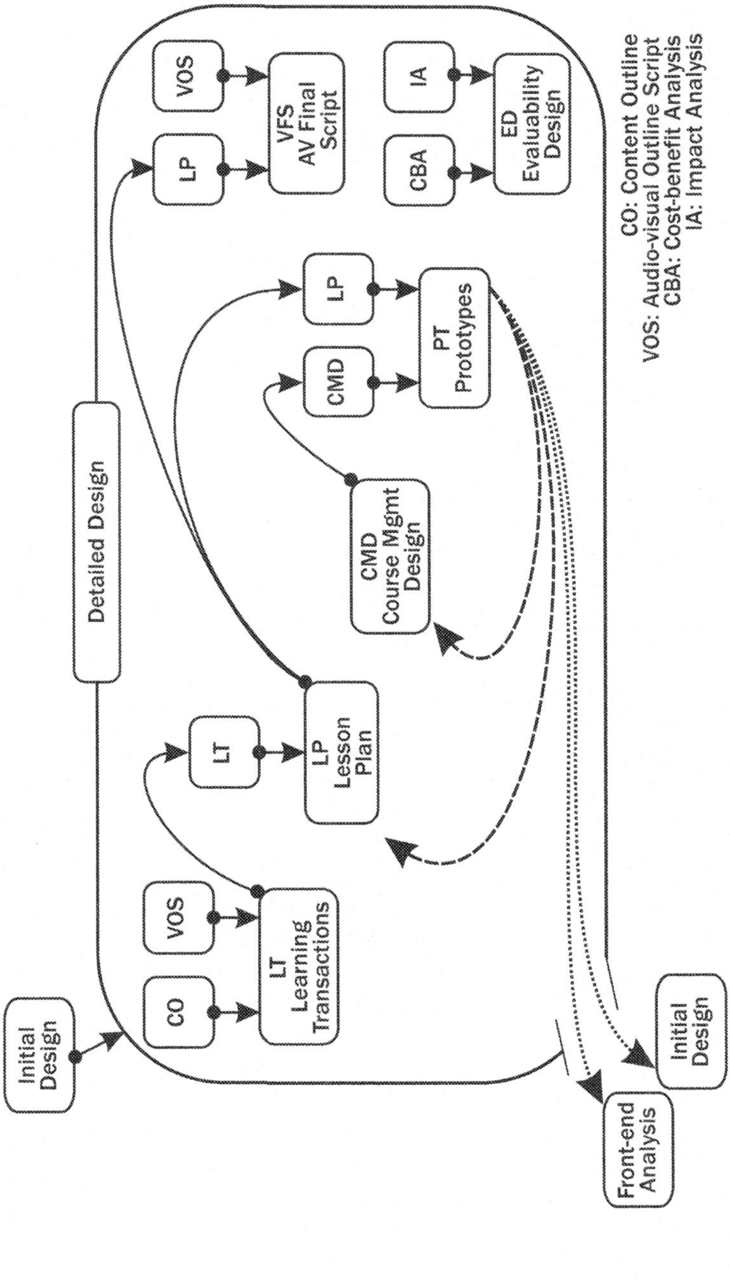

Each of these categories has a specific technical definition, summarised in Table 9.1.

- A *fact* consists of two specifics, 'A' and 'B', and is called a 'fact pair' in CDT. For example, there is the fact that the Battle of Hastings was fought in 1066. 'The Battle of Hastings' is A, and '1066' is B. The key feature of a fact is that it simply consists of two specifics.
- A *concept* involves the name of the concept, 'X', a superordinate class 'Y' of which X is a member, and a list of attribute-value pairs 'A' and 'V' which serve to classify various objects 'O' according to the concept in question. For example, there is the concept of a predator as an animal that hunts and eats other animals. The concept, and its name X, is 'predator'. The superordinate class to which a predator belongs is 'animal', Y. One of the attribute-value pairs of a predator is that its 'feeding behaviour', A1, is 'hunting', V1. Another attribute-value

Table 9.1 Definition of CDT categories of subject matter

Fact	Fact pair	A + B
Concept	Concept definition	Name of concept, X Superordinate concept class, Y Attribute An – value Vn pairs That classify objects, O An X is a Y which has V1 on A1, V2 on A2, ...
Procedure	Activity definition	Name of procedure, X Used in situation S To achieve a goal G Via a set of steps E Using tools T To X when S to achieve G, E using T
Principle	Proposition definition	Name of principle, X Applied in situation S Involves cause-effect relationships CERn Between objects or events E The CERs observed between E in S is called X

pair is that its 'food', A2, is 'other animals', V2. The concept serves to classify or sort objects O such as birds, apes or dinosaurs. The key feature of a concept is that a number of attributes are used to classify or categorise things according to their values on those attributes. 'Is a' is the key phrase that distinguishes a concept from a fact.

- A *procedure* has a name, 'X', and is used in a situation 'S' to achieve a goal 'G' via a set of steps 'E', possibly using some specified tools 'T'. For example, market research on the street to get information involves dressing in business clothes and then approaching strangers and asking them to complete a survey. The procedure, and its name X, 'market research', is used in situation S 'on the street' to achieve the goal G of 'getting information'. The steps E involve 'dressing in business clothes', 'approaching strangers' and 'asking them to complete a survey'. The 'survey' is the tool T. The key feature of a procedure is that it involves a series of steps or actions.
- A *principle* has a name, 'X', is applied in a situation 'S' and involves the specification of cause-effect relationships 'CERs' between objects or events 'E'. For example, the principle of gravity applies to two or more bodies in a region of space such that they mutually attract each other in relation to their mass and to the inverse of the square of the distance between them. The principle, and its name X, is that of 'gravity', applicable in the situation S 'when two or more bodies occupy a region of space', so that there is a CER-1 between 'mass of body' and 'mutual attraction' of 'directly related', and another CER-2 between 'distance between bodies' and 'mutual attraction' of 'inversely related to its square', where the events and objects E are 'bodies' and 'attraction'. The key feature of a principle is that it involves cause-effect relationships that can usually be expressed as some sort of an equation.

Some analyses of subject matter suggest that, in addition to the above four categories, there is a fifth, called 'process' (Clark and Kwinn, 2007). Because a process, at heart, comprises a series of steps, CDT tends to include it within the category of procedure. There are some processes, however, which are better treated as concepts or principles, because their steps cannot be carried out by people. Examples are typically scientific and include processes such as evolution and continental drift.

CDT also distinguishes between subject matter that contains specific instances and subject matter that contains generalisations or general statements. The point of this distinction will become apparent in the next section.

Presentation mode

An individual act of teaching may be done in one of two modes – expository or inquisitory. The student is either told the subject matter or asked to do something with the subject matter. CDT calls these two approaches the 'presentation mode'.

When the two modes of presenting the subject matter are combined with the two kinds of subject matter (either specific instances or general statements), four different 'primary presentation forms' or PPFs result, as shown in Figure 9.3.

CDT labels subject matter generality as 'G', and subject matter specific instances as 'eg'. The expository presentation mode is labelled 'E', and the inquisitory presentation mode is labelled 'I'. The resulting four PPFs are thus 'EG', 'IG', 'Eeg' and 'Ieg'.

The EG PPF involves telling the student a generality, usually by providing the definition of a concept, procedure or principle. The Eeg PPF involves showing the student a specific instance, usually by providing an example of the concept or a demonstration of the procedure or principle in action. The

Figure 9.3 Primary presentation forms

Primary presentation form (PPF)		Presentation mode	
		Expository (Tell)	Inquisitory (Ask)
Subject matter content	Generality	EG (Tell the definition)	IG (Ask for the definition)
	Instance	Eeg (Show an example)	Ieg (Ask for an example)

Ieg PPF involves asking the student something specific, usually asking them to name a concept, rehearse a procedure or explain the principle in action. The IG PPF involves asking the student something general, usually asking them to recall the definition of a concept, procedure or principle.

These PPF labels and names of EG, IG, Eeg and Ieg need not be considered further. The ideas that they label, however, are important, and these are used in the next few sections to yield very useful ways of designing e-learning transactions.

Types of e-learning objective

Merrill takes a simple approach to e-learning objectives and cognitive abilities. These are classified as 'recall/remember', 'use' or 'find'. The objective taxonomies of Bloom and Gagné are illustrated in Table 9.2 for comparison.

- The ability to *remember* something is the lowest objective and the lowest cognitive skill.
- The ability to *use* something is expected to comprise the majority of the objectives and cognitive skills in any unit of e-learning.

Table 9.2 CDT types of objective or cognitive skill

Merrill	Bloom	Gagné
Find	Synthesis	Problem-solving
Use	Analysis Evaluation Application Comprehension	Rules Concepts
Recall	Knowledge	Discriminations

- The ability to *find* is to find something new, and is a shorthand way of saying 'invent' or 'create'. Explicitly attempting to teach inventive or creative skills is notoriously difficult, and it would be expected that such objectives would be unusual in most e-learning.

CDT teaching acts

The combination of four kinds of subject content, three types of cognitive ability and four primary presentation forms yields the 23 CDT teaching acts, summarised in Table 9.3. There are not 48 acts, as might be thought (4 × 3 × 4), because some of the combinations do not make sense.

In developing these teaching acts, CDT distinguishes between working with new material with students and working with old material. The following sections expand on each of the 23 CDT teaching acts.

CDT teaching acts for facts

There are two CDT teaching acts for facts, 'fact pair' and 'fact name', both at the level of the 'remember' cognitive skill, as shown in Table 9.4. There are no teaching acts for

Table 9.3 **Summary of 23 CDT teaching acts**

		Primary presentation form			
Subject content	**Cognitive ability**	**Tell definition**	**Show example**	**Ask for instance**	**Ask for definition**
Fact	Remember		Fact pair	Fact name	
Concept	Remember Use Find	Concept definition	Example	Name Classify Explore categories	State definition Invent definition
Procedure	Remember Use Find	Activity definition	Demons-tration	Rehearse Demons-trate Explore procedures	State steps Devise procedure
Principle	Remember Use Find	Proposition definition	Explana-tion	Explain Predict Explore problems	State cause-effect relation-ships Discover principle

Table 9.4 **Teaching acts for facts**

Presentation form		**Teaching act**	**Description**
Show example	Tell	Fact pair	Present the fact, A + B
Ask for example	Ask remember previous	Fact name	Ask for B, given A Ask for A, given B

the 'use' of facts or for 'finding' facts, since facts cannot be 'used' or 'found' in isolation. There are also no teaching acts for generality presentation forms, since facts are always specific instances in presentation form.

The expository teaching act for facts is 'fact pair'.

- In *fact pair*, the student is simply told or presented with the fact, 'A + B'. For example, 'The Battle of Hastings was in 1066.'

The inquisitory teaching act for facts is 'fact name'.

- In *fact name*, the student is asked to recall or name the fact, either by being prompted with the 'A' part or by being prompted with the 'B' part. For example, 'When was the Battle of Hastings?' or 'What battle took place in 1066?'

CDT teaching acts for concepts

There are seven CDT teaching acts for concepts, as shown in Table 9.5.

The expository teaching acts for concepts are 'concept definition' and 'example'.

- In *concept definition*, the student is told the definition of the concept in its full form: an X is a Y which classifies Os according to their V1 on A1, V2 on A2 and so on. For example, 'A predator is an animal whose feeding behaviour is hunting and whose food is other animals.'
- In *example*, the student is told of an example of the concept by being given or shown a specific O which illustrates the relevant values Vn on the various attributes An of the concept. For example, the student might be shown a video clip of an eagle hunting and eating a rabbit.

The inquisitory teaching acts for concepts are 'name', 'classify', 'state definition', 'explore categories' and 'invent'.

- In *name*, the student is asked to recall the objects O that were previously shown to satisfy the given concept X, or is asked to recall the concept X that was previously shown to apply to the given objects O. For example, the student might

Table 9.5 **Teaching acts for concepts**

Presentation form		Teaching act	Description
Tell definition	Tell	Concept definition	Present the concept name X, the superordinate concept class Y and the attribute-value pairs A1-V1, A2-V2, ... to be used in classifying objects O
Show example	Tell	Example	Show specific O which illustrates V1 on A1, V2 on A2, ...
Ask for example	Ask remember previous	Name	Ask for previous O, given X Ask for previous X, given O
Ask for example	Ask use new	Classify	Ask for new O, given X Ask for X, given new O
Ask for definition	Ask	State concept definition	Ask for definition of concept X
Ask for example	Ask find	Explore categories	Ask for new sorting or classification given new Os
Ask for definition	Ask find	Invent concept definition	Ask for new concept definition with new sorting or classification for various Os

be asked to recall the names of specific predators, or be asked to say what was common to eagles, lions and sharks.

- In *classify*, the student is asked to use the concept X to classify new objects O, or to identify the appropriate concept X to apply to new objects O. For example, the student might be shown a variety of insects and asked which of them were predators, or shown a beetle and asked what kind of animal it was. In these teaching scenarios the objects are new to the student, in the sense that they were not previously introduced or explicitly taught as instances of the concept. This requires the student to 'use' the concept on new material rather than 'remember' previously taught material.

- In *state definition*, the student is asked for the definition of the concept in its full form: an X is a Y which classifies Os according to their V1 on A1, V2 on A2 and so on. For example, the student might be asked to define 'predator', and would then be corrected or marked according to whether the superordinate and the attribute and value pairs were correctly given.
- In *explore categories*, the student is asked to develop a new way of sorting or classifying new objects. The task for the student is to develop new attribute-value pairs that would sort the new objects appropriately. For example, the student might be given a Venus fly-trap plant, and asked to develop new attribute-value pairs which would allow such a plant to be called a 'predator', or which would differentiate such a plant from existing 'predators'.
- In *invent*, the student is asked to invent a new concept and give a name to a new way of sorting or classifying objects. The task for the student is to invent and name a set of new attribute-value pairs that would sort objects appropriately. For example, the student might be asked to define and name a new concept that would recognise the predatory element of plants which eat insects and small animals.

CDT teaching acts for procedures

There are seven CDT teaching acts for procedures, as shown in Table 9.6. These methods closely parallel the teaching acts for concepts.

The expository teaching acts for procedures are 'activity definition' and 'demonstration'.

- In *activity definition*, the student is told the definition of the procedure in its full form: procedure X involves steps E in situation S to achieve goals G using tools T. For example,

Table 9.6 **Teaching acts for procedures**

Presentation form		Teaching act	Description
Tell definition	Tell	Activity definition	Present name of procedure X to be used in situation S to achieve a goal G and describe the steps E involved and the tools T used
Show example	Tell	Demonstration	Show execution of steps E using the tools T in situation S to achieve goal G
Ask for example	Ask remember previous	Rehearse	Ask for execution of steps E using T in situation S to achieve goal G where T, S and G have been previously shown
Ask for example	Ask use new	Demonstrate	Ask for execution of steps E where one or more of T, S and G is new
Ask for definition	Ask	State procedure steps	Ask for the definition of procedure X
Ask for example	Ask find	Explore procedures	Ask for new steps E or new tools T to achieve goal G in situation S
Ask for definition	Ask find	Devise procedure	Ask for new activity definition with new E or T for various S and G

'Conducting market research on the street involves dressing smartly, approaching strangers and asking them to complete a survey, in order to get information.'

- In *demonstration*, the student is shown the procedure being executed with specific tools T in the specific situation S to obtain specific goals G. For example, the student might watch the tutor role-play a market researcher approaching strangers to obtain a completed survey.

The inquisitory teaching acts for procedures are 'rehearse', 'demonstrate', 'state procedure steps', 'explore procedure' and 'devise procedure'.

- In *rehearse*, the student is asked to execute the procedure using previously provided tools in previously taught situations to achieve previously taught goals. For example, the student might role-play a market researcher approaching strangers to obtain a completed survey, if this had previously been role-played by the tutor.
- In *demonstrate*, the student is asked to carry out the procedure using new tools or in a new situation or to achieve a new goal. For example, the student might be asked to role-play researching inside a railway station rather than on the street, or while dressed in casual clothes rather than business clothes.
- In *state procedure steps*, the student is asked to state the procedure in its full form. For example, the student might be asked to state the procedure of 'market survey researching', and would then be corrected or marked according to whether the tools, goals, situation and steps were correctly given.
- In *explore procedure*, the student is asked to develop new steps to achieve specific goals in specific situations using specific tools. For example, the student might be asked to modify the researching procedure so as to obtain help rather than a completed survey.
- In *devise procedure*, the student is asked to devise a new procedure and give a name to a new set of steps to achieve goals G in situation S using tools T. The task for the student is to devise and name a procedure that would achieve relevant goals. For example, the student might be asked to devise and name a procedure for obtaining help from strangers in the street.

CDT teaching acts for principles

There are seven CDT teaching acts for principles, as shown in Table 9.7. These methods closely parallel the teaching acts for procedures and concepts.

The expository teaching acts for principles are 'proposition definition' and 'explanation'.

- In *proposition definition*, the student is told the definition of the principle in its full form: principle X applies in situation S to objects or events E involving cause-effect

Table 9.7 **Teaching acts for principles**

Presentation form		Teaching act	Description
Tell definition	Tell	Proposition definition	Present name of principle X that is applied in situation S which involves cause-effect relationships CERn between objects or events E
Show example	Tell	Explanation	Show the CERs between E in S
Ask for example	Ask remember previous	Explain	Ask for CERs that show how X applies to previous S between previous Es
Ask for example	Ask use new	Predict	Ask for CERs that will occur given new S and/ or Es
Ask for definition	Ask	State cause-effect relationships	Ask for definition of principle X
Ask for example	Ask find	Explore problems	Ask for new CERs (explanations) for different Es or S
Ask for definition	Ask find	Discover principle	Ask for new principle definition involving new CERs that apply in situations S between Es

relationships CERn. This definition may involve an equation. For example, 'Gravity applies to two or more bodies in a region of space such that they mutually attract each other in relation to their mass and to the inverse of the square of the distance between them.'

- In *explanation*, the student is told or shown how the CERs affect the Es in S; for example, the falling of an apple to the ground. The tutor may apply the relevant equation to a specific problem.

The inquisitory teaching acts for procedures are 'explain', 'predict', 'state cause-effect relationships', 'explore problems' and 'discover principle'.

- In *explain*, the student is asked to specify the CERs that are involved in S between the Es. For example, the student might be asked what happens when an apple comes loose from a tree. The S and Es have been previously taught.
- In *predict*, the student is asked to specify how the CERs are involved with a new S or new Es. For example, the student might be asked what happens when a comet approaches the earth. The student might be asked to calculate the gravitational attraction in this case using the formula previously given.
- In *state cause-effect relationships*, the student is asked to state the principle in its full form, and would then be corrected or marked according to whether the cause-effect relationships, situation and objects or events were correctly given. For example, the student might be asked to state the equation for gravitational attraction between two bodies in space.

- In *explore problems*, the student is asked to provide different CERs for different cases. For example, the student might be asked to state what would happen if a third body was added to the situation.
- In *discover principle*, the student is asked to discover a new principle and give a name to a new set of CERs that apply in situation S to objects or events E. The task for the student is to devise and name a principle (often, derive a new equation) that would apply. For example, the student might be asked to discover the equation that deals with the three-body problem.

The e-learning transaction

An e-learning transaction is considered to be the unit of e-learning in this discussion, where teacher and student engage in a Laurillardian conversation in pursuit of an understanding of the answer to a particular question of interest. The e-learning transaction is considered to consist of five key teaching acts, summarised as 'tell', 'show', 'ask', 'respond' and 'give feedback'. The structure of a general e-learning transaction is illustrated in Figure 9.4.

The question of interest (question A.x.y.z), the purpose of the e-learning transaction, is generally given by the enabling objectives for this part of the e-learning, as specified in the content outline from the initial design stage (Chapter 8). The subject matter of the transaction for this part of the e-learning is also as specified in the content outline, where it is matched or paired with its corresponding enabling objective(s). CDT provides a minimum set of e-learning transactions designed according to the type of subject matter and the kind of enabling objective involved.

Figure 9.4 Structure of an e-learning transaction

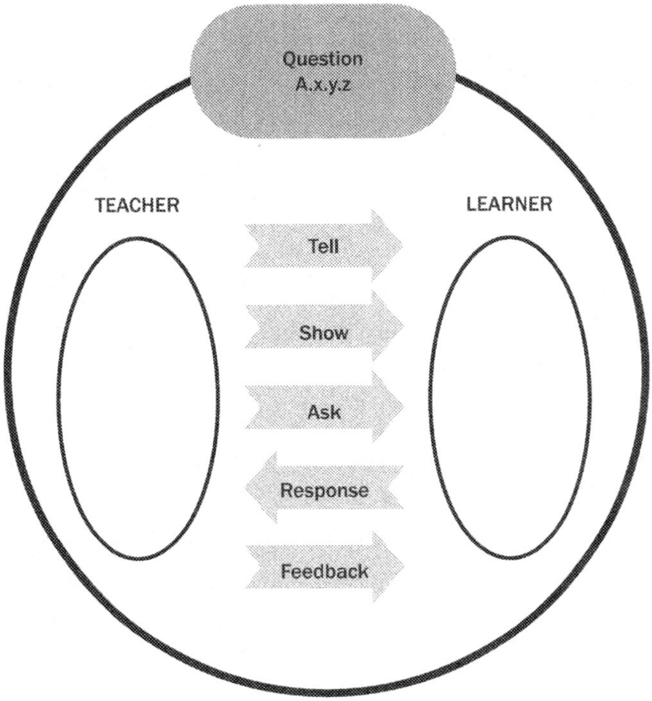

CDT e-learning transactions

Given a variety of different teaching acts, CDT finally offers a set of prescriptions that specify which combination of teaching acts should be used in which circumstances. These prescriptions are summarised in Table 9.8, and are what will now be called e-learning transactions.

The CDT e-learning transaction depends upon the kinds of subject matter, of which there are four types, and upon the e-learning objective or cognitive ability being taught, of which four kinds are also identified. There are 13 CDT e-learning transactions, since three of the fours kinds of e-learning objective do not apply to facts.

The four types of subject matter are 'facts', 'concepts', 'procedures' and 'principles'. The four kinds of e-learning

Table 9.8 **CDT e-learning transactions summary**

Subject content	E-learning objective/cognitive ability: Remember instance	Remember generality	Use	Find
Fact	Fact pair Name			
Concept	Example Name	Definition Example State definition	Definition Examples Classify	Explore categories Invent definition
Procedure	Demonstration Rehearse	Definition Demonstration State steps	Definition Demon-strations Demonstrate	Explore procedures Devise procedure
Principle	Explanation Explain	Definition Explanation State cause-effect relationships	Definition Explanations Predict	Explore problems Discover principle

objective relevant to CDT e-learning transactions are 'find', 'use' and 'remember', divided into 'remember instance' and 'remember generality'.

Each CDT e-learning transaction involves two or three teaching acts. Each transaction involves at least one inquisitory teaching act, and, where the e-learning objective is at the 'find' level, two. Finally, every e-learning transaction involves feedback to the student following the inquisitory teaching act. More detail on the nature and structure of effective feedback is provided in Chapter 10 on lesson plans.

CDT e-learning transaction for facts

The only e-learning objective or cognitive ability relevant to facts is 'remember instance'. Table 9.9 lists the CDT e-learning transaction for teaching facts, which consists of:

Table 9.9 CDT e-learning transaction for facts

Cognitive ability	Mode	PPF	Teaching act
Remember instance	Present Ask	Show example Ask for example	Fact pair Fact name

- presenting the fact (fact pair);
- asking the student to recall one or other part of the fact (fact name).

A diagrammatic representation of the transaction is presented in Figure 9.5.

Table 9.10 provides an example CDT e-learning transaction for facts, drawn from the subject matter of

Figure 9.5 The e-learning transaction to remember a fact

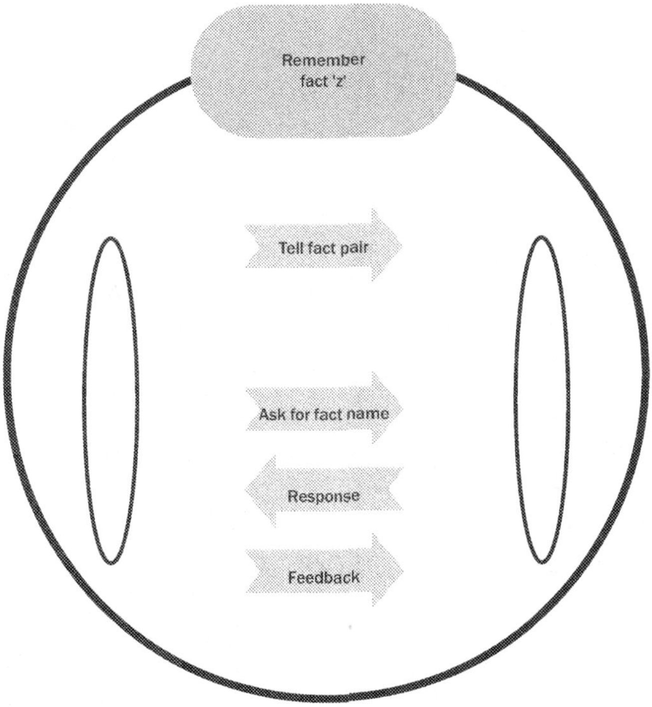

Table 9.10 **Example CDT e-learning transaction to remember a fact**

Enabling objective	Subject content	CDT e-learning transaction
Define nodes, edges (remember instance)	Node is a numbered circle or oval (fact) Edge is an arrow-headed line (fact)	Present a flow graph and identify nodes and edges (fact pair) Ask student to identify nodes and edges in a different flow graph (fact name) Give feedback on performance

graph theory. What is relevant to note is that the enabling objective is categorised as one of the four kinds of CDT e-learning objective, and the subject content is categorised as one of the four kinds of subject matter. The CDT e-learning transaction is then derived to yield a statement of how that subject matter could be taught.

CDT e-learning transactions for concepts

Table 9.11 lists the CDT e-learning transactions for teaching concepts, and these are shown diagrammatically in Figure 9.6.

If the student is to remember an instance of a concept, this is taught by:

- presenting an example of the concept (example);
- asking the student to recall instances of the concept or to recall the concept exemplified by a particular instance (name).

If the student is to remember a general concept, this is taught by:

- presenting the definition of the concept (definition);
- giving an example of the concept (example);
- asking for the definition of the concept (state definition).

Table 9.11 CDT e-learning transactions for concepts

Cognitive ability	Mode	PPF	E-learning transaction
Remember instance	Present Ask	Show example Ask for example	Example Name
Remember generality	Present Present Ask	Tell definition Show example Ask for definition	Concept definition Example State concept definition
Use	Present Present Ask	Tell definition Show examples Ask for examples	Concept definition Example Example Example Classify Classify Classify
Find	Ask Ask	Ask for examples Ask for definition	Explore categories Explore categories Explore categoreis Invent definition

If the student is to use a concept, this is taught by:

- presenting the definition of the concept (definition);
- giving numerous examples of the concept (example);
- asking for the concept to be used to classify numerous new instances, or asking for the appropriate concepts which apply to numerous new instances (classify).

If the student is to be able to find a new concept, this is taught by:

- asking for new ways of sorting or classifying numerous new examples (explore categories);
- asking for the name and definition of the new way of sorting or classifying objects (invent definition).

Figure 9.6 The e-learning transactions for concepts

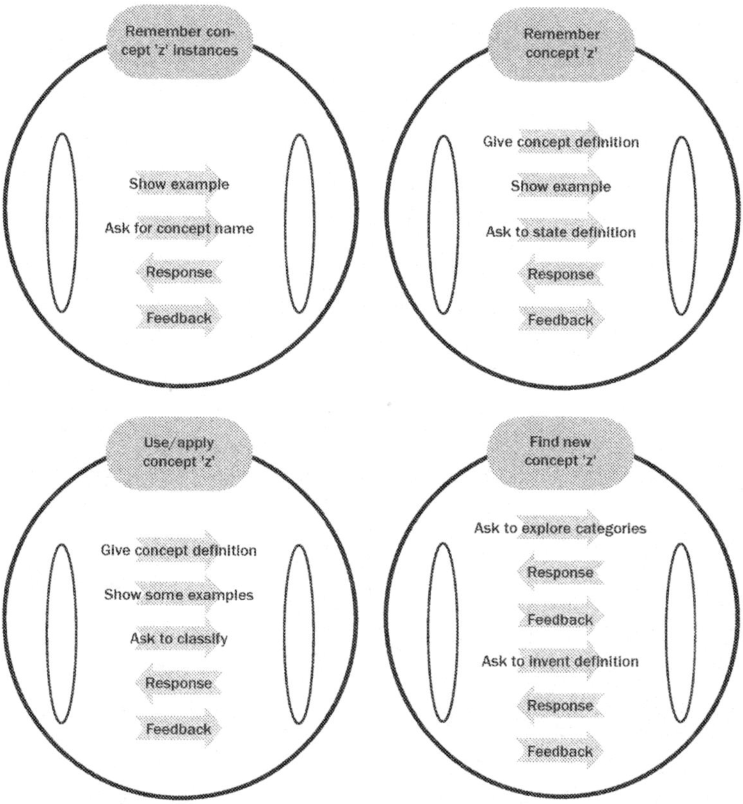

In all cases, feedback is provided to the student on their performance when asked to undertake any task.

Table 9.12 provides an example CDT e-learning transaction for the use of a concept, again drawn from graph theory. The enabling objective is categorised as 'use' and the subject content is categorised as 'concept'. The CDT prescription of 'concept definition', 'example, example, example', 'classify, classify, classify' is then applied to the subject content to yield a statement of how the use of the concept could be taught.

Table 9.12 Example CDT e-learning transaction to use a concept

Enabling objective	Subject content	CDT e-learning transaction
Decompose compound logical conditions (use)	Compound logical condition involves logical connectives (AND, OR) between simple conditions (concept)	Present definition of a compound condition (concept definition) Present examples of compound conditions (example) Ask student to provide new example compound conditions (classify) Give feedback on performance

CDT e-learning transactions for procedures

Table 9.13 shows the CDT e-learning transactions for teaching procedures, and Figure 9.7 illustrates this in diagram form.

Table 9.13 CDT e-learning transactions for procedures

Cognitive ability	Mode	PPF	E-learning transaction
Remember instance	Present Ask	Show example Ask for example	Demonstration Rehearse
Remember generality	Present Present Ask	Tell definition Show example Ask for definition	Activity definition Demonstration State procedure steps
Use	Present Present Ask	Tell definition Show examples Ask for examples	Activity definition Demonstration Demonstration Demonstration Demonstrate Demonstrate Demonstrate
Find	Ask Ask	Ask for examples Ask for definition	Explore procedures Explore procedures Explore procedures Devise procedure

Figure 9.7 The e-learning transactions for procedures

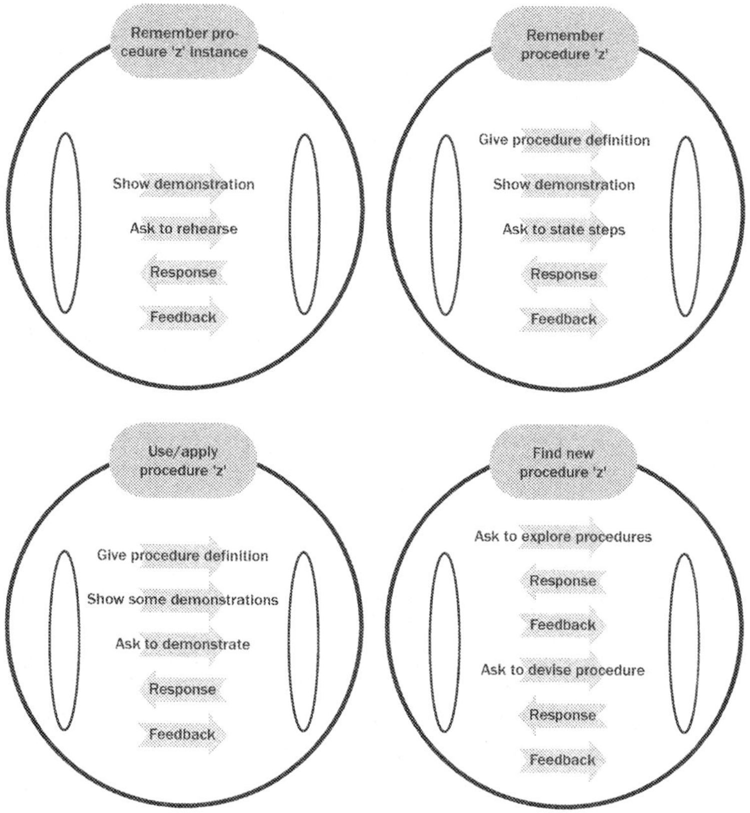

If the student is to remember an instance of a procedure, this is taught by:

- showing the procedure being executed (demonstration);
- asking for the procedure to be carried out on familiar materials (rehearse).

If the student is to remember a general procedure, this is taught by:

- presenting the definition of the procedure (definition);
- showing the procedure being executed (demonstration);

Table 9.14 **Example CDT e-learning transaction to use a procedure**

Enabling objective	Subject content	CDT e-learning transaction
Draw nodes and edges (use)	Draw one node for every line of code; connect each node in sequence with an edge (procedure)	Present procedure for drawing nodes and edges (procedure definition) Demonstrate construction of nodes and edges of a flow graph (demonstration) Ask student to construct nodes and edges of a flow graph from a simple fragment of sequential line-numbered code (demonstrate) Give feedback on performance

- asking for the procedure to be stated (state steps).

If the student is to use a procedure, this is taught by:

- presenting the definition of the procedure (definition);
- showing the procedure being executed a number of times in a variety of situations (demonstration);
- asking for the procedure to be carried out using a variety of new tools, new situations or new goals (demonstrate).

If the student is to be able to find a new procedure, this is taught by:

- asking for a number of new steps to be tried (explore procedure);
- asking for a new procedure name and definition for the new set of steps (devise procedure).

In all cases, feedback is provided to the student on their performance when asked to undertake any task.

Table 9.14 provides an example CDT e-learning transaction for the use of a procedure, again drawn from graph theory.

Table 9.15 **CDT e-learning transactions for principles**

Cognitive ability	Mode	PPF	E-learning transaction
Remember instance	Present Ask	Show example Ask for example	Explanation Explain
Remember generality	Present Present Ask	Tell definition Show example Ask for definition	Proposition definition Explanation State relationships
Use	Present Present Ask	Tell definition Show examples Ask for examples	Proposition definition Explanation Explanation Explanation Make prediction Make prediction Make prediction
Find	Ask Ask	Ask for examples Ask for definition	Explore problem Explore problem Explore problem Discover principle

The enabling objective is categorised as 'use' and the subject content is categorised as 'procedure'. The CDT prescription of 'procedure definition', 'demonstration, demonstration, demonstration', 'demonstrate, demonstrate, demonstrate' is then applied to the subject content to yield a statement of how the use of the procedure could be taught.

CDT e-learning transactions for principles

Table 9.15 shows the CDT e-learning transactions for teaching principles, illustrated diagrammatically in Figure 9.8.

If the student is to remember an instance of a principle, this is taught by:

- telling how the principle applies in a given situation (explanation);
- asking for an explanation of how the cause-effect relationships apply in a known situation (explain).

Figure 9.8 The e-learning transaction for principles

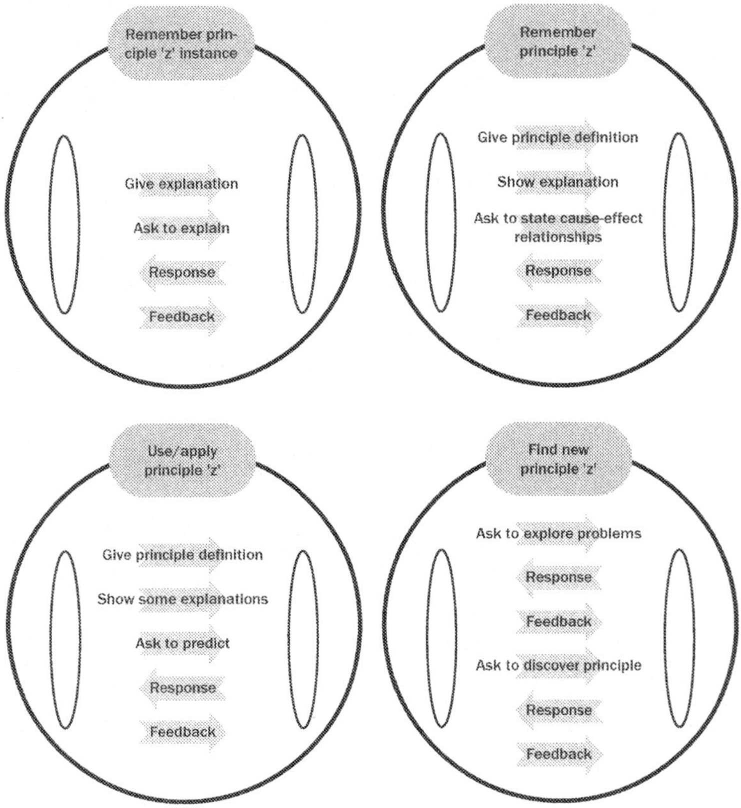

If the student is to remember a general principle, this is taught by:

- presenting the definition of the principle (definition);
- telling how the principle applies (explanation);
- asking for a statement of the principle (state relationships).

If the student is to use a principle, this is taught by:

- presenting the definition of the principle (definition);
- telling how the principle applies in a variety of situations (explanation);

Table 9.16 **Example CDT e-learning transaction to remember a principle**

Enabling objective	Subject content	CDT e-learning transaction
State formula for cyclomatic complexity (remember generality)	Cyclomatic complexity = Edges – Nodes + 2 (principle)	Present formula for cyclomatic complexity (proposition definition) Show how formula calculates cyclomatic complexity for a particular flow graph (explanation) Ask student to state formula for cyclomatic complexity (state relationships) Give feedback on performance

- asking for a prediction of how the cause-effect relationships apply in a variety of new situations (make prediction).

If the student is to be able to find a new principle, this is taught by:

- asking for the application of different cause-effect relationships in a variety of new situations (explore problem);
- asking for the new principle to be named and defined (discover principle).

In all cases, feedback is provided to the student on their performance when asked to undertake any task.

Table 9.16 provides an example CDT e-learning transaction for the student being able to recall a principle, again drawn from graph theory. The enabling objective is categorised as 'remember generality' and the subject content is categorised as 'principle'. The CDT prescription of 'proposition definition', 'explanation', 'state relationships' is then applied to the subject content to yield a statement of how the ability to recall the principle could be taught.

10

Detailed design: lesson plans

Lesson plan

The second major step of the detailed design stage is the preparation of the lesson plans. During the lesson plan step, the e-learning transactions, products of the prescriptions of component display theory and the first major step of the detailed design stage, are augmented with:

- secondary presentation forms (SPFs) from CDT;
- designs for student interaction.

They are then arranged into:

- structures which provide a complete learning and teaching experience, an e-learning lesson.

If there is audio or video, the relevant detail from the lesson plan is extracted and added to the AV outline script to yield the AV final script, a complete word-for-word and shot-by-shot list of everything that must be recorded.

The inputs to the lesson plan are illustrated in Figure 10.1.

The structure of an e-learning lesson is shown in Figure 10.2. Such a lesson contains a number of e-learning transactions focused upon a particular problem, 'y'. The bulk of the e-learning transactions are concerned with the various questions 'z' associated with problem 'y', and these transactions were developed in the e-learning transactions

Figure 10.1 Techniques for lesson plan development

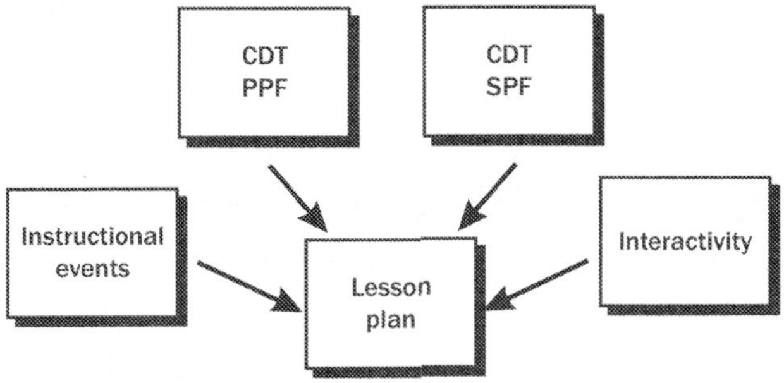

Figure 10.2 E-learning lesson

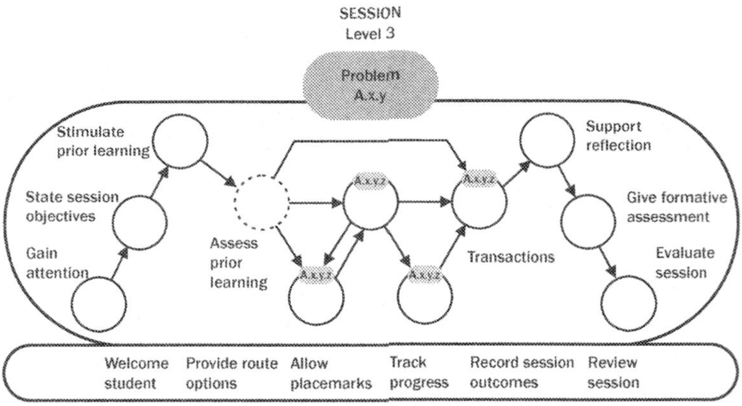

step earlier in the detailed design stage. In addition to these subject matter or content-oriented transactions, an e-learning lesson incorporates a number of other transactions, such as gaining student attention and assessing prior learning.

The particular problem 'y' addressed by the e-learning lesson derives from the e-learning objective for the lesson identified during the initial design stage.

CDT secondary presentation forms

The CDT *secondary presentation forms* are components that enhance or improve the presentation and teaching for the student, elaborating and enhancing the e-learning transactions identified earlier. SPFs are arranged according to the *primary presentation form* (PPF) employed in the e-learning transaction (Table 10.1). For example, if the student is being given a PPF *explanation*, in the context of an e-learning transaction on using a principle, then an appropriate SPF is to provide some definition of the terms employed.

Mnemonic aids

A mnemonic aid is anything that helps the student remember the material being presented. For example, to remember the order of the colours in a rainbow, the mnemonic ROYGBIV (Richard Of York Gained Battles In Vain) may be provided.

Mnemonics are most useful, according to CDT, when the student is being 'told' or 'shown' something; that is, being given a PPF definition, example, demonstration or explanation.

Table 10.1 CDT secondary presentation forms

	Primary presentation form			
	Tell definition	Show example, demonstration, explanation	Ask to classify, demonstrate, predict, explore	Ask to define, invent, devise, discover
Mnemonic aid	✓	✓	✓	✓
Define terms	✓	✓	✓	✓
Provide context	✓	✓	✓	✓
Focus attention	✓	✓	✓	✓
Provide alternative representation	✓	✓	✓	✓
Provide feedback			✓	✓
Provide suggestions			✓	✓

Define terms

The definition of new terms should be provided whenever they occur, and the student should be reminded of the definition of key terms whenever these are required. It may also be useful to provide a glossary.

The definition of terms is appropriate for all PPFs: definition, example, demonstration, explanation, classifies, demonstrates, predicts, explores, states definition, invents, devises and discovers.

Provide context

Information and teaching are most readily processed when presented in a context that the student is likely to find interesting and of which they are likely to have some previous experience. At the least, the material should be elaborated as necessary with connections to who, where, when and why. More usefully, the relevance of the material should be emphasised with some discussion on why it is important. For most audiences, it is also very useful to embed the material within a story, scenario or case study.

Again, providing a context is appropriate for all PPFs: definition, example, demonstration, explanation, classifies, demonstrates, predicts, explores, states definition, invents, devises and discovers.

Focus attention

In presentations it is important to draw the student's attention to the distinctive features of the material, using graphic elements such as arrows and colour, textual elements such as different typography or eye-catching elements such as animation.

It is important to recognise that this SPF is concerned with focus, and with focus upon significant or key features of the material. For example, if the material concerns the drawing of a data flow diagram, the various symbols employed in such a diagram might be presented with a red outline while the remainder of the material consists of normal black text and graphics. This SPF is not concerned with general presentation issues such as the colour of the background to all screens or the kind of font to be used in body text.

Attention-focusing devices are most useful, according to CDT, when the student is being 'told' or 'shown' something; that is, being given a PPF definition, example, demonstration or explanation.

Provide alternative representation

To help the student process and understand the material, this SPF suggests finding another way of providing or presenting it. Characteristically, most information is provided as text or words; alternative representations such as graphs, drawings, charts, tables, formulas or flowcharts serve to augment and consolidate learning.

Providing alternative representations is appropriate for all PPFs: definition, example, demonstration, explanation, classifies, demonstrates, predicts, explores, states definition, invents, devises and discovers.

Provide feedback

The last two SPFs are concerned with those parts of the lesson where the student is asked to do something. In these cases it is vital that the student be given feedback on their performance, and hence on their understanding, by way of the correct answer or a working or reworking of the problem.

Providing feedback is appropriate for PPFs which 'ask' the student to do something: classifies, demonstrates, predicts, explores, states definition, invents, devises and discovers.

Provide help

Where a student is asked to do something, it is useful for them to have access to some help if they feel they need it. This might consist of an example of what is required, a paraphrase of the question or problem or hints on how to proceed.

Providing help is most appropriate for 'ask' PPFs: classifies, demonstrates, predicts, explores, states definition, invents, devises and discovers.

Interactivity

Since the first commercial release of graphics-intensive CD-ROMs and the first availability of websites, these media have been marketed as 'interactive multimedia'. Nothing could be further from the truth for many of these products, unless a completely impoverished definition of 'interactive' is intended.

Almost all these media involve what might be called 'electronic page-turning', where their 'interactivity' consists of clicking on 'Back' or 'Next' buttons. From an e-learning point of view, such materials have the same level of interactivity as reading a novel – more or less none.

At one level, of course, the issue is simply one of definition. However, 'interactivity' in an e-learning systems context has a very clear and specific meaning that is completely different from that used in marketing hype. This meaning is outlined below, where a cycle of student engagement is presented based upon principles from the psychology of learning.

Perhaps closer to the common notion of 'interactive multimedia' is the issue of student control over the material and its presentation. This is discussed as a separate concern in the next section.

Control of learning

The degree to which the student can exercise control over the e-learning materials can be recast as a consideration of the control to be imposed by the course or program. Table 10.2 illustrates typical areas of control.

Both kinds of control are needed in any lesson. The question of how to bias the relative degrees of program and student control can be considered from the audience analysis, illustrated in Table 10.3; it can also be considered from the point of view of the demands of the subject matter content, revealed in the task analysis, illustrated in Table 10.4.

Table 10.2 Program versus student control

Program-initiated	Commands	Press <Enter> Click on 'Next' Turn to chapter X
	Choices	Choose the topic to study next
	Questions	Which of the following is true?
	Feedback	Remedial routing through extra material
Student-initiated	Commands	Repeat the topic Give me a practice example
	Seek help	Give me a hint What's the best way to do this?
	Manipulate variables	What if X changed from 2 to 3?

Table 10.3 Audience analysis for control of materials

Program control best for audience which	Has little or no knowledge Has low motivation Sees little relevance Is inexperienced in the subject Is used to structured and directed learning Is inexperienced in independent learning Does not know what it needs or wants to know Has low confidence Is inexperienced with the medium of delivery Prefers being told what to do
Student control best for audience which	Knows what it needs or wants to know Is motivated Sees the relevance of the material Is experienced in the subject Is used to independent learning Resists structure Has high confidence Is experienced in the medium of delivery

Table 10.4 Task analysis for control of materials

Program control best when	Content requires a specific sequence There is no pre-test of student competence Content required for certification
Student control best when	Content is not linear Learning sequence is not critical Students can assess their own mastery level at entry No requirement for certification Learning is discretionary

In a number of ways the issue of student or program control is related to whether the audience is an 'expert' or a 'beginner' audience. 'Experts' can be given, and indeed would expect, greater control over the e-learning materials and the learning and teaching process.

The cycle of interactivity

'Interactivity' in an e-learning systems context means that the student is presented with a number of choices to make which require them to process the course information and materials actively, and that they are then given prompt and specific feedback about their particular choice.

This model of interactivity is based upon principles from the psychology of learning, where the student operates upon their environment and receives feedback as a result of such operations. It is presumed that the most effective learning takes place when the materials are interactive and the student is required to be interactive. The relevant conditions of 'interactivity' are illustrated in Figure 10.3, the 'interactivity cycle'.

The 'interactivity' discussed in this section is interactivity that is to be added to the e-learning transaction. That is, having developed the e-learning transaction, it is now necessary to make as many of these transactions as possible 'interactive', to enhance and ensure effective learning.

In fact, the e-learning transaction already has interactivity included, if it was developed using CDT. Each of the PPFs of classifies, demonstrates, predicts, explores, states definition, invents, devises and discovers is a point of interactivity in the lesson.

- As a preliminary, then, the student receives guidance on learning. The guidance primarily covers what to learn,

Figure 10.3 Interactivity cycle

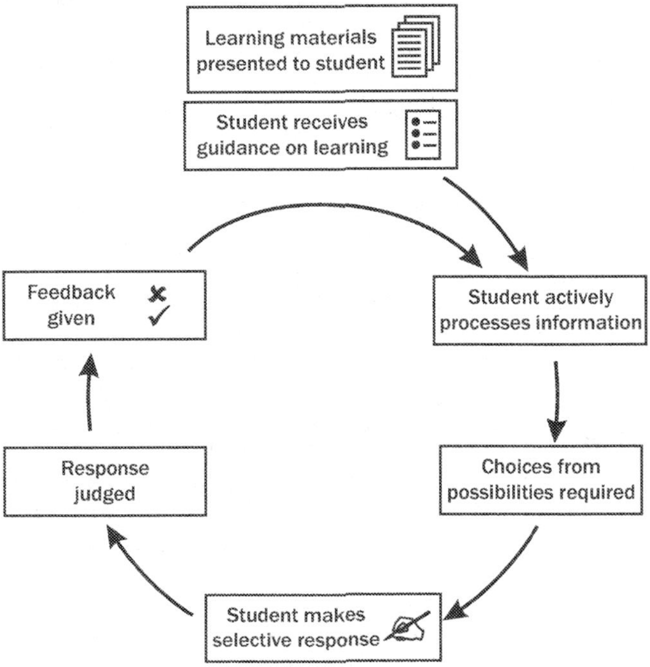

but may also be concerned with how to learn. This 'guidance' comprises the bulk of the subject matter content, and is contained in the e-learning transactions developed so far.

- Interactivity begins with the student being required to process the materials and information actively.
- In order to ensure active processing of the materials, the student is posed a problem, question or situation that offers a number of options or choices.
- The student responds to the problem, question or situation by making a choice and selecting one of the options.
- The response of the student (the option selected) is judged and assessed.

- Feedback is given to the student on their response, and if necessary remedial help is given.
- The student moves on to the next interaction.

This cycle of interactivity is presented in a general form, to ensure it is applicable to most forms of learning in addition to cognitive skills, including the learning of motor skills and moral values, for example. Figure 10.4 illustrates some of the key characteristics of the interactivity cycle.

- *Student receives guidance on learning.* This means that the student is being taught. There are circumstances in which the student may be learning without being explicitly

Figure 10.4 Characteristics of the interactivity cycle

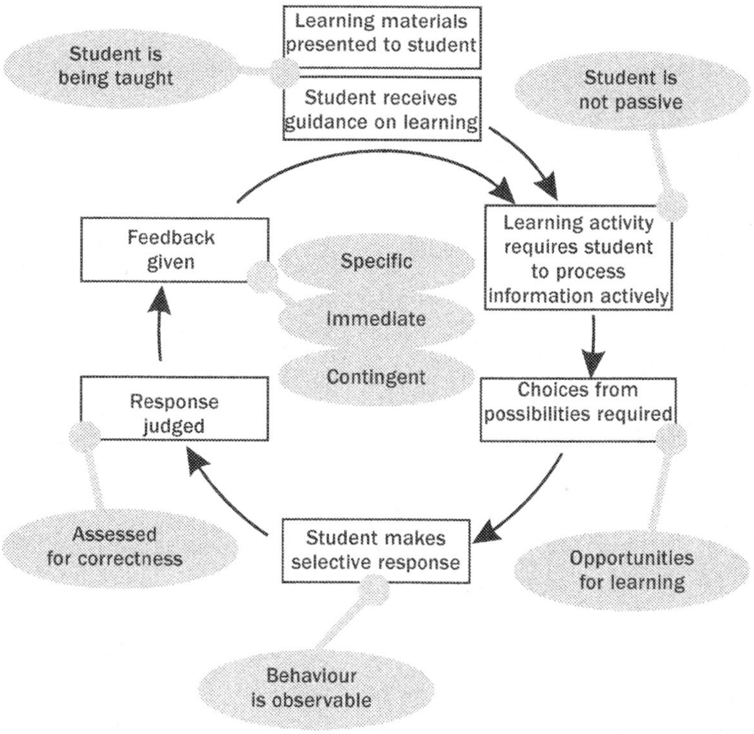

taught, and the interactivity cycle is presumed to operate here as well. For example, 'learning from experience' means that the student makes choices, receives feedback and is said to have learned if they then modify their behaviour appropriately.

- *Student actively processes information.* The point here is that the student is not passive. There are unusual circumstances in which learning seems to take place when the student is passive, but it must be presumed that there are nevertheless internal, active processes taking place in the student for learning to occur. It seems clear that effective e-learning requires the active participation of the student.
- *Choices from possibilities required.* The key point here is that various possibilities are made available to the student, and that these possibilities provide opportunities for learning. Strictly speaking, learning cannot take place without choices, options and possibilities.
- *Student makes selective response.* This is the crux of interactivity, where, in order to make a 'good' choice, the student has to process and think about what they are being and have been taught.
- *Response judged.* A mechanism is needed to assess the 'goodness', 'quality', 'correctness' or 'fitness' of the student's choice. In most circumstances the subject matter expert specifies the 'correct' answer or criteria for judging whether an answer is correct.
- *Feedback given.* There are three established conditions that make feedback most effective and usable by the student: it is immediate, specific and contingent.

With regard to the last item, generally feedback must be given immediately, or as soon as possible. Delayed feedback is usually less useful the more it is delayed, and is of course completely useless if it never arrives. There are situations when feedback can usefully be delayed for a period of time. Usually these situations tend to involve the maintenance of motivation and expectation. There is one area where delayed feedback may be important in the learning and teaching of cognitive skills, and that is where the student needs time to absorb, consider, reflect and then restructure or reintegrate what they have just learned with what they have previously learned.

Feedback must be specific if it is to be maximally effective. It is the specificity of the feedback that allows the student to focus on exactly those aspects of their learning that could do with improvement. Without such specificity, the student has little idea on where or how to progress.

Most importantly, feedback must be contingent. This is a technical term that means the feedback must be functionally dependent upon, must follow and be linked to, the student's selective response. If the student is given the answer to the problem without having made a choice, the answer is not contingent upon the student making a choice.

Question and feedback

It should be clear that, in materials that are designed to teach a cognitive skill, 'interactivity' is very much equivalent to asking the student a question. If the materials are being developed using CDT, the required interactions have already been identified at every point in the e-learning transaction where the PPF requires the acts of classifies, demonstrates, predicts, explores, states definition, invents, devises or discovers. When the designer produces the lesson plan from such an e-learning transaction, each of these PPFs is augmented by a specification of the exact form of the question to be put to the student, and, more importantly, a specification of the correct or acceptable answers and of the way in which feedback is to be given.

If the e-learning transaction was not developed using CDT PPFs, the designer and subject matter expert need to agree on the lesson key points. For each key point an interaction is then devised, having due regard to the thoroughness with which the subject content must be taught. Posing a question for the student, specifying the acceptable answer(s) and specifying the way in which feedback is to be given generally identify an acceptable interaction.

Table 10.5 illustrates some of the issues involved in constructing an interaction. The level of detail in the interactions of the instruction is one of the prime determinants of that instruction's cost to design and produce.

Restricted-choice kinds of questions can be computer-judged, while free-response questions must be tutor-judged. The design of the interactions must thus consider the e-learning concept and the media and methods contemplated. The kinds of computer-judged questions were discussed in Chapter 8 dealing with the student test step, part of the initial design stage.

Table 10.5 **Characteristics of questions, answers and feedback**

Question complexity	Restricted choice versus free response
Answer analysis	Anticipated answers can be programmed Unanticipated answers can be accommodated High tolerance and flexibility for unanticipated answers
Feedback	Depth and detail Specific to incorrect choices

The major issue in answer analysis is dealing with unanticipated responses. While it is normally straightforward to specify and judge a set of conventionally correct answers, it is not possible to enumerate every possible incorrect answer. For tutor-presented courses, criteria can be laid out to help in judging students' answers.

Providing feedback that is relevant and specific for each incorrect response is both time-consuming and often tedious. As the discussion on the interactivity cycle above emphasises, however, it is the quality of such feedback that distinguishes an effective course from other courses.

Gagné's e-learning events

Gagné et al. (2004) outlined nine events that an effective lesson must include. These are outlined below and illustrated in Figure 10.5. These events are developed from theories and research in the psychology of learning, and are used to structure the lesson plan. The lesson plan is augmented by the addition of a further two e-learning events to the list of nine Gagné events, as outlined below. The illustration suggests where any particular event of instruction could be interactive, shown by incorporating a '?' against it. It also suggests where a particular learning event might involve a number of pages or screens, by showing the event as a multiple stack of e-learning transactions.

Gain attention

Any lesson should begin by gaining the attention of the student with one or more e-learning transactions. The presumption is that an alert and interested student will benefit more than one who is not. Attention can be gained in a number of ways, and an appropriate method will depend upon the audience analysis.

Figure 10.5 The events of instruction

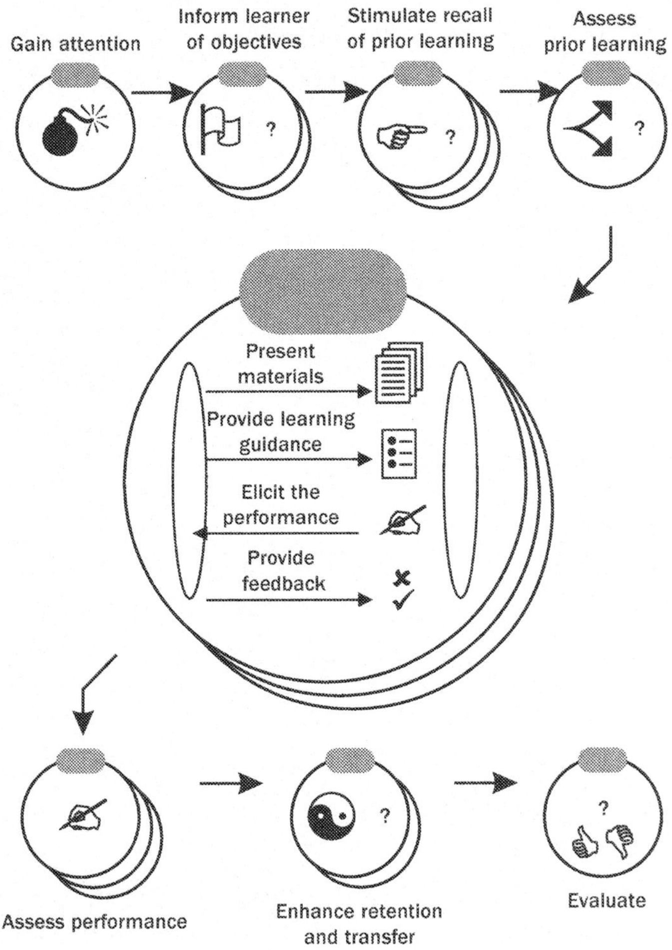

For example, a lesson on calculating the amount of fuel needed by a jumbo jet for a transatlantic crossing might quote a newspaper report of a flight that was forced to crash-land because inadequate reserve fuel had been allowed for strong headwinds. More dramatically, and perhaps less tastefully, the lesson might incorporate graphic stills from or video footage of a crash-landing.

This is also the place to explain to the student why they should want to learn – colloquially called WIIFM, 'What's in it for me?'

Inform learner of objectives

The lesson should then incorporate e-learning transactions which tell the student not what the lesson content is to be, but what the lesson objectives or intended e-learning outcomes are – that is, what the student will be able to do. In general, these would be paraphrases of the top-level objectives. As the illustration in Figure 10.5 shows, this should be done in an interactive manner if possible, to engage the student in the learning and teaching process.

For example, the lesson might say that by the end of it the student would be able to calculate the fuel requirements of a flight. It might then go on to ask the student to select the kind of flight they expected the lesson to deal with: a fully loaded transatlantic jumbo jet, a partially loaded cross-Channel turboprop or a ten-seater business jet flying in the tropics. Each of the responses could be used to provide feedback to the student on the specifics of the lesson objectives.

Stimulate recall of prior learning

A number of enabling objectives will have been labelled as 'prerequisite' during the initial design stage, and these represent prior learning that the student needs in order to tackle the current lesson properly. The student should not only be reminded of this prior learning, but also helped to recall it. Such e-learning transactions could take the form of a pre-test for the lesson with full feedback, or a more informal set of interactions.

For example, the flight fuel-planning lesson might need the student to know already that the volume occupied by a given weight of fuel depends upon the temperature. The recall of this prerequisite knowledge could be stimulated by asking the student to identify the circumstances under which an aircraft may not be permitted to fly with its maximum number of passengers when fuelling in tropical countries: if it is winter and there is a chance of snow on the runway; if it is summer; or if a significant number of passengers have checked in with excess baggage.

Assess prior learning

The first of the non-Gagné e-learning events, the assessment of prior learning, is significant for any instruction where the student may be routed to different parts of the lesson or unit depending upon their current level of understanding and skill. Although this event obviously has points in common with the previous event, the stimulation of prior learning recall, it has a subtly different focus. In particular, the assessment of prior learning here is to check whether the student is already capable of meeting the lesson objectives or intended learning outcomes. That is, although the prior learning being assessed is not the prerequisite learning of the student which is required to support their learning in the current lesson, the question is whether the student needs to undertake the study of the remainder of the lesson at all or whether they can proceed directly to the end of the lesson for formative assessment.

Strictly speaking, the assessment of prior learning is not an e-learning event but a lesson or unit management process. It nevertheless requires explicit attention at this step in the detailed design stage. There are lesson plans where this event of instruction would not be included because every student would be required to progress through the lesson content. In others, this assessment would greatly enhance the value of the lesson by directing more capable students, as identified in the audience analysis, to other e-learning transactions better suited to their current state of learning. Of course, these other transactions require analysis, design and production, and there are issues of cost and cost-effectiveness to consider.

Present materials

This is the point in the lesson where the subject matter is presented. If the lesson has been developed with CDT and interactivity, this event and the following three e-learning events will already have been incorporated into a set of e-learning transactions. While Gagné calls this and the following three components 'events of instruction', they are identified in the present discussion as 'teaching acts', components of a e-learning transaction. The other Gagné events of instruction are identified here as complete e-learning transactions in themselves.

Provide learning guidance

If the lesson has not been designed with CDT to yield e-learning transactions, this event is to remind the designer to include teaching acts which tell the student both what to learn and how to learn, as well as to help the student learn more effectively by providing examples, definitions of terms, supporting context and the other relevant elements of SPFs.

Elicit the performance

If the lesson has not been designed with CDT and the interactivity cycle, this event is to remind the designer to include teaching acts which ensure that the student is asked to demonstrate the skills called for by the lesson's objectives.

Provide feedback

If the lesson has not been designed with the interactivity cycle, this event is to remind the designer to include teaching acts which ensure that the student receives immediate, specific and contingent feedback on their performance.

Assess performance

This is the point in the lesson where certain of the student test items are presented. If the lesson has not been fully designed according to the ELSYE life cycle, the event is to remind the designer to incorporate e-learning transactions involving test items to help the student and instructor determine and ensure that the lesson objectives have been met.

This event of instruction is also labelled 'formative assessment' in this discussion. For some lesson plans the assessment of performance at this point might be in fact be summative. However, the presumption is that, in general, summative assessment is given at the end of a larger block of instruction, the e-learning unit, which consists of a number of e-learning lessons.

Enhance retention and transfer, support reflection

The final Gagné e-learning event comes towards the end of the lesson, where attention is given to designing e-learning transactions to help the student retain the lessons learned or skills gained and use them in other circumstances or situations.

It is possible to debate the exact location of this event, as to whether it precedes formative assessment or follows it. Either position may be appropriate, depending upon the particulars of the instruction under consideration.

For example, one of the key learning points of the flight fuel-planning lesson might be that allowance must be made for a 30-minute hold at the destination airport. A question could then be asked about which of the following situations would also probably require a 30-minute hold: a fully loaded transatlantic cargo jet; a partially loaded cross-Channel passenger turboprop; or a ten-seater business jet flying between regional and not international airports.

Evaluate lesson

The second non-Gagné event of instruction comes at the end of the lesson. Again, it is strictly a lesson management event rather than an e-learning event. In it, attention is given to gathering, recording and analysing data to help in the tutor review and quality assurance of the instruction. Depending upon the nature and extent of the higher-level e-learning units and programmes of which the lesson is a part, this event and its associated e-learning transactions might not formally be designed to be part of the lesson, but incorporated into the higher-level unit or programme instead.

Lesson plan storyboard and script

Storyboard: screen and page mock-ups

From the design point of view, the lesson plan is a sketch of the kind of treatment to be given to the instruction and its materials. Wherever a certain kind of interaction is required or a certain kind of presentation is planned, a lesson storyboard should show it so that it can be prototyped and confirmed or improved. In this case the storyboard – screen and page layouts – need only treat each kind of interaction or presentation once.

Figure 10.6 Screen mock-up

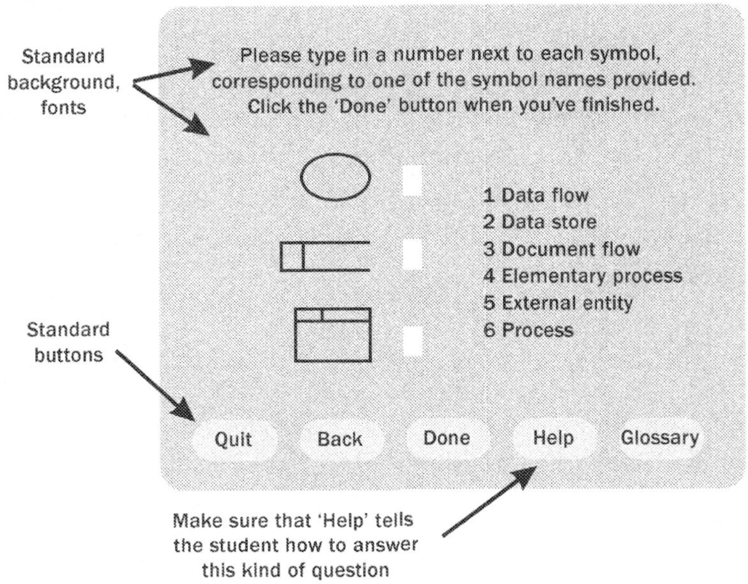

A sketch of the kind of treatment to be given to the lesson materials is usually shown as a series of mocked-up screens or pages. Figure 10.5 suggests where mock-ups might be required in the lesson storyboard – for each e-learning transaction shown as a circle. Around each mocked-up screen would be numerous annotations pointing out the characteristics and significance of the elements shown. An example of a mocked-up screen is given in Figure 10.6.

The screen or page mock-ups are sketched with guidance from the technical, presentation and design standards from the initial design stage (Chapter 8).

Lesson script

From the production point of view, and from the customer's point of view, *every* interaction and *every* presentation must be specified. These cannot be left to the programmer or graphic

Table 10.6 **Lesson script layout**

Subject matter	CDT e-learning transaction	SPF, control, interactivity
Symbols for data stores, data flows, document flows, external entities, processes and elementary processes	Present each symbol with its name Ask the student to name some of the symbols when presented Give feedback on performance	(Enter the names in the glossary. [define terms]) (Draw each symbol in red. For an elementary process, draw the '/*' device in blue. [focus attention]) (Provide a button that allows the student to display an example data flow diagram. [provide context and student control]) (Present a graphic of each of the data store, external entity and process symbols.) (Present the possible names in a numbered list: 1 data store, 2 data flow, 3 document flow, 4 external entity, 5 process, 6 elementary process. Ask the student to type the appropriate number next to each symbol, and to click on the 'Done' button when finished. [interactivity]) (For each symbol correctly named, display below the symbol and the student's answer 'Correct, this is a/an X'. For each symbol incorrectly named, display 'No, this is a/an Y', and redisplay the incorrect number highlighted in red. [feedback])

Notes: Elements in () are instructions for production.
Elements in [] provide cross-references to the detailed design components and would not normally be shown on a lesson script.

artist to complete. The type of treatment for the various interactions and presentations can be specified by reference to the storyboard, but the specifics are still required. For example, every interaction must specify the question wording, the acceptable answers and their feedback, anticipated incorrect answers and their feedback, other answers and their feedback and the different routes to be followed through the material if dependent upon these answers.

The lesson plan thus consists of two components:

- the *storyboard*, a visual sketch of the lesson using mocked-up screens or pages;
- the *script* for the lesson detailing the content of every interaction and every presentation.

The *lesson script* is the fully detailed specification of the e-learning transactions where all SPFs and interactions are identified, with the details of the events of instruction added where required. The layout of a lesson script is shown in Table 10.6.

Audio-visual final script

The AV final script provides a complete word-for-word and shot-by-shot list of everything that must be recorded. On the video side three lists are required: the shot list, the stills list and the special effects. On the audio side there are two lists: the audio script broken down into each take, and the list of audio effects that need to be recorded.

Video sequence storyboards

Each planned video sequence should be mocked-up as a storyboard, similar to the lesson storyboard. This form of prototyping is intended to portray the live action shot by shot so that it can be evaluated, confirmed and/or improved.

Video stills

The lesson plans will identify where still shots may be required from certain of the video sequences, and the storyboards will help identify where other stills are required at the start and end of sequences.

Additionally, there will usually be extensive lists of stills required for the subject matter content.

Video special effects

Where indicated by the design, special effects may be required. These special effects are generally computer-generated sequences which provide transitions from one live-action take to another, titling and overlays, or animation.

Audio script

The lesson plans will identify where audio may be required, either as voice-over or re-recorded in studio conditions to replace live-action audio which may suffer due to the environmental circumstances of the shoot.

Audio effects

As for video, where indicated by the design there may be special audio effects. These special effects are generally computer-generated or studio-generated.

11

Detailed design: remaining steps

Course management design

Course management is concerned with the management issues involved in any course, and the course management design step is concerned with the specification of these issues, which may be best presented as a series of questions.

Will students register, or be registered, to take the course? Will students log on by supplying a user ID and password? Will progress to further parts of the course depend on completing earlier parts? Can parts of the course previously taken be taken again?

Will the system track student progress, with dates and times of access? Will the scores on student tests be recorded? Analysed? Will the individual responses of a student to course interactions be recorded?

How will access to student data be protected? How will student data be amended or deleted?

Prototypes

It is suggested in Chapter 14 on quality management that producing samples or prototypes of materials is an effective method of exposing the planned materials to inspection and review. The issues are taken up in more detail below.

Problems with simple ELSYE

Following the simple linear sequence of the ELSYE stages from feasibility to operation is known in software engineering as the 'waterfall' model. Such a simple sequence has problems.

- A 'big bang' installation (i.e. rolled out to all users at the same time) may lead to problems, particularly with user resistance. If the 'big bang' installation and operation experience difficulties, these are usually in proportion to the size of the bang. It is usually unwise to wait until operation for the user to experience all of the materials and systems that have been developed.
- Requirements change unpredictably as the materials and systems are designed, produced and piloted. It is usually wise to involve the user early and often throughout each stage, and then iterate back to previous stages as needed based upon their input.
- The assumption of complete, concise, consistent e-learning requirements being available prior to development is usually invalid. Most users will change their expectations and understanding of what they want and what is achievable as the project progresses.
- A linear development sequence makes it difficult to ensure effective feedback between stages. This is illustrated in Figure 11.1, where the early stages of development are shown as being at a considerable remove from the evidence and feedback that would show whether those stages have been correctly done.

Figure 11.1 Linear development with feedback

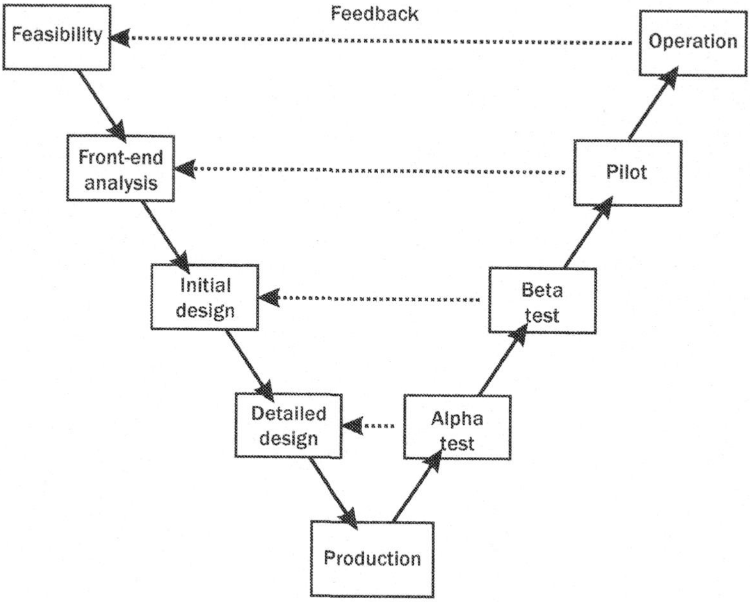

- Associated with the distance between decisions made in the early stages of development and knowledge of their effects, early errors are expensive to correct and may make the materials and systems ineffective or useless.

Solution: prototypes

These difficulties with a simple linear development sequence can be overcome by providing opportunities for effective feedback at the stage this feedback is required. The idea is to provide prototypes or simulations (sketches, mock-ups, etc.) at each stage of development. This is illustrated in Figure 11.2, where the 'V' of the linear model has been replaced by the 'W' of the prototyping model.

Figure 11.2 **Development with prototypes and feedback opportunities**

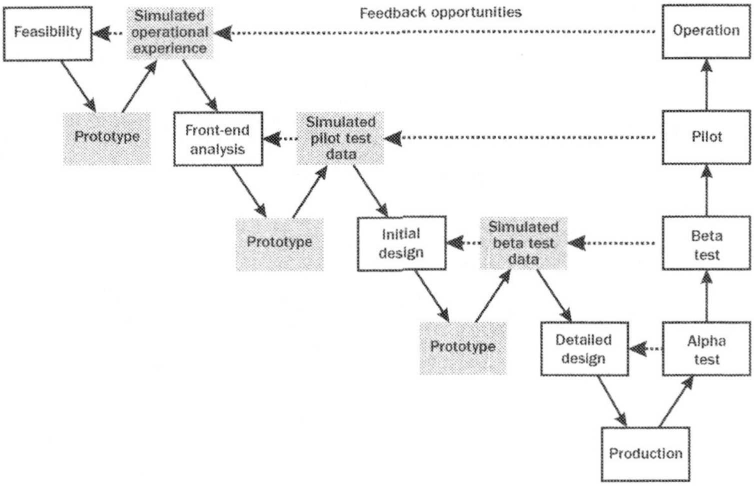

While the 'W' model of Figure 11.2 shows prototypes at every stage, the ELSYE life-cycle model only shows explicit prototypes towards the end of detailed design. The issue is simply one of scale. The formal ELSYE model assumes projects of small to medium size, and therefore an explicit requirement for prototypes is really only necessary in preparation for the next stage of (expensive) production. For larger projects, prototypes should indeed be produced as part of the stages of front-end analysis and initial design.

Prototyping drawbacks

While in general it can be said that prototyping is advantageous, there are some drawbacks to consider.

- Users may think the final product is almost ready.
- Developers may be reluctant to discard (hard) work.
- Iterations may be difficult to control and document.

- Resource planning and management may be difficult.
- Limits of the prototype or prototyping tool may give a misleading impression of the end result or fail to expose problems.

Evaluability design

The point of evaluating a course is to secure incremental quality improvements over successive implementations. Evaluation is not an end in itself, but only one part of the ELSYE life cycle. Many people and organisations operate a simple 'analyse – plan – implement' trajectory, where there is no real interest in learning from the outcome. Undertaking evaluation indicates that the interest is in learning from and improving upon the outcome in successive iterations. If there is an activity that is more important than the others, that key activity is 'plan' rather than 'evaluate'. The 'plan' includes planning for evaluation, after all, as well as for implementation.

As discussed in Chapter 14, the quality management of a course involves two separate activities: quality assurance of the course products, both interim and final, and continuous quality improvement of the course development process. An effective institutionalised quality improvement process must therefore provide for the inspection of course products and materials, and for the definition of the applicable standards in and the processes of course development.

It is possible to limit an evaluation of e-learning to the question of the achievement of its objectives (goal-oriented), and to avoid evaluation of the myriad other outcomes which were not formally intended (known as 'goal-free' outcomes). Until experience and expertise is gained, it may be necessary to restrict evaluation to the goal-oriented variety. In many cases, however, the real impact of e-learning may well be found in outcomes not formally intended.

Input to the concerns of the evaluability design step comes from the steps of the project plan stage of cost-benefit analysis and impact analysis (Chapter 7), as well as from the top-level objectives step of the front-end analysis stage (Chapter 6). In those steps it was assumed that the course would have certain benefits and certain impacts, as well as achieving its e-learning objectives.

In the pilot step of the production stage, and in the evaluation stage (Chapter 13), two kinds of evaluation are considered. 'Validation' is a process which answers the question 'Is the right product built?', while 'verification' answers a subtly different question, 'Is the product built right?'. The step of evaluability design needs to consider the design of instruments to provide answers to both kinds of evaluation.

A useful classification of the kinds of information to seek from an evaluation is associated with the work of Kirkpatrick (outlined in Buckley and Caple, 2007):

- reaction;
- learning;
- performance change;
- organisational benefit.

Reaction information is typically the information gathered by course evaluation questionnaires – essentially questions around the issue of how much the students liked the e-learning. This information is readily obtained through questionnaires and is readily analysed in quantitative and statistical terms, as discussed later in this section.

Learning information concerns the effectiveness of the e-learning – questions around the issues of how much, and how well, the students actually learned what was intended, and possibly around the issue of how much they learned that was unintended.

Performance change information is concerned with whether the learning which took place as a result of the e-learning educational or training experience led to actual performance changes and improvements on the part of the students.

Organisational benefit information concerns the overall value of the e-learning for both the organisation and the stakeholders. It may be worth recalling that the cost-benefit analysis step of the project plan stage (Chapter 7) has identified the value of the e-learning to the stakeholders, and evaluation would seek to establish evidence for the extent to which such value had indeed been obtained.

Evaluation instrument design

At the least, the evaluation instrument is specifically designed to gather data that reflect upon the achievement of specific e-learning goals (aims and objectives). To this extent, every evaluation instrument is a bespoke design, tailored for a particular and unique purpose. These comments apply, of course, where evaluation is part of a problem-solving approach to a problem situation. Where no particular problem situation exists and no problem-solving is being undertaken, the process is one of monitoring and control and not of evaluation.

There is an analogy with Gödel's incompleteness theorem, which states that any formal system is incomplete (Hofstadter, 2000). In the case of evaluation, we may anticipate that there are always outcomes that cannot be predicted. At a simple level, this means that any evaluation instrument should make provision for some open-ended responses, since even the longest and apparently most exhaustive list of questions is, in principle, incomplete. At a deeper level, it means that an evaluation's results are never the whole story relevant to the quality of e-learning.

Baseline metrics

While a 'standard' evaluation form does not address the specific objectives and teaching needs of e-learning, there are some standard questions that should be part of any course evaluation. The point of these standard questions is to provide some baseline measures that allow comparison of changes across e-learning units, student groups and times of delivery. Without the baseline, the comparative outcomes of changes cannot be assessed.

Where continuous quality improvements are installed, repeated evaluation with forms that have 'standard' questions will lead to these questions being used to define the key measures of quality and the key criteria by which the e-learning is judged. Because of this, very particular care needs to be given to the exact nature and wording of questions and criteria which form the baseline metrics.

Evaluation is not necessarily restricted to occurring at the end of a process. Interim or mid-course evaluation may be usefully sought to guide development or change during the delivery of an e-learning unit, or simply to confirm that the e-learning is working well.

The Scottish Higher Education Funding Council has developed a set of criteria relevant to the quality of a course. These criteria, shown in Table 11.1, may be used to formulate a set of 'standard' questions in any evaluation instrument.

Data concerning the effectiveness of the e-learning will be gathered in the last stage of the ELSYE project life cycle, evaluation (Chapter 13). At this point in the detailed design

Table 11.1 **Scottish Higher Education Funding Council quality criteria**

The course objectives are explicit and known
The course objectives match the needs of the student, customer and other interested stakeholders
The course content reflects and matches the course objectives
The course structure matches and meets student needs in terms of the course's length or duration, modes of attendance, location, structure, sequence and optional elements
The course accommodation is sufficient
The specialist facilities are sufficient
The ancillary facilities are adequate
The course structure is clearly laid out, logically sequenced and communicated
The course assessments are clearly scheduled and coordinated
Feedback on the course is regularly obtained
Action is taken on the feedback received
Student advisory services are provided
There is effective liaison between support providers
Information and advice are provided for potential students
Tutors and other staff are concerned for student well-being
A successful learning and teaching experience is shown in student performance and attitudes
There is a commitment to excellence by staff and students
The subject matter experts and tutors have suitable qualifications, experience and status
The course's delivery methods relate to its objectives
Course delivery is properly paced
The approach taken in the course encourages independent learning and student responsibility
The course content is enriched by cross-curricular, research and industrial links
The course assessments and course work correspond to the course objectives

Table 11.1 Scottish Higher Education Funding Council quality criteria (*Cont'd*)

Assessments and course work are regularly required
An appropriate standard of work is required
Students' achievement is comparable to that elsewhere
Course assessments use an appropriate range of diagnostic, formative and summative methods
The scope and weighting of every assessment are known in advance
The standard of work expected is explicitly specified and consistently applied
The assessment procedures ensure validity, reliability and fairness
Feedback on assessment results is given to students in reasonable time
The appeal procedures are reasonable and readily available
The correct level of prior/prerequisite knowledge is assumed

stage, effort is made to ensure that suitable data can be gathered and analysed. In particular, one or more course evaluation forms are designed, and their possible forms of analysis sketched.

Where the e-learning involves a summative assessment of student achievement, this may be used as evidence for the effectiveness of the e-learning. Where a module or course does not include a post-test, this is the place to construct one in preparation for the evaluation stage.

In addition to information on the effectiveness of the e-learning, other questions within an organisational context might involve the impact of the e-learning on job performance, and the views and opinions of both co-workers and managers on this impact.

Figure 11.3 illustrates an evaluation form where the student is asked for their opinions using closed questions. Figure 11.4 illustrates open questions. Both types of question may, of course, be used in the same evaluation instrument.

Figure 11.3 Example evaluation form, closed questions

Student Opinion Form

Course / Date

	Strongly agree	Agree	No opinion	Disagree	Strongly disagree
Lecturer's presentation is clear, explanations are good	☐	☐	☐	☐	☐
I feel I can easily ask the lecturer questions if I want or need to	☐	☐	☐	☐	☐
The material is pitched to suit my background knowledge and skills	☐	☐	☐	☐	☐
I find the material interesting and involving	☐	☐	☐	☐	☐
The difficulty level of the work is fine for me	☐	☐	☐	☐	☐
The amount of material and its pace of delivery is fine for me	☐	☐	☐	☐	☐

Figure 11.4 Sample evaluation form, open questions

Final Course Evaluation

Course / Date

If you didn't rate this course highly on a particular question, please say what it could do better.

What would you change in this course? Mention the most significant item.

What would you keep in this course; what was the best bit? Mention the most significant item.

Finally, it is always useful to provide contact or forwarding information on any questionnaire for those students who may prefer to provide their comments after due reflection.

Analysis of evaluation data

It is relatively easy to concoct and administer an evaluation questionnaire. What may be less obvious are the statistical and graphical analyses of the data necessary in order to obtain valid and repeatable interpretations of the 'meaning' of the results. The effort of data analysis far exceeds the effort of questionnaire design and delivery. Inadequate data analysis makes the whole exercise pointless, and so part of the point of the evaluability design step is to ensure that adequate attention is paid to the method of analysis of the results.

It is difficult to perform a quantitative analysis of the responses to open questions. The procedure usually followed is to code the various responses into a limited number of categories, from which histograms can be drawn.

For a qualitative analysis of the evaluation, logging the opinions exactly as offered allows a useful comparison of the (usually) divergent comments. In the example of Figure 11.5, one comment is that things are too slow and another that they

Figure 11.5 List of open-question responses

Opinions Offered

Course / Date

N = number of respondents

Pace needs to be faster

Things are moving fairly fast, seem unrelated
I'm not convinced I have grasped something before we move on
Too much work in too short a timespan

Teaching method is fine (x3)

Teaching method discourages questions
Discussion as a tool is not sufficiently utilised

Little outside reading
Presentation clear only after thought and work
Need clear examples to follow (x2)

are too fast. Judgement is always required in considering open-question responses, in particular following reflection on whether the comments are relevant to the stakeholder requirements of, or the standards applicable to, the e-learning.

The students' responses may be shown as histograms. In the example analysis shown in Figure 11.6, the class average opinion rating for each question is shown in a shaded rectangle, based on converting the ratings to a scale from 1 to 5, with 1 being 'strongly agree' or 'the most'.

These averages need to be interpreted in the light of the actual distribution of opinion on each question. For example, the statement 'I feel I can ask the lecturer questions

Figure 11.6 Histogram analysis of evaluation data

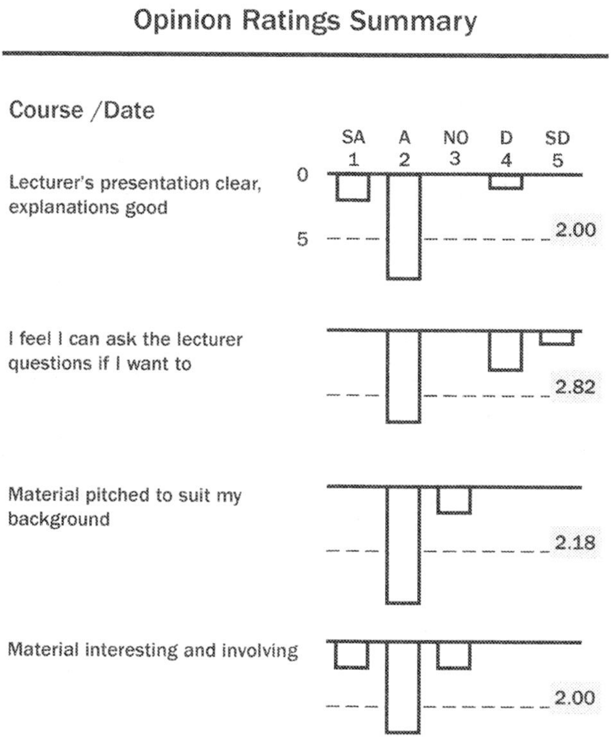

if I want to' shows the majority of the class to be quite happy, but a minority not so. The bimodal distribution yields an average of 2.82 that is probably somewhat underestimating the 'true' degree of satisfaction with the issue. The median might be a better measure in such a case.

It is important to compare baseline or 'standard' measures between different deliveries of a course in order to track the effectiveness of planned (or otherwise) changes. Of course, differences of opinion are to be expected, but how big a difference is needed before it 'really counts'? The illustrated box plot (Figure 11.7) provides a box which is approximately plus and minus one standard error wide. Average class opinions which fall within the box are comparable and not 'really different'. In the example of Figure 11.7 it is clear that the 95/96 class had a significantly poorer opinion of their ability to ask questions of the lecturer, while the 97/98 class was significantly happier on this issue.

Figure 11.7 Box plot for repeated evaluations

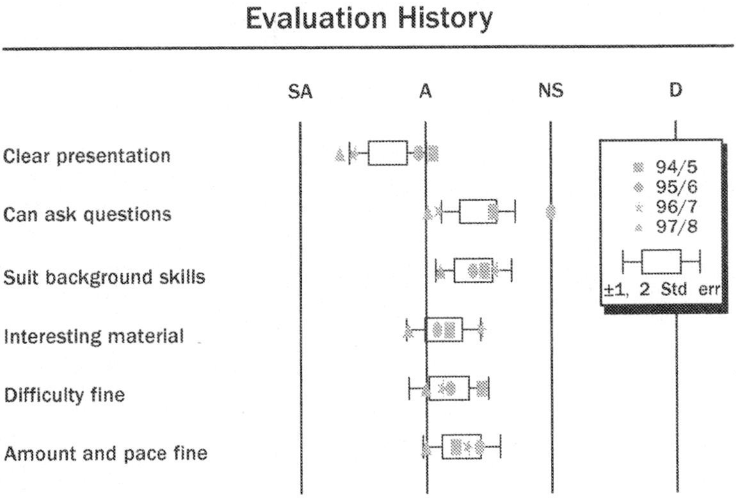

The analyses presented so far have examined each question in turn and considered the class's response. A correlational analysis can help shed light on the pattern of response – for example, if the class thought the material was difficult, did they also think the explanations were poor?

A dendogram is a simple method for seeing which questions tend to be answered in agreement – clustered – with which other questions, and which are not. In the example of Figure 11.8, the students' opinion of the difficulty of the material is closely associated with their opinion about its interest. Not a surprising result, which tends to give credence to the class's opinions as a whole.

A factor analysis is a more sophisticated analysis which shows how the agreement between questions is clustered on to

Figure 11.8 Dendogram analysis

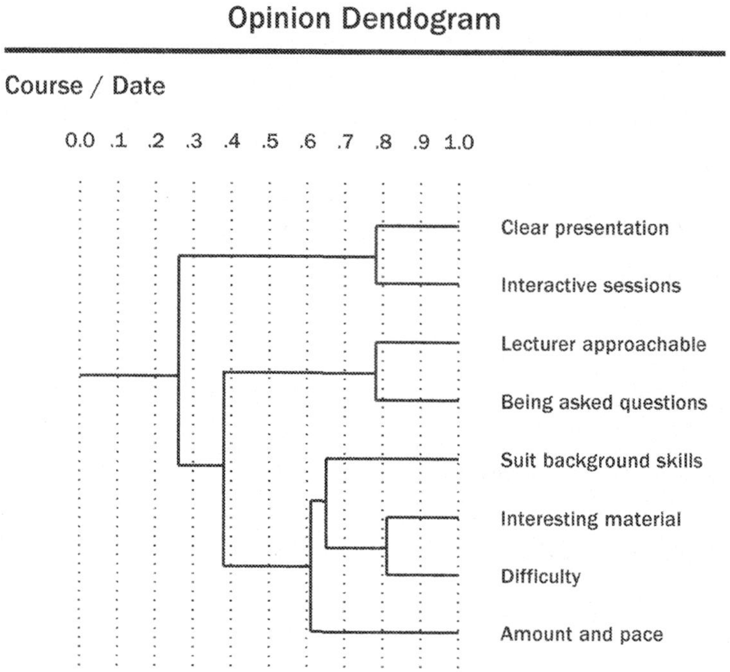

Figure 11.9 Factor analysis

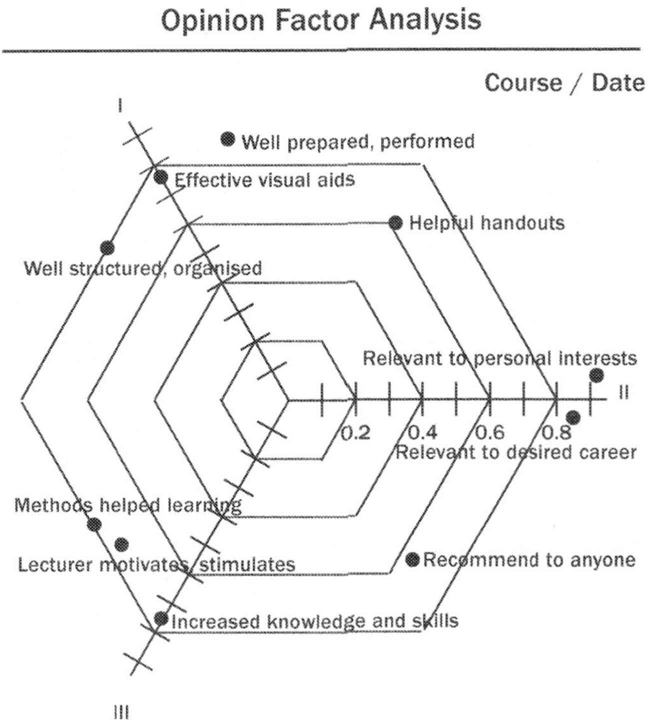

discrete dimensions or components. In the example of Figure 11.9, three dimensions of response have been identified. The first, Factor I, relates to the delivery of the course, where the questions of performance, organisation and visual aids cluster together. The second, Factor II, is a dimension of relevance to the student. Interestingly, their view of the handouts is shared between delivery issues and relevance issues. The third dimension, Factor III, relates to their actual learning or understanding, quite distinct from the delivery mechanisms or the relevance of the material. Interestingly, whether they would recommend the course depends both on whether they felt they learned anything and on whether they thought the course to be relevant to their interests.

12

Production

The stage of production is located within the construction phase of the ELSYE life cycle, as illustrated in Figure 12.1, and its steps are shown in Figure 12.2. During the production stage, the audio-video final script from the detailed design stage is taken into AV production. The student test from initial design and the lesson plan from detailed design feed into materials production, informed by the technical and presentation design standards of initial design. The AV products and the materials are then integrated in the next step of programs and integration, informed by the course management design from detailed design. The completed product is then subject to alpha testing before transfer into the next stage of piloting.

Outcomes from alpha testing feed back within the stage to programs or materials, and to the earlier stage of detailed design if necessary. Note that alpha testing does not feed back to AV production. If issues are uncovered with AV production as a result of alpha testing, they need to be addressed by an iteration through detailed design, since their impact upon budget and schedule will be very significant.

Figure 12.1 **Production stage in the ELSYE life cycle**

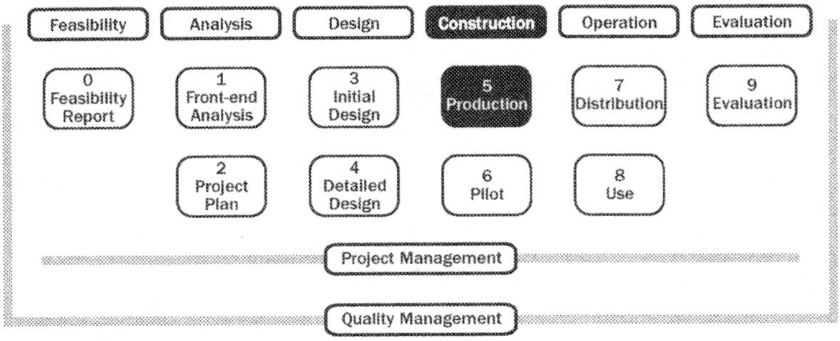

Audio-visual production

AV production is usually the preserve of specialists, certainly in the case of e-learning materials intended for commercial use. While talented amateur staff might be able to construct an attractive graphic or write an engaging paragraph for the materials step, they are unlikely to have either the equipment or the skills to shoot well-lit, well-paced, well-acted video sequences or record well-balanced noise-free expressive audio tracks. The following paragraphs on AV production are therefore short notes intended to help the project manager and staff appreciate the components of the stage rather than assist them in actual production.

AV pre-production

Among many detailed matters which require attention in preparation for AV production, the pre-production step involves the major tasks of casting, location reconnaissance, booking of post-production facilities and preparing shot lists.

During detailed design, the AV final script step will provide a list of the audio and video takes required in lesson plan sequence. This sequence is not likely to be the sequence

Figure 12.2 Steps of the production stage

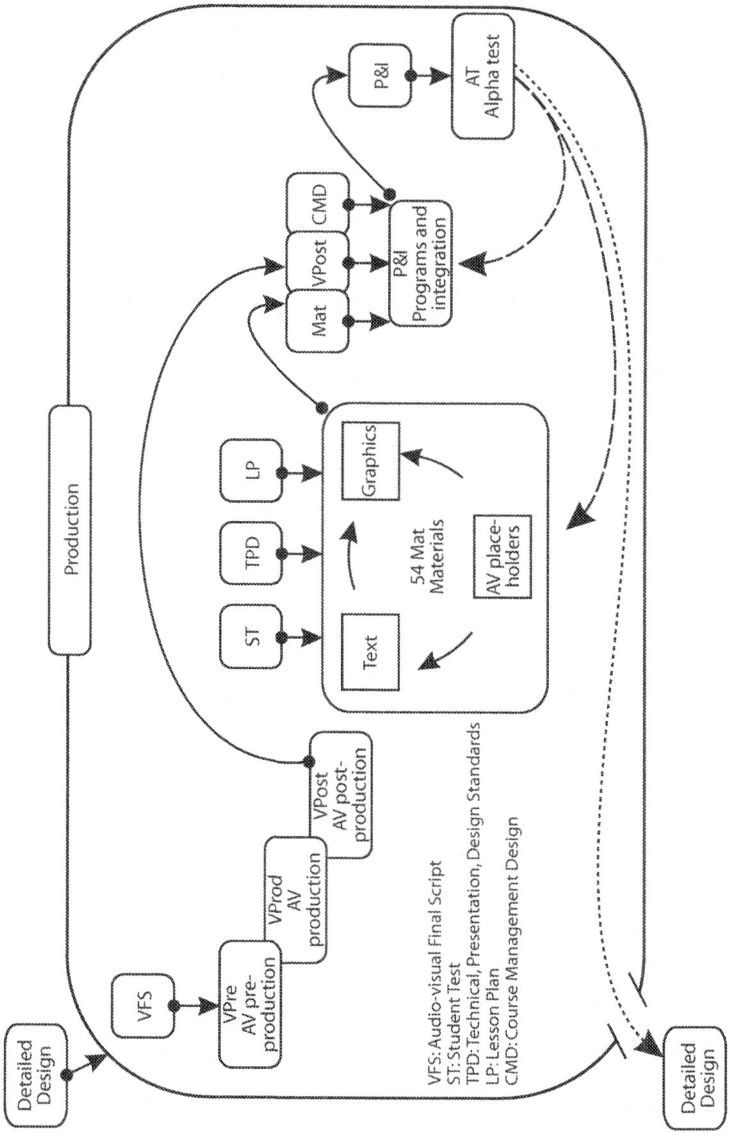

that the director will require for location or studio shooting or recording. Instead, the shot list would be completely reordered. If there are a number of locations, all shots at a particular location would be grouped together. Within a shot list, sequencing is then likely to be driven by set-up requirements, such that the use of actors and props follows a progression which minimises changes between shots.

AV production

Location and studio recording is usually an intensive, short period of time where expensive resources are brought together to achieve the required footage. Because of this, the scripts and shot lists must be immaculately prepared, since there is little chance of correcting significant errors or omissions on the day.

AV post-production

Following the pressured and controlled semi-chaos of production, the post-production step involves assembling the results into the materials required for integration into the end product. The tasks here are the offline editing of the materials for customer review and approval; the online edit of materials to produce a master; and the transformation of the master into the parts needed for CD-ROM or DVD production, or into the resources needed for programming and integration into the end e-learning product.

Materials

The production of materials essentially refers to the production of the text and graphic images required by the lesson plan. Where AV materials (video and audio) are required, placeholders are provided in the text and graphics.

The production stage can be a highly variable process, depending upon the production team and the way the project has been set up. At one extreme, the detailed design may be so thorough and complete that production simply involves the creation of the text and graphics specified. At the other extreme, detailed design may be sketchy and 'outline only', leaving it up to the production team (who may well be the designers undertaking a new role) to complete both processes of design and production in one stage. In this case the production of materials is usually an iterative process, as design decisions are made on the fly about the relative balance between textual and visual presentation.

The following comments on materials production rely heavily on the treatment given by Clark and Mayer (2003). Where the e-learning development involves a thorough detailed design, the following sections properly belong within the detailed design stage, since they deal with design issues fundamental to textual and graphic requirements. Where the e-learning development involves a less complete detailed design, perhaps extending only to the specification of the learning transactions, such that the remainder of the design activity is addressed during production, the following sections may be taken to provide the foundations necessary at this point.

The role and positioning of graphics

It is always possible to describe and explain concepts, procedures or principles using text. In general terms, where a concept, procedure or principle can be shown visually, it should be shown visually as well. Static images may show facts and concepts, while moving images (animation, video) may be used to illustrate procedures and principles.

Given a textual and a graphic representation, these two components should be integrated and placed in proximity and not separated into different pages or links.

The role of audio

Reading text occupies two modalities – vision and hearing. Listening to audio occupies one – hearing alone. In general, where material involves text and images such that both need to be processed at the same time, it may be better to present the text as audio, leaving the visual modality to concentrate on the images alone. Audio usually provides explanation and description for graphic content.

Sometimes the material is needed for reference, and in this case it should be provided as text rather than audio. Sometimes it seems necessary to have both text and graphics on screen or on a page as well as providing audio, but this should be avoided if the audio is simply a restatement of the text. Narration (audio delivery of the text) may, however, be desirable in special circumstances, typically when student attention needs to be focused upon the words of the text, such as in language learning.

Coherence

Text, graphics, video and audio should always be relevant, and not decorative or extraneous. For any topic there will always be related (and probably interesting) matters and issues. Leave these out of the e-learning lesson plan, and focus instead on the learning of the key points.

Programs and integration

Depending upon the authoring environment being used and the nature of the e-learning materials and systems, some programming may be necessary. In any case, the materials and AV resources are integrated in this step into the final product or deliverable. Prior to pilot, the final product is tested in the next step.

Alpha test

The testing of the final e-learning product by the developers is known as alpha testing. Testing by users is usually called beta testing, and is central to the next stage, pilot (Chapter 13).

Broadly, alpha testing seeks to ensure that the e-learning product works, and there are two techniques for the construction of test cases which may be most useful: boundary value analysis and basis paths.

Principles of testing

In testing an e-learning product, the intention is to find errors. A good test is one that is likely to expose errors, and a successful test is one that finds new errors. An unsuccessful test is one that fails to find any errors at all. The point of testing is *not* to demonstrate correctness of the product in operation. Such an approach is likely to yield a self-fulfilling prophecy; that is, the product is likely to be found correct. The point of testing is to find the errors that are inevitably in the product, perfection not being a routine attribute of many human artefacts.

These are some guidelines for testing.

- *Use independent testing staff.* Do not use the programmers who programmed the software, the designers who designed the materials or systems, the users who helped specify them, or any others who have vested interests in finding that the product is correct.
- *Test that the system meets the customer's requirements.* It is very easy to slip into the practice of testing to see if the product meets (often unexpressed) intentions, whether they are of the programmers or the designers. In an e-learning product the overall requirements are found in the top-level objectives, while the detailed requirements may be found in the lesson plans.
- *Plan and design tests as soon as the customer requirements are known.* That is, do not leave test planning until it is time to run the tests. When the lesson plan is known, test-case construction can begin.
- *Start small, work up to big.* Start with screens and pages, work up to lessons, modules or units and finish with the whole e-learning product.

Test cases

The heart of testing involves the construction and execution of a number of test cases. A test case consists of two components: a specified set of inputs and an expected result. A test case is usually a sequence of written instructions for the tester to follow, with a statement or image of the expected outcome, and needs to be constructed on the assumption that the tester is an independent member of staff who has no previous connection with the project.

It is usually quite easy to identify the input for a test case. More difficult, and needing particular attention, is the statement of the expected result. For every test input, the expected result is a statement of what the system *should* do, from the point of view of a satisfied customer or user. For example, it is easy to say that the input of an incorrect value should result in an error message. This is not a satisfactory test case until the content of the error message has been spelled out. What should happen is that the error message identifies the nature of the error and provides some help towards correcting it, and this requirement needs to be written into the test-case instructions.

Boundary value analysis

The technique of boundary value analysis (BVA) is used to generate test cases based upon a systematic consideration of how the system should handle valid and invalid inputs. Usually it is possible to identify a range of values which could be input, and to identify some part of that range as valid. The remainder of the range is thus invalid. These parts may be called valid and invalid partitions, and are illustrated in Figure 12.3. The valid partition is illustrated as having boundary values of 'C' and 'D'. BVA suggests exactly three test-case inputs for the lower boundary of the valid partition: values of 'C–1', 'C' and 'C+1'. In a similar way, BVA suggests values of 'D–1', 'D' and 'D+1' as test input data for the upper boundary of the valid partition, 'B–1', 'B' and 'B+1' for the upper boundary of the lower invalid partition, and so on.

For example, suppose an e-learning product asked the user to input his or her age, and because the product was for use in higher education, suppose that the designer had

Figure 12.3 Boundary value analysis

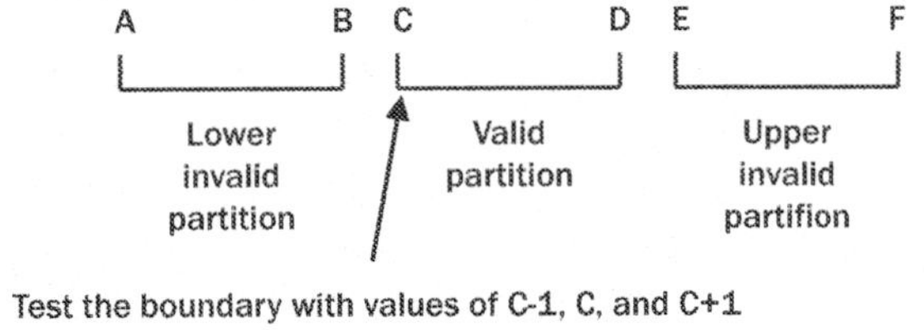

determined that the lowest valid age for a student was 16 years. In this case, the three test input values for the lower boundary of the valid partition would be '15', '16' and '17'.

Basis paths

Basis paths testing is used to generate test cases which test whether all possible paths through a study program work correctly. The technique guarantees to find a certain minimum set of test inputs which will exhaustively test all possible combinations of program or software routes.

The technique uses a notation, illustrated in Figure 12.4, which expresses the flow of control logic in a program or item of software. Program statements are called nodes, and they are connected by edges. A predicate node, shown shaded in the figure, is a node where the program flow can branch.

For example, an assessment item allows the student three attempts, at each attempt displaying feedback, and exiting when the student either provides the correct answer or uses up the three allowed attempts. The program for this process might be as shown in Figure 12.5.

The corresponding flow graph for this program is shown in Figure 12.6. Each line of the program is numbered for reference, and this reference inserted into the relevant node. Note that where one program statement follows another in

Figure 12.4 Flow graph notation for basis path testing

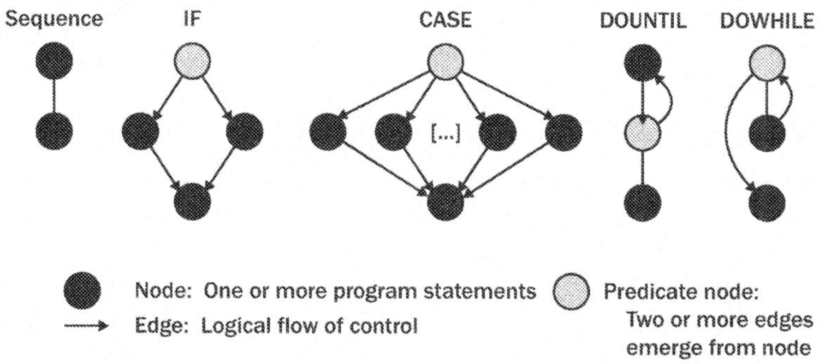

Figure 12.5 Example program for basis path testing

```
TryCount:= 0
DO
   Present question
   Mark response
   IF correct THEN
      GotIt = TRUE
      Give "correct" feedback
      ELSE GotIt = FALSE
      Give "wrong" feedback
   ENDIF
   TryCount:= TryCount +1
UNTIL TryCount = 3 OR GotIt
END
```

Figure 12.6 Flow graph for example program

```
TryCount:= 0
DO
   Present question
   Mark response
   IF correct THEN
      GotIt = TRUE
      Give "correct" feedback
      ELSE GotIt = FALSE
      Give "wrong" feedback
   ENDIF
   TryCount:= TryCount +1
UNTIL TryCount = 3 OR GotIt
END
```

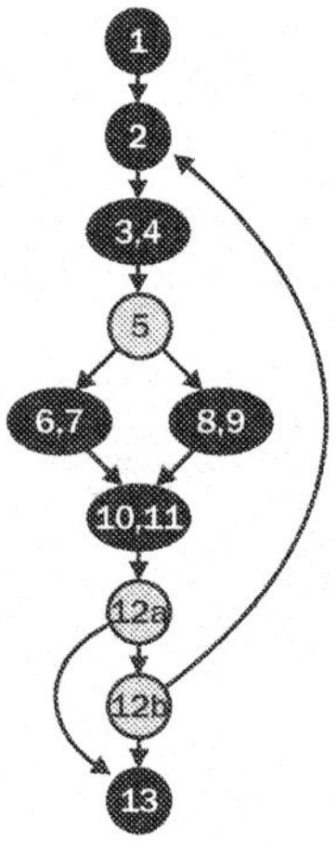

sequence, these statements may be gathered together and represented with one node, as illustrated for statements 3 and 4, 6 and 7, and so on.

Also note how the compound condition of the UNTIL statement has been broken down into its elementary conditions, labelled 12a and 12b in the example. This is necessary to preserve the structure of the flow graph and its ability to show clearly the points at which program control may branch.

Given the flow graph for any program, the upper limit on the number of distinct and unique paths through that program is given by the cyclomatic complexity of the graph. The cyclomatic complexity of a flow graph may be calculated using three methods.

- *Count the number of regions of the graph.* A region is any area enclosed by edges. By convention, the 'sheet of paper' on which the graph is drawn counts as a region. Figure 12.7 illustrates the four regions of the example flow graph, hence the cyclomatic complexity is 4.
- *Count the number of edges and nodes.* The cyclomatic complexity is given as the number of edges less the number of nodes plus 2:

$$\text{Cyclomatic complexity} = \text{Edges} - \text{Nodes} + 2$$

Figure 12.7 Regions of the example flow graph

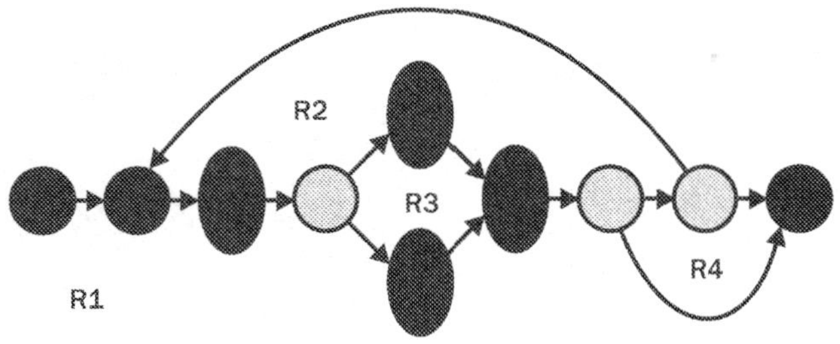

In the example flow graph there are 12 edges and 10 nodes. Hence the cyclomatic complexity is 12 – 10 + 2 = 4.

- *Count the number of predicate nodes.* The cyclomatic complexity is given as the number of predicate nodes plus 1:

Cyclomatic complexity = Predicate nodes + 1

In the example flow graph there are 3 predicate nodes, hence the cyclomatic complexity is 3 + 1 = 4.

Given that the cyclomatic complexity places an upper bound on the number of distinct and unique paths that can be traced through the flow graph, the next task is to identify these paths. For the example flow graph, Figure 12.8 illustrates one possible set of four distinct paths. These distinct paths are called basis paths.

Note that there are a number of different alternative sets of four basis paths. For instance, in basis paths C and D, the program flow could be shown from node 5 through 6,7 instead of through 8,9. What is significant and important is

Figure 12.8 **Distinct paths through the example flow graph**

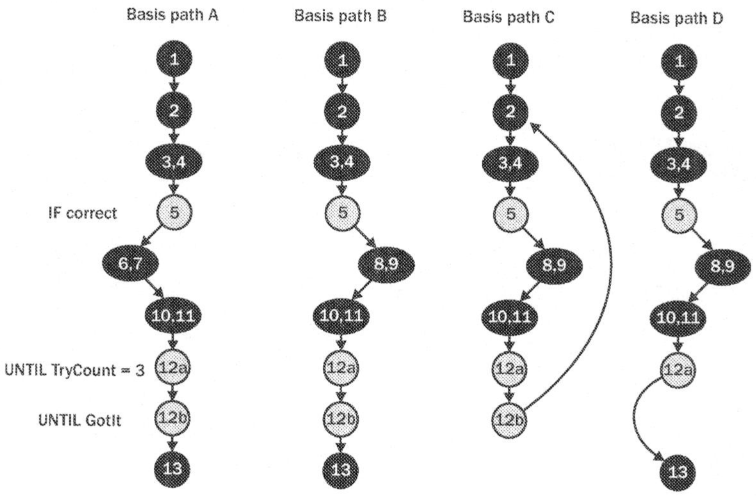

Figure 12.9 Test-case data for example basis paths

	Basis path A	Basis path B	Basis path C	Basis path D
IF correct	correct = TRUE	correct = FALSE	correct = FALSE	correct = FALSE
UNTIL TryCount = 3	TryCount = 1	TryCount = 1	TryCount = 1	TryCount = 3
UNTIL GotIt	GotIt = TRUE	GotIt = TRUE	GotIt = FALSE	GotIt = N/A

that, in any particular set of four basis paths, every edge of the flow graph is traversed at least once.

Finally, a set of test cases is constructed: one test case per basis path. Each test case is intended to exercise its particular path and hence to check that particular flow of program control and execution. The test cases corresponding to the basis paths of Figure 12.8 are shown in Figure 12.9.

For example, for basis path A the test-case instructions are: 'When presented with the assessment, answer correctly on the first attempt.'

Note that basis path B cannot be tested directly. It requires the question to be answered incorrectly, but then requires the variable 'GotIt' to be set to TRUE. This is not possible given the program, since an incorrectly answered question necessarily means that 'GotIt' is set to FALSE. It is not uncommon to find one or other basis path cannot be tested in reality, and this requires a closer inspection of the basis

Figure 12.10 Every possible combination to test example program

	Test case A	Test case B	Test case C	Test case D
IF correct	correct = TRUE	correct = FALSE	correct = TRUE	correct = FALSE
UNTIL TryCount = 3	TryCount = 1	TryCount = 1	TryCount = 3	TryCount = 3
UNTIL GotIt	GotIt = TRUE	GotIt = TRUE	GotIt = TRUE	GotIt = TRUE

	Test case E	Test case F	Test case G	Test case H
IF correct	correct = TRUE	correct = FALSE	correct = TRUE	correct = FALSE
UNTIL TryCount = 3	TryCount = 1	TryCount = 1	TryCount = 3	TryCount = 3
UNTIL GotIt	GotIt = FALSE	GotIt = FALSE	GotIt = FALSE	GotIt = FALSE

path to check whether it contains an edge that would otherwise remain untraversed in all other basis paths. Comparing basis path B to basis path A, it can be seen that its distinctive edges are between nodes 5 and 8,9 and between nodes 8,9 and 10,11. It turns out that these four edges are traversed in both basis paths C and D, and so there is no problem: just the three test cases for basis paths A, C and D will ensure exhaustive testing of the program.

It might be thought that a comprehensive test of this program would require every possible combination of answering the question correctly or not and of having three attempts or not. The resulting eight combinations are illustrated in Figure 12.10. As the basis paths testing example shows, however, at most four combinations will serve to test the program exhaustively.

13

Pilot, distribution, use and evaluation

Earlier stages of the ELSYE life cycle, from feasibility to production, have been presented in Chapters 5 to 12. This chapter gathers together and discusses the remaining stages of pilot, distribution, use and evaluation.

Pilot stage

The pilot stage is located within the construction phase of the ELSYE life cycle, as illustrated in Figure 13.1, and its steps are shown in Figure 13.2. During pilot, the alpha-tested product from production is validated and beta tested. The final product is then taken into the next phase, operation, for the stages of distribution and then use.

Outcomes from pilot (as a result of either validation or beta testing), if changes are not minor and readily made, feed back to the earlier stages of production for larger-scale changes to materials, or further back to detailed design or even initial design if necessary for structural design changes. As with the alpha test in the production stage, if the pilot uncovers issues with AV production they will probably need to be addressed by an iteration through detailed design, since their impact upon budget and schedule will be very significant.

Figure 13.1 Pilot stage in the ELSYE life cycle

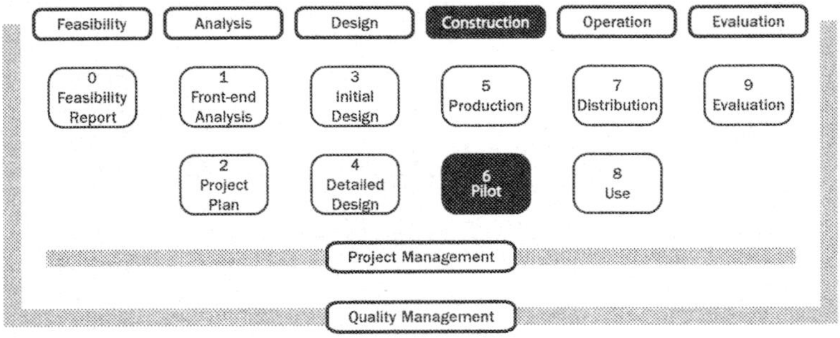

Validation

The intention of the pilot stage is twofold: to validate the e-learning products, and to verify them. 'Validation' is a process which answers the question 'Is the right product built?', while 'verification' answers a subtly different question, 'Is the product built right?'. The two processes are closely connected, since both are quality management issues. Validation focuses upon the e-learning requirements identified during front-end analysis and initial design (top-level objectives, task analysis, enabling objectives) and checks that the product meets them. Verification tends o focus upon the standards which the product should meet (the project and quality management standards from front-end analysis and the technical, presentation and design standards from initial design), and asks questions about completeness, consistency and coherence, as well as questions about correctness, clarity and conciseness.

There are a series of quality reviews during the ELSYE life cycle, illustrated in the diagram of the development 'V' (introduced in Figure 11.1) which has been modified to make the links back to the earlier life-cycle stages more explicit (Figure 13.3). Validation is mainly a review of how the

Figure 13.2 Steps of the pilot stage

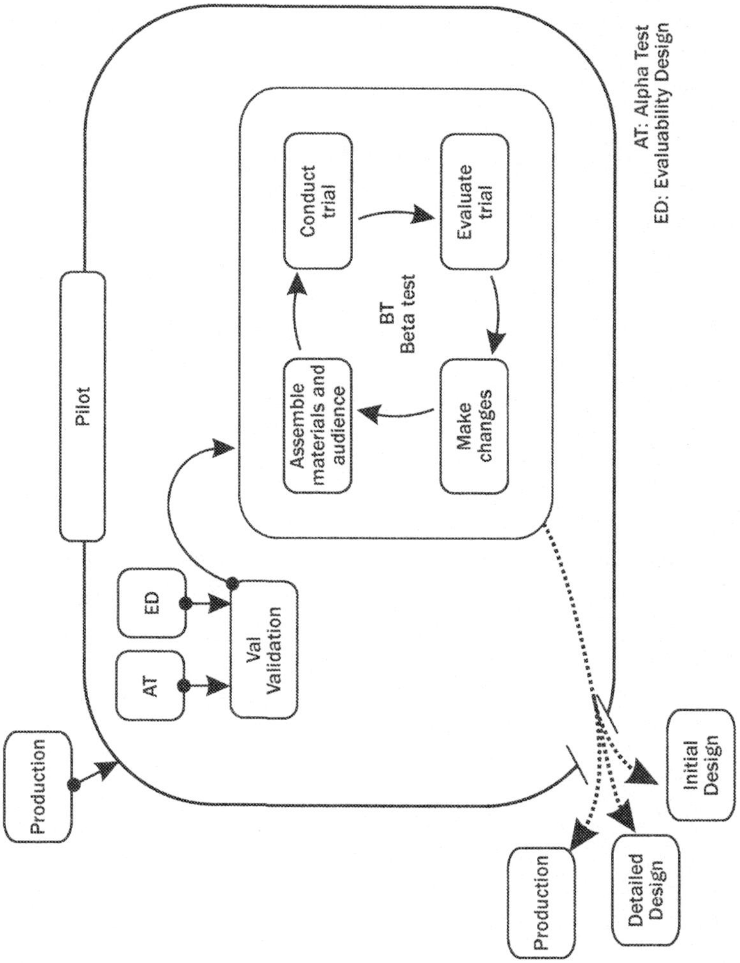

Figure 13.3 Review points in the ELSYE life cycle

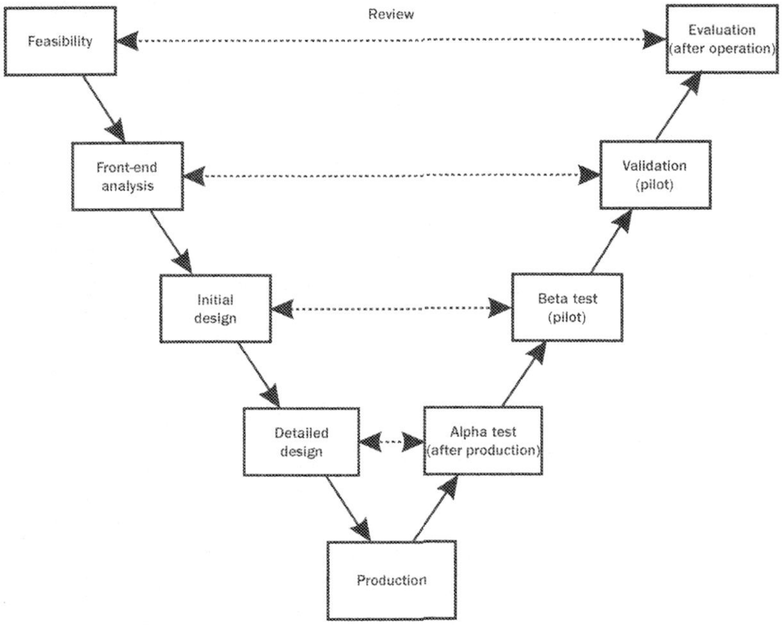

e-learning products have implemented the decisions taken during front-end analysis, while verification, in the form of the beta test, is mainly a review of how the products have implemented the decisions taken during initial design.

The validation step involves one or more review meetings, usually structured inspections as discussed in Chapter 14 on quality management. In order to keep the review focused on relevant issues, one or more checklists are used; these checklists would have been developed during, or would derive from, the evaluability design step of the detailed design phase.

Beta test

The beta test step involves one or more iterations through the tasks of assembling the e-learning products and a sample of the audience, conducting the beta test trial, evaluating the outcomes and making any necessary changes or amendments.

Select the pilot audience

There may be a number of beta test trials, each focused on a particular kind of evaluation with a particular kind of user.

- A small group of representative users from the target audience might be assembled for a detailed qualitative evaluation using participative observation.
- A larger group of representative users might be assembled for a quantitative evaluation using questionnaires.
- A group of 'high performers' might be assembled to check that the e-learning product agrees with the learning points (they have already achieved the objectives and do not have needs from a learning point of view), and to provide feedback in their views of how well the needs of more representative users have been met.
- One or more groups of supervisors and managers might be asked to use the materials and give feedback on how well the needs of their students have been met.

Conduct a trial

The kind of information to seek from a trial was discussed in Chapter 11 in the section on evaluability design:

- reaction;
- learning;
- performance change;
- organisational benefit.

A beta test is likely to seek information in the first two categories, while the evaluation stage is likely to seek information in the last two categories.

Certain varieties of e-learning might be more educational than training, and may not have an end-of-lesson or end-of-session student test incorporated into the product. If the quality of the student learning is to be assessed, it may be necessary for a test or quiz to be constructed for use during the beta testing. Such a test or quiz would be based upon the top-level and enabling objectives, following the discussion in Chapter 8 on the student test step.

What students actually do with the e-learning, how they navigate it, how long they take doing it and whether they seem to have learned anything by the end are usually best explored by *participative observation*. The intention here is first to observe a student closely as they interact with the e-learning, and then to participate in their interactions seeking clarity and explanation as to where, how and why the e-learning was used. These are some of the kinds of questions and issues that might be observed and explored.

- What questions does the user ask of the teacher or, much more interestingly, of a peer?
- Where in the e-learning does the user seem to move quickly through, and where slowly?
- Where does the user skip the instructions?
- Where do any misunderstandings or misinterpretations (of instructions or content) occur?
- What observable use is made of the e-learning (e.g. taking notes, placing finger on the screen, looking up other resources, etc.)?

Evaluate a trial and make changes

Information from a beta test will usually suggest changes in one or more of the following areas.

- Relatively minor changes may require an iteration through parts of the production stage, involving changes to materials or programming (changes to AV resources are unlikely to be minor). Such minor changes should not have significant budgetary or schedule impacts.

- More major changes are those requiring a revisit to the design of the e-learning, either detailed design or initial design. Because these changes will have serious impacts, they will usually require management approval.
- In addition, beta test information may indicate that changes are required to the development processes or the standards employed. These changes may not directly affect the current project, but will concern future projects. Such information is often the most valuable outcome of the beta tests, but because it may not directly affect the current project, it is the information most likely to be lost or ignored. As discussed in Chapter 14, process change and improvement are the most important kinds of quality improvement (otherwise future projects simply repeat time and again the mistakes of earlier ones).

Given agreed changes to the e-learning product, a question always arises about related changes to the e-learning analysis and design documentation, particularly the detailed design documents such as the storyboards. Whether product changes during pilot should be propagated back into design documents will depend upon the size of the project, the requirement for future maintenance and enhancement, contractual arrangements among the stakeholders and so on.

Some guidance might be given in terms of the nature of the e-learning actually produced. If this is predominantly linear, it is likely that any changes will be visible to anyone who runs through the e-learning, and so changing the design documentation is less important. However, if the e-learning involves numerous branch and decision points, such that a particular run through may only reveal a fraction of the product, then changing the design documentation becomes much more important. The number of decision and branch points would have been revealed if the e-learning had been subject to basis path analysis during alpha testing at the end of the production stage (Chapter 12). If the resulting measure of cyclomatic complexity yielded a number greater than, say, 3 (or whatever policy might be set by the project manager), then changing design documentation as well as the product would be indicated.

Distribution

The distribution stage is located within the operation phase of the ELSYE life cycle, and its steps are illustrated in Figure 13.4. During distribution, the beta-tested product from pilot is first taken into manufacturing and packaged if it is intended for mass distribution. A distribution plan is then developed, along with an installation plan and a user training plan.

Figure 13.4 Steps of the distribution stage

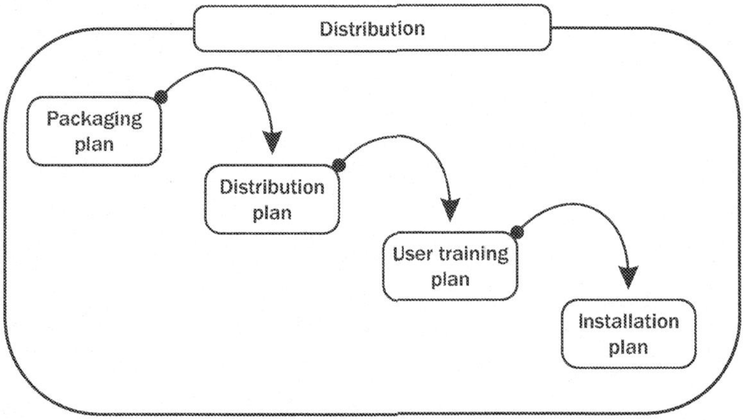

An issue to consider in the packaging plan is the importance of keeping materials and resources together. This is particularly significant if some of the resources are web-based, some print-based and so on.

If the e-learning product is intended for a large audience and multiple sites, marketing issues may be relevant. In particular, marketing information and messages may need to be developed to ensure adequate interest and take-up. Comments from the pilot stage may be useful, along with the ability to give explicit guidance on timing as estimated from the pilot runs.

Use

The use stage is located within the operation phase of the ELSYE life cycle, and its steps are illustrated in Figure 13.5. During use, plans should be developed for three kinds of product and user attention: supporting users, maintaining the product and enhancing the product.

Figure 13.5 **Steps of the use stage**

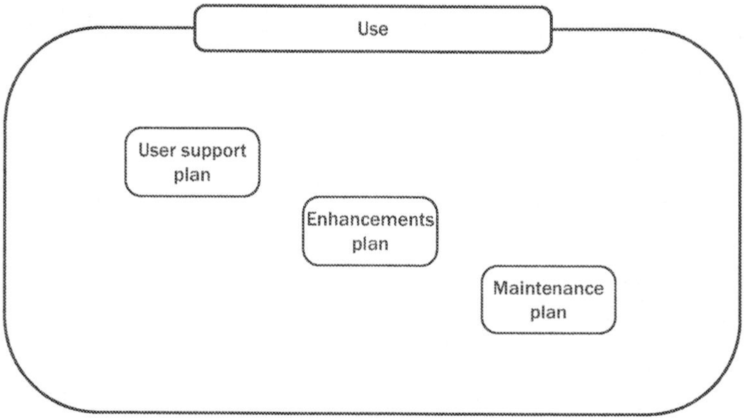

Figure 13.6 Steps of the evaluation stage

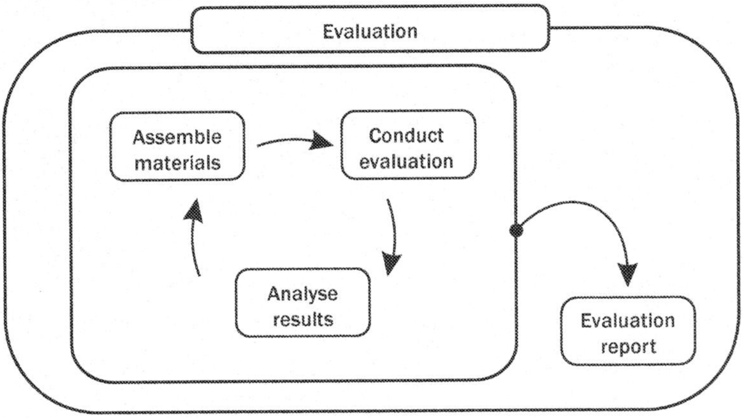

It is inevitable that issues will arise with the e-learning product during use, and the level of reaction needs to be planned in advance rather than worked out under pressure at the time. At the least, if no maintenance and no enhancement are planned, users will need to be advised of work-arounds and may well need a sympathetic contact point which will log issues anyway.

For materials which age or date, possibly through legislative or professional society changes, a maintenance plan is required to keep them up to date. And, if the e-learning product is an important part of business processes, an enhancement plan would be required to ensure it continues to serve needs which are inevitably subject to change and development.

Evaluation

Evaluation is the last stage and review point in the ELSYE life cycle, as illustrated in Figure 13.6, and deals with the issue first addressed during the feasibility phase – 'Has the e-learning project achieved the value intended?'; that is, has it been worth it? It involves the conventional steps of conducting the evaluations and then reporting on them.

Given the earlier classification of the kind of information to seek from a review of the e-learning products (Buckley and Caple, 2007), the evaluation stage focuses upon performance change and organisational benefit – has it met stakeholder needs, and has it delivered value?

The issues to explore in the evaluation stage will have been identified, and appropriate instruments designed, during the evaluability design step of detailed design (Chapter 11).

14

Quality management

The place of quality management in the ELSYE life cycle is illustrated in Figure 14.1. This chapter focuses on some general approaches to quality management in ELSYE. It begins by considering some philosophical issues, and distinguishes between product quality assurance and process quality improvement. It then moves on to consider Fagan's structured inspection as a generally applicable technique of product quality management, and the capability maturity model as a guide to process quality management.

The quality management issues outlined here are those considered necessary and basic to the repeated development of substantial e-learning systems by professional teams to commercial standards of merchantability and fitness for purpose. Where e-learning materials are to be developed as a one-off project, for example, the considerations of process quality and the capability maturity model are less relevant. Where individuals develop occasional, modest e-learning materials for local use, the full formality and documentation requirements of the quality management procedures described here would not be necessary.

Some philosophical issues

Among the many considerations of 'quality' which can be found in recent texts, this chapter makes two points. The

Figure 14.1 Quality management in the ELSYE life cycle

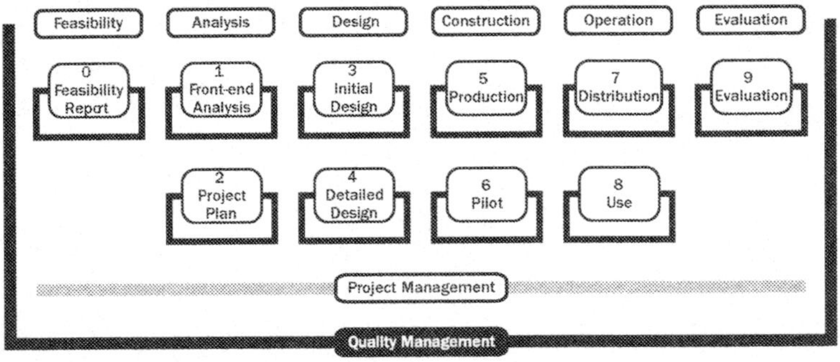

first is that there is no algorithm or procedure which can guarantee the quality of any product; any such algorithm or procedure is inherently incomplete and limited. The second point is that, while the quality of a product *can* nonetheless be quite successfully judged to within acceptable tolerances, it cannot be so judged by the person or persons who originated the product; independent inspection is strictly necessary. The section concludes by distinguishing between the quality management of products and that of the processes which produce the products.

The incompleteness of quality criteria

'Quality' involves meeting a requirement or expectation to an explicit or implicit standard of excellence. The quality of a particular product or service is judged with reference to the requirement it is intended to meet and the standard that applies to it meeting that requirement. From an engineering point of view, this approach to quality is well expressed by the slogan 'Quality is conformance to requirements' (Crosby, 1995), and the approach has certain practical use. The difficulty here is that the quality of a product depends upon its requirements and the applicable standards; for a 'quality' product, therefore, 'quality' requirements and 'quality' standards are needed. But 'quality' requirements and 'quality' standards themselves need 'quality' requirements of requirements, 'quality' standards of requirements, 'quality' requirements of standards and so on. There is an infinite regress that prevents any final assessment of 'quality', illustrated in Figure 14.2.

Gödel's 'incompleteness' theorem

This infinite regress shows that the notion of 'quality' is inherently incomplete. Any assessment of 'quality' which purports to be exhaustive cannot be so, and there can be no procedure or algorithm that provides a final or absolute judgement. Like Gödel's theorem on the incompleteness of any formal system (Hofstadter, 2000), however, the incompleteness of any quality system does not mean that such systems are worthless; simply that they are limited. Some practical consequences of this are discussed later.

Judging quality requires outsiders

One of the best 'primers' on quality is Pirsig's (1999) bestseller *Zen and the Art of Motorcycle Maintenance*, and one of the points Pirsig makes is that, while 'quality' is essentially indefinable, it is nonetheless easily recognised; you know it when you see it. The point needs to be clarified, however, since your recognition of something's quality is generally restricted to things which result from others' effort and not your own. You are generally a rather poor judge of your own products and services, though you are generally a much better judge of those of others. The phenomenon is

Figure 14.2 Infinite regress of quality criteria

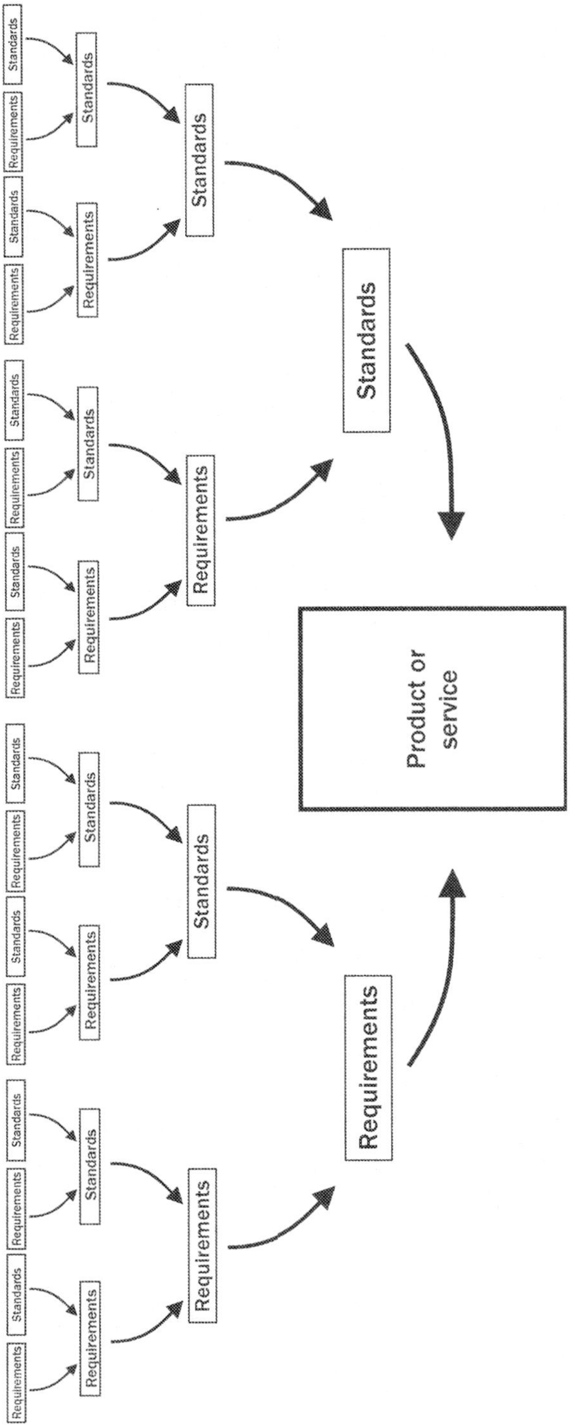

related to the biblical issue of seeing the speck in another's eye and not the plank in your own. Figure 14.3 provides an illustration of why judging your own work is problematic: the objective deliverable item 'fits' what is in the author's head, but does not fit what is in the reviewer's mind.

The reason why judging your own work is so difficult and uncertain is because of its necessarily excellent fit to your own ideas and approaches. After all, it is only in the most unusual circumstances that one does not do or try one's best, and hence one generally feels that the result is at least reasonable if not really rather good. The reason judging someone else's work is so much easier is that, in all those places where it does not fit your own ideas and approaches, you can objectively identify and weigh the work's strengths and weaknesses.

As a consequence, this phenomenon has a profound impact on appropriate quality assurance procedures in ELSYE. Essentially, it implies that outsiders – independent inspectors – are required to judge the quality of e-learning

Figure 14.3 The plank in your eye and the speck in others' eyes

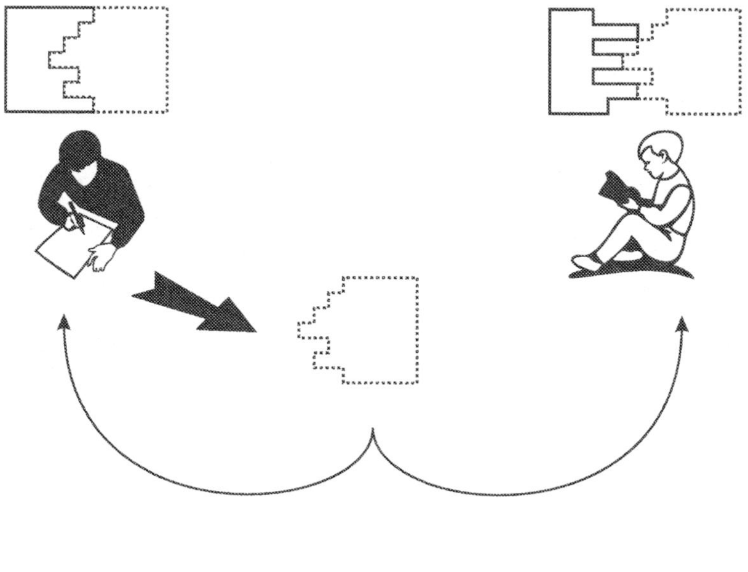

designs and materials adequately and to evaluate e-learning outcomes. It also implies that these independent inspectors are not required to be experts in ELSYE. These points will be developed in later discussion.

Product and process

Managing *product* quality involves the traditional aspects of quality assurance: review, inspect and test. Figure 14.4 illustrates product quality management. In each phase or stage of development and production, the products and materials are inspected and any product defects are fixed. This approach is perfectly sound and always necessary, but it has a central difficulty: the development and production process could cause product defects as much as any other causes. A quality management approach that simply focuses on product defects finds itself fixing the same kinds of defects time and again, project after project.

Figure 14.4 **Product quality management**

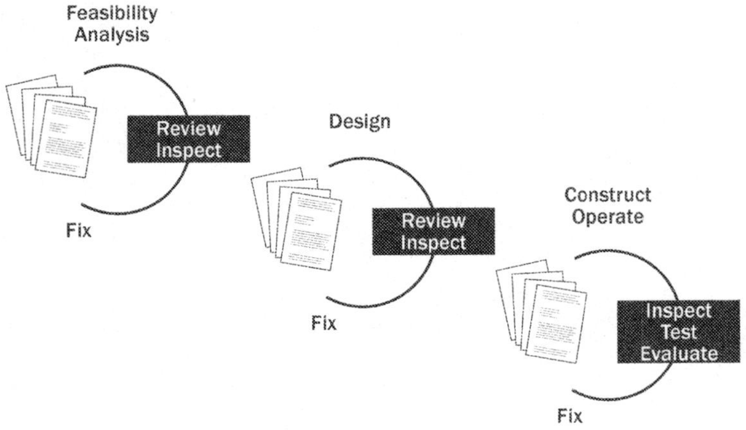

Managing *process* quality involves the more recent emphasis on continuous improvement, where the methods by which the product is developed are evaluated and improved. A second focus is thus necessary, upon the development and production processes themselves. Figure 14.5 illustrates this focus upon process quality assurance. The same principles of inspection and defect correction apply, but to the process rather than to the product. In this way, product defects which result from the production process are systematically eliminated, and as each project is completed the defects list shrinks and the same errors are not repeated.

Any project comprises three major activities: technical, managerial and quality. This is illustrated in Figure 14.6. The key quality management activities are shown in Figure 14.7 as enclosing the technical and project management activities.

Figure 14.5 **Process quality management**

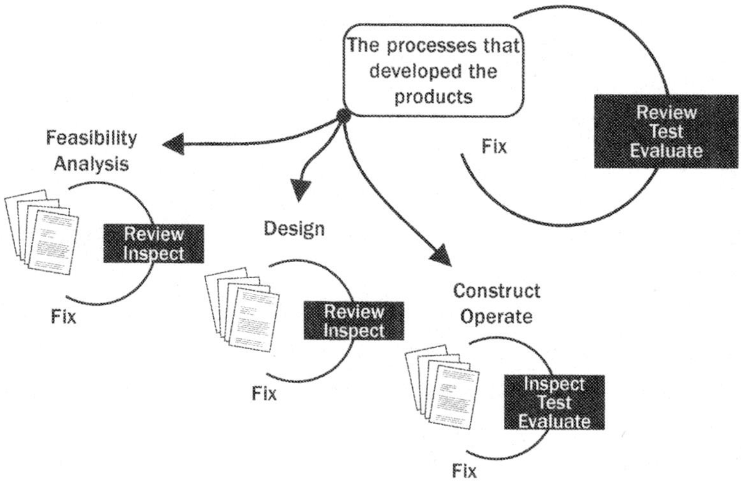

Figure 14.6 Component activities of a project

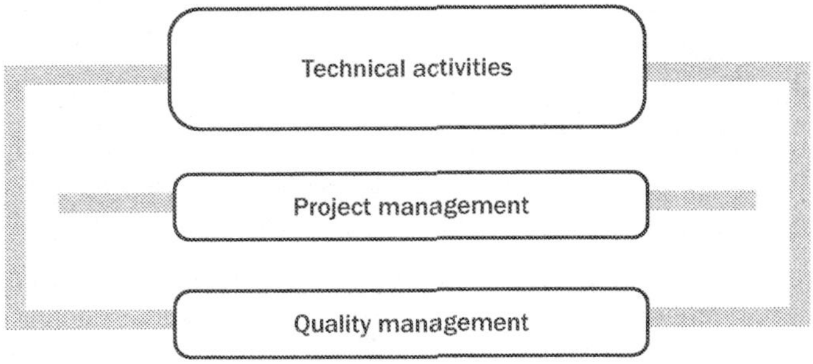

Figure 14.7 Quality management concerns

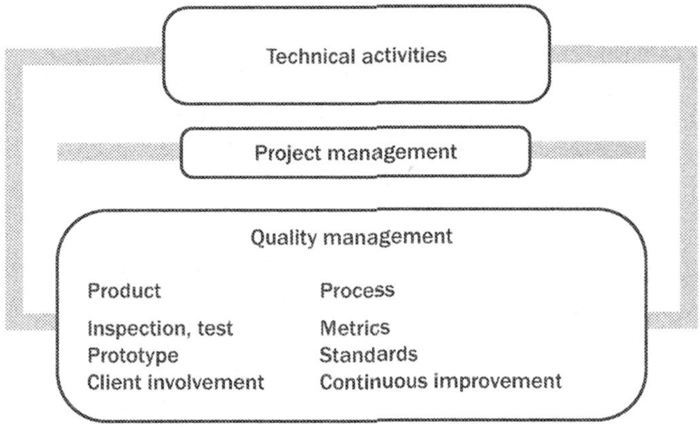

A general approach to quality assurance in ELSYE

The general approach to quality management taken in this book is shown in Figure 14.8. The figure specifies project management activities as well as quality management activities. While it is often difficult to distinguish the two, since both are managerial as opposed to technical concerns, it is usually unnecessary, since effective project management

Figure 14.8 Generic project and quality management activities

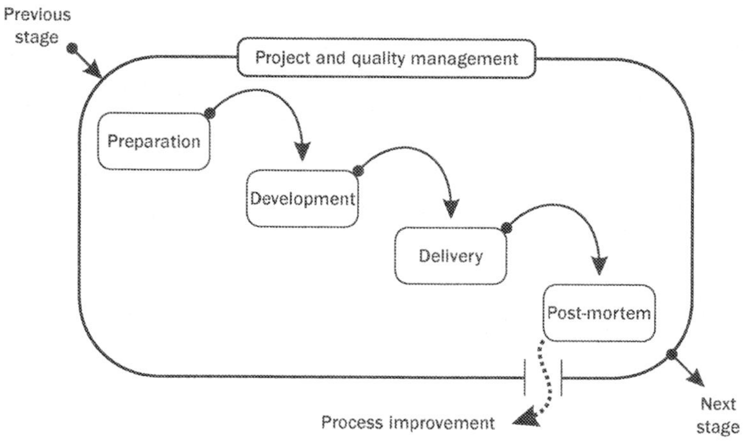

is in fact essential to quality management, and can be considered part of it. The project management issues are considered in the next chapter.

One consequence of the fact that one is generally not good at judging the quality of one's own work is the need to make that work available and accessible for others to judge. This must occur as early as possible and as often as possible. As elaborated in Figure 14.9, every ELSYE product, whether it is a technical product such as a needs analysis, a management product such as a Gantt chart, or some e-learning materials, can be usefully inspected at three points before it is finalised: when it is in outline form, when some samples are available and when it is in draft form.

- *Product outline.* Each product has its contents (and possibly its approach or treatment) outlined before work on the product starts. To facilitate this, pertinent information such as previous technical documents, designs or standards needs to be reviewed. Figure 14.9

Figure 14.9 General quality management activities

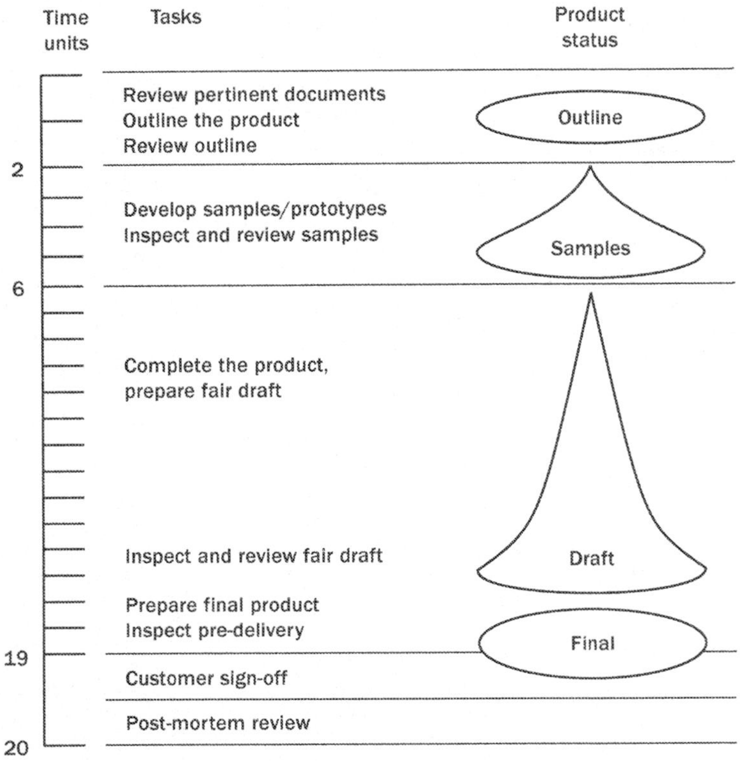

suggests that about two or three units of time (out of 20) are devoted to these preparatory tasks.

- *Product samples or prototypes.* Samples, models or prototypes of the product are developed, reviewed and evaluated before full-scale work is undertaken or completed. Figure 14.9 suggests that such samples should be produced within the first third of the time set aside for the product's production, and might take about three or four units of time (out of 20) to produce. Samples or prototypes are particularly suited to inspection and comment by the customer.

- *Product draft.* Finally, a product draft is inspected before delivery to the customer. The draft should be available for internal inspection after about 17 units of time (out of 20), and the remaining two or three units of time should be spent on the customer sign-off and post-mortem review.

At each of these inspection points the customer may be involved in the review process as an interested and affected party. For some projects customer involvement at a lower level may be acceptable, in which case only samples or prototypes need be presented for the customer's consideration. The customer's acceptance and sign-off of the final product represents a fourth point at which it is reviewed; this is a formality if the previous three review points were properly carried out. After customer acceptance, there should be a post-mortem that considers the lessons to be learned and the process improvements that may be desirable.

This approach to product quality management applies generally at both micro and macro levels. It is applied in ELSYE to both the macro stages of the life cycle and the micro steps of which each stage consists. Figure 14.10 illustrates these general quality and project management components.

Product quality: structured inspection

A very useful and systematic approach to product inspection, particularly the inspection of analysis and design materials, has been developed within IBM and is in wide use in software engineering. The following discussion is based on the work of Fagan (Pressman, 2004).

Figure 14.10 General quality and project management steps at each ELSYE stage

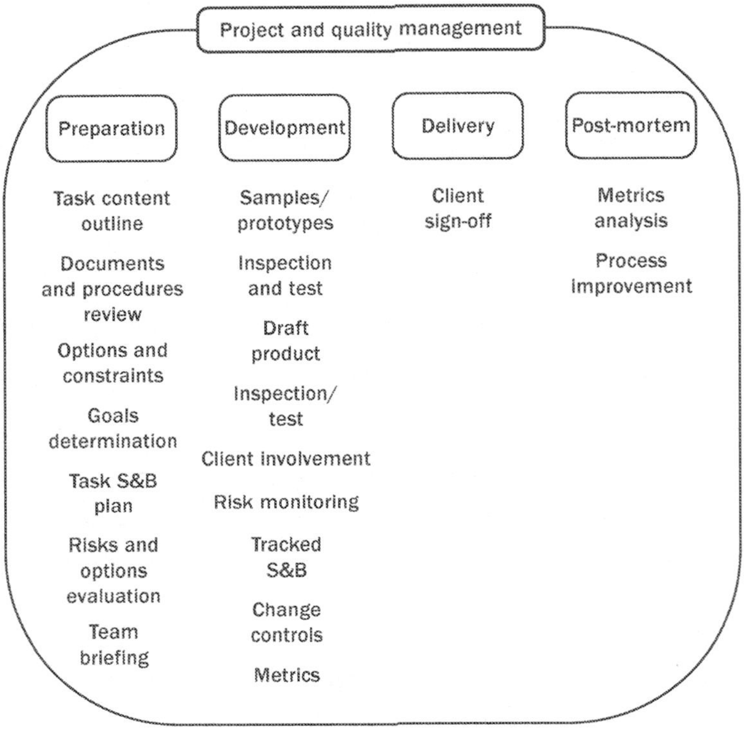

Structured inspections consider all classes or types of defect in product form and content, at all points in the ELSYE life cycle: the spelling, grammar, layout and mechanics; the sequence, logic, coherence and consistency of the product's components; the applicability and appropriateness of notation and other conventions used; and the general accuracy, validity and applicability of the contents.

A structured inspection involves a moderator or chairperson, a panel of two to four inspectors, the product materials to be inspected and the supporting documentation. The moderator receives the product material for inspection; determines who will inspect, where and when; and distributes

Figure 14.11 **Structured inspection**

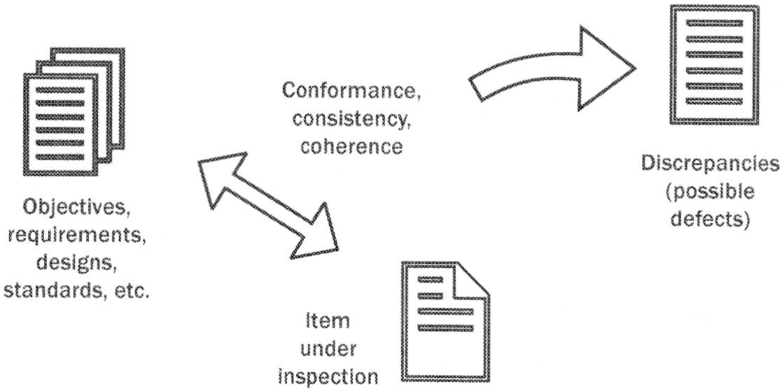

the materials to the inspection panel. The materials consist of the item(s) for inspection and all supporting project documentation and other information, including project and organisational standards, organisational documents on goals and objectives, quality checklists and so on. The process is illustrated in Figure 14.11. In the following discussion, an ELSYE product inspection might have the project manager as the moderator, two inspectors who are practising teachers (trainers, lecturers and so on), an inspector who is a technical expert in one or other aspect of e-learning development (graphics artist, software programmer, etc.) and an inspector who is a subject matter expert.

Preparation

The panel of inspectors familiarise themselves with the materials beforehand. During preparation, inspectors typically spend 1.5 hours preparing a list of presumed defects. This individual written list is important, since research shows that inspectors are more committed to their findings and less likely simply to agree with whatever is said in the inspection meeting if they write down their individual thoughts beforehand.

Inspection meeting

The inspectors spend about two hours working through the product materials, discussing their individual lists of presumed defects and agreeing a collective definitive list. No originators of the materials are present; this is important since it is known that originators have a poor ability to detect their own errors and are likely to be emotionally involved with their creation.

No attempt is made by the inspectors to correct or improve any of the defects they identify. More significantly, there is no discussion of whether a defect is 'real'. It simply requires the inspectors to agree that 'something' is wrong for it to be logged as a presumed defect in need of attention.

Key inspection technique

During preparation for the inspection meeting, and in the inspection meeting itself, the inspectors operate the key inspection technique illustrated in Figure 14.12. During inspection the item under inspection is compared against all its relevant precursor documents and materials, particularly documents which specify the requirements of the item and the standards applicable. The inspection focus is on the item's conformance to standards, consistency with precursors and its own internal coherence. Inspection does not particularly demand technical knowledge of or expertise in the item being inspected, since the relevant and necessary background materials are bundled with the item.

Figure 14.12 Inspection process

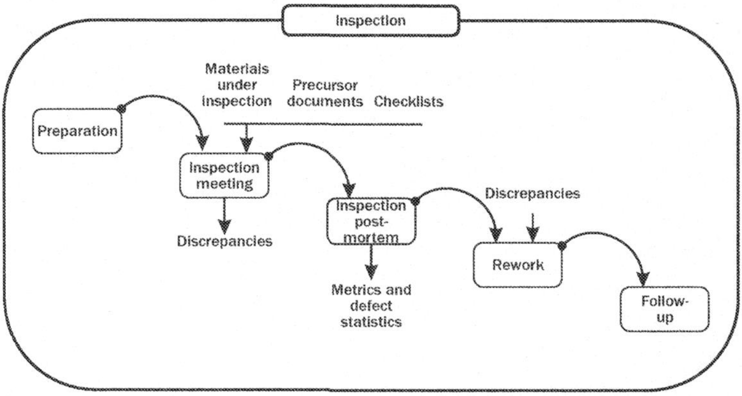

Checklists

It is a characteristic feature of structured inspection that it develops and uses checklists relevant to the material under review. A well-developed checklist instantiates and makes explicit the quality criteria to be applied to the product.

Inspection post-mortem

A post-mortem to the inspection meeting is optional. If it does take place, usually immediately after the inspection, there are two activities involved. First, suggestions and ideas for good repairs may be noted. Second, defect statistics (metrics) may be gathered and analysed.

Defect statistics (metrics)

Inspections should develop and use statistics to measure the defectiveness of the products inspected and monitor the effectiveness of the inspection process. Example metrics include the number of pages of documentation inspected, the number of defects logged, the defect density (defects per page), the number of hours spent undertaking inspection (preparation and meeting), the defect detection rate (defects per hour), the cost of the inspection, the cost of defect detection per defect logged, the inspection rate (pages per hour) and so on.

Rework

The moderator arranges for the product material to be assigned, probably to its originators, for repair. There are at least two good reasons to pick out the originators as the most suitable persons to carry out repairs: they need to bear responsibility for their work; and they are most familiar with the product, minimising communications and handover problems.

Follow-up

The moderator ensures all listed defects are addressed. There is no need to judge the correctness of the repairs, but the moderator may choose to do so. Notice that there is no formal requirement for the repaired material to be resubmitted for inspection.

Process quality: capability maturity model

While structured inspection has been primarily developed for the quality management of analysis and design products, the capability maturity model (CMM) was developed to address the quality management of the process of software development.

The general concerns and prescriptions of the standard software CMM (Humphrey, 1990) can be extrapolated to e-learning systems engineering. The development of software systems and the development of e-learning systems have considerable similarities at the macro level, particularly for e-learning systems that use technology for delivery.

What may now be called the ELSYE CMM, which is an interpretation of the software CMM, describes five levels of capability that refer to the general ability of an e-learning development or engineering environment to translate a set of e-learning objectives effectively into a completed e-learning system.

Level 1: chaos

Level 1 capability in the ELSYE CMM could be called the 'chaos' level, and is illustrated in Figure 14.13. At this level of capability, the process which takes an e-learning intention and produces some e-learning materials is effectively

Figure 14.13 **'Chaos': level 1 of the ELSYE capability maturity model**

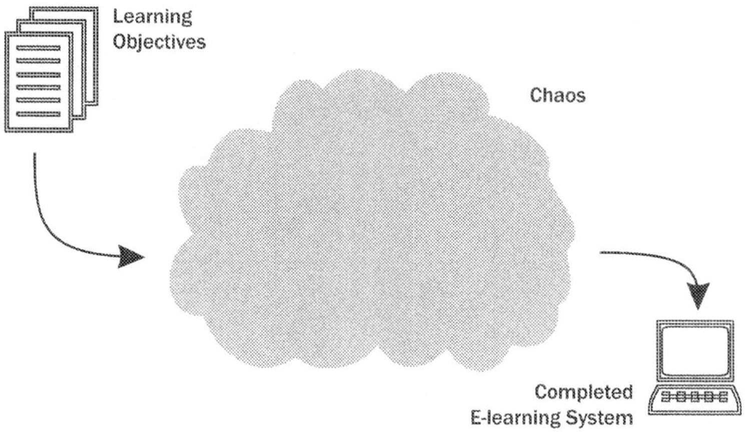

unknown, unsystematic, unpredictable and undefined. Level 1 capability probably characterises the efforts of first-time developers. Of course, the results of level 1 capability might be perfectly adequate; but this would be by accident rather than by design.

Level 2: repeatable

Level 2 capability is called 'repeatable' and is illustrated in Figure 14.14, where the cloud of the chaos of level 1 has parted somewhat to reveal the key feature of level 2, the presence of project management. At this level of capability, the process that takes an e-learning intention and produces some e-learning materials can be generally repeated and the outcome is somewhat more predictable. This is not to say that the outcome is necessarily of good quality; a repeatable process may simply repeatedly produce poor-quality products. Nevertheless, a process which can be reliably

Figure 14.14 'Repeatable': level 2 of the ELSYE capability maturity model

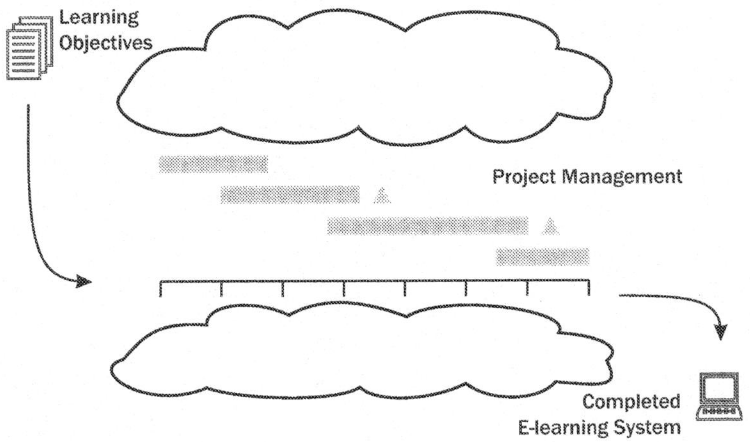

repeated is the basis of a process which can be made to produce quality products; the reverse is not true.

The key capabilities of a level 2 ELSYE CMM process are listed in Table 14.1. The focus is on the management and planning of the project as a whole. Developers exhibiting level 2 capability may be thought of as showing good intentions, particularly on the project management side, but are still unsure of the correct technical components of e-learning systems development.

Table 14.1 **Level 2 ELSYE CMM capabilities**

Level 2 'repeatable' components	
Objectives management	E-learning objectives baselined and controlled Plans, products and activities consistent with e-learning objectives
Managing e-learning materials	Configuration management planned E-learning materials identified and controlled Changes controlled Baseline status and content disseminated
Project planning	Estimates, activities and commitments documented Stakeholder commitments agreed
Project tracking	Actuals tracked against plan Corrective actions taken to closure Changes agreed by stakeholders
Subcontract management	Qualified subcontractors selected Commitments agreed Ongoing communications maintained Prime contractor tracks subcontractor performance and actuals

Level 3: managed

The capability at level 3 of the ELSYE CMM is called 'managed' and is illustrated in Figure 14.15, where the clouds of uncertainty and imprecision which attended level 2 have dissipated further. The theme running through the capability of a level 3 CMM process is that of standards, particularly standards related to the development process itself and the ways in which the standardised process can be modified to cater for different kinds of project. At this level of capability, the process that takes an e-learning intention and produces some e-learning materials is under active project and product quality management. The process is generally repeatable and predictable, and additionally the standards and product quality assurance activities ensure the production of good-quality products.

Table 14.2 lists the level 3 capabilities in more detail. Developers operating at level 3 capability are operating an ELSYE development process that is technically and managerially well specified.

Figure 14.15 'Managed': level 3 of the ELSYE capability maturity model

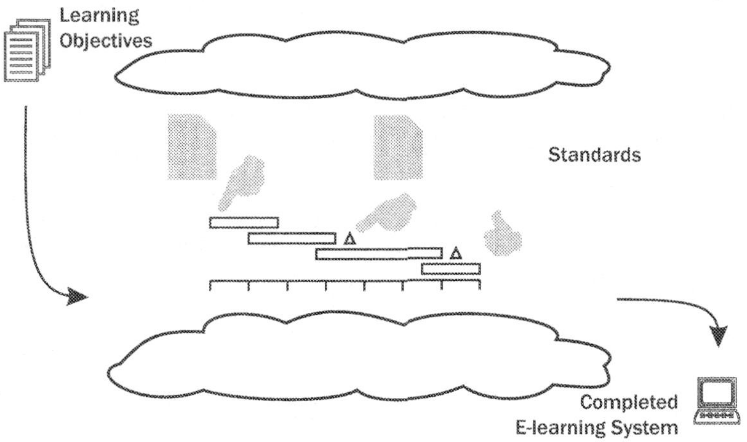

Table 14.2 **Level 3 ELSYE CMM capabilities**

Level 3 'managed' components	
Process focus	ELSYE process development and improvement activities planned and coordinated across organisation Process strengths and weaknesses identified
Process definition	Standard ELSYE process developed and maintained Information on use of standard process is collected and disseminated
Integrated software management	Particular project's process is tailored from organisation's standard ELSYE process Project is planned and managed according to its defined process
Product engineering	Tasks are defined, integrated and consistently performed Products are consistent with each other
Coordination	All stakeholders agree requirements and commitments Intergroup issues are identified, tracked and resolved
Quality assurance	QA activities planned Adherence to standards verified QA results disseminated Non-compliance addressed by senior management
Reviews	Peer reviews are planned Defects in products are identified and removed
Training	Training is planned, provided and taken by those who need it

Level 4: quantified

At level 4 CMM the ELSYE process is called 'quantified', illustrated in Figure 14.16. Here the project and quality management processes are quantified and measured.

Figure 14.16 'Quantified': level 4 of the ELSYE capability maturity model

Quantifying, measuring and managing projects using measurements are known as metrics. The key idea at level 4 is that all the good practices of levels 2 and 3 are subjected to measurement so that improvement can be managed: numerical targets can be set, the process can be controlled numerically and the effects of changes to the process can be measured and statistically analysed. In the same way that the ELSYE process could not deliver quality products unless effective project management was in place, the process cannot be reliably improved unless metrics are in place and the improvement activities use the metrics to measure and control the required changes.

Table 14.3 lists the capabilities of a level 4 process in more detail. The emphasis here is on the quantification of project and quality management procedures and standards to permit managed improvement in these processes and standards. Developers operating an ELSYE process of level 4 capability are able to estimate with considerable accuracy, for example, the man-days needed to produce a multimedia course of e-learning, the number of defects such a course would exhibit on its release and the costs of

Table 14.3 Level 4 ELSYE CMM capabilities

Level 4 'quantified' components	
Quantitative process management	Quantitative process management activities planned Project's process performance controlled quantitatively Organisation's standard ELSYE process capability is quantified
Quality management	Quality management activities are planned Measurable product quality goals defined and prioritised Actual progress on achieving goals is quantified and managed

increasing materials inspection and piloting to reduce such defects by 50 per cent.

Level 5: optimised

The highest level of ELSYE process capability is called 'optimised', illustrated in Figure 14.17. Based on the

Figure 14.17 'Optimised': level 5 of the ELSYE capability maturity model

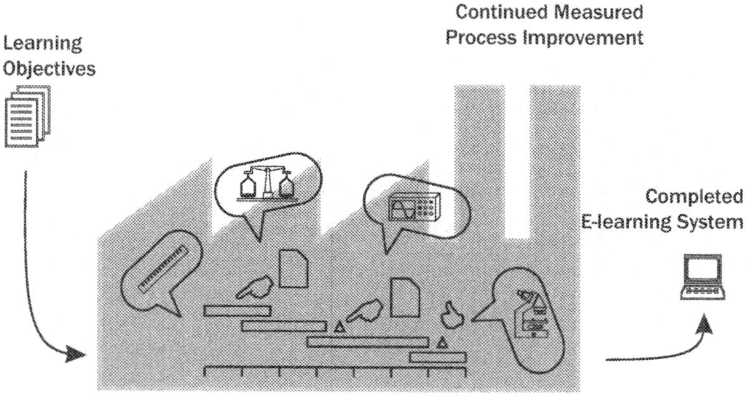

Table 14.4 **Level 5 ELSYE CMM capabilities**

Level 5 'optimised' components	
Defect prevention	Defect prevention activities planned Common causes of defects sought out and identified Causes of defects are prioritised and systematically eliminated
Technology change management	Incorporation of technology changes planned New technology impact on quality and productivity evaluated Appropriate new technology transferred into normal practice
Process change management	Continuous process improvement planned Organisation-wide participation in process improvement Organisation's standard ELSYE process and projects' defined processes continuously improved

quantification of the ELSYE process achieved in level 4, the capability of the level 5 process is to undertake quality and process optimisation. While the various stages and steps of the ELSYE process were fine-tuned and incrementally improved at level 4, at level 5 this tuning and improvement optimises production for a variety of different kinds of project, so the result resembles an engineering 'factory' for the efficient and optimum production of high-quality e-learning materials.

Developers operating a level 5 ELSYE process are using a process that is under continuous improvement, where the effectiveness of changes to the process can be estimated and demonstrated and where process changes are optimised. Table 14.4 shows the detailed capabilities of a level 5 ELSYE process.

15

Project management

A characteristic feature of ELSYE projects is the variety of skills required in the design and production of e-learning materials. A characteristic feature of poor or failed ELSYE projects is their lack of awareness and lack of deployment of the necessary e-learning design, graphic design and writing skills, among others. (These different roles are detailed in Table 15.5.) Another feature of failed projects in general is their lack of appreciation of the process and impact of organisational power and politics. This chapter is concerned with the role of the project manager; other chapters make clear where and why the other skills are required in the ELSYE life cycle.

In this chapter the estimating, preparation and tracking of schedules and budgets are outlined, along with the collection and use of process and product metrics. Change control and configuration management are also discussed, while the topic of risk analysis is treated in Chapter 7 on the project plan step.

Finally, issues relating to the structuring of project teams are discussed later in this chapter, and the political (as in organisational politics) dimension to project management is discussed last.

Project stages

Figures 15.1 and 15.2 illustrate the place of project management activities in the ELSYE life cycle, alongside the

Figure 15.1 Project management within the ELSYE life cycle

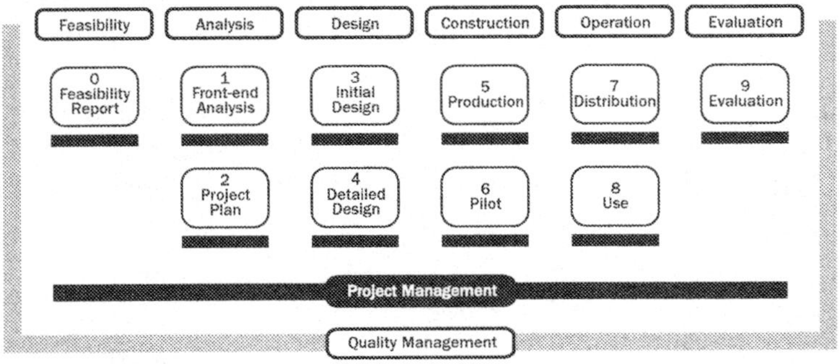

Figure 15.2 Project management general activities

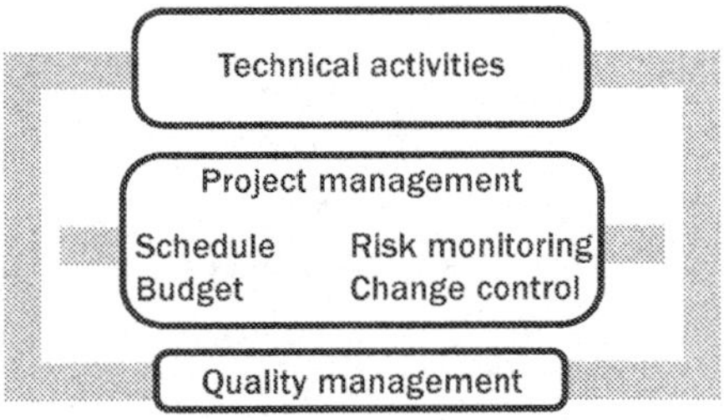

two other major components of technical work and quality management. Project management at the level of the ELSYE life cycle focuses upon the very general tasks of preparing and tracking the project budget and schedule, monitoring the project risks and controlling the inevitable pressure for changes and modifications as the project progresses. Project management within each stage focuses upon the appropriate structuring and execution of the stage's tasks.

Figure 15.3 illustrates the general structure of each ELSYE stage, and expands upon the nature of the project and quality management activities which generally occur at each stage. It is clear from Figure 15.3 that, operationally, project management and quality management activities are difficult to distinguish, and in practice the project manager is also the quality manager, undertaking all those management roles

Figure 15.3 Generic structure of the ELSYE life-cycle stage

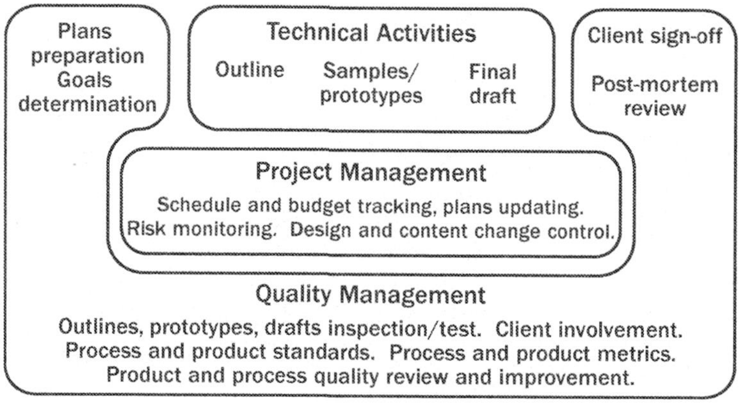

necessary to manage the project successfully. At the level of the ELSYE stage, the project management tasks can be a little more differentiated. The ELSYE stage is the major building-block of an ELSYE project, and involves in particular the major customer reviews and sign-offs of the various stage products: the feasibility report, the front-end analysis, the initial and detailed designs and the finished materials from production.

Within each stage there are usually between two and five steps. The general project management tasks common to every stage in an ELSYE project are illustrated in Figure 15.4. Each stage involves the step of preparation for the stage, then the step of technical development of the stage's technical products, followed by the step of delivery of the product to the customer and finally the step of post-mortem. It may be useful to recall from Figure 15.3 and the earlier discussion of quality management (Chapter 14) that, within technical development, the stage's technical products will be made inspectable and externally visible for managerial and quality purposes in the form of outlines, some samples or prototypes and drafts.

Figure 15.4 **Project management overview: activities within each technical stage**

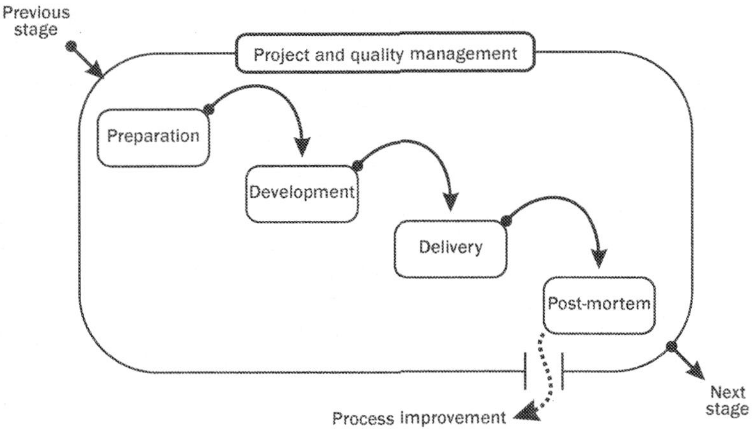

Preparation

Figure 15.5 illustrates the tasks within the step of preparation. During preparation for the stage, the project manager updates the project plans based on current estimates and briefs the project team.

The first task in the preparation step is that of documents and procedures review. The project manager reviews the standards set down for the conduct and management of the stage (the project and quality management standards, prepared during the stage of front-end analysis), and reviews the technical products from the previous stage. The result of this task is the preparation of a task content outline: an outline of the technical tasks to be undertaken in the stage. This outline corresponds to the 'outline' identified in Chapter 14 on quality management.

The project manager then identifies the options and constraints that affect the stage concerned. These options and constraints are both technical and managerial.

Figure 15.5 Preparation

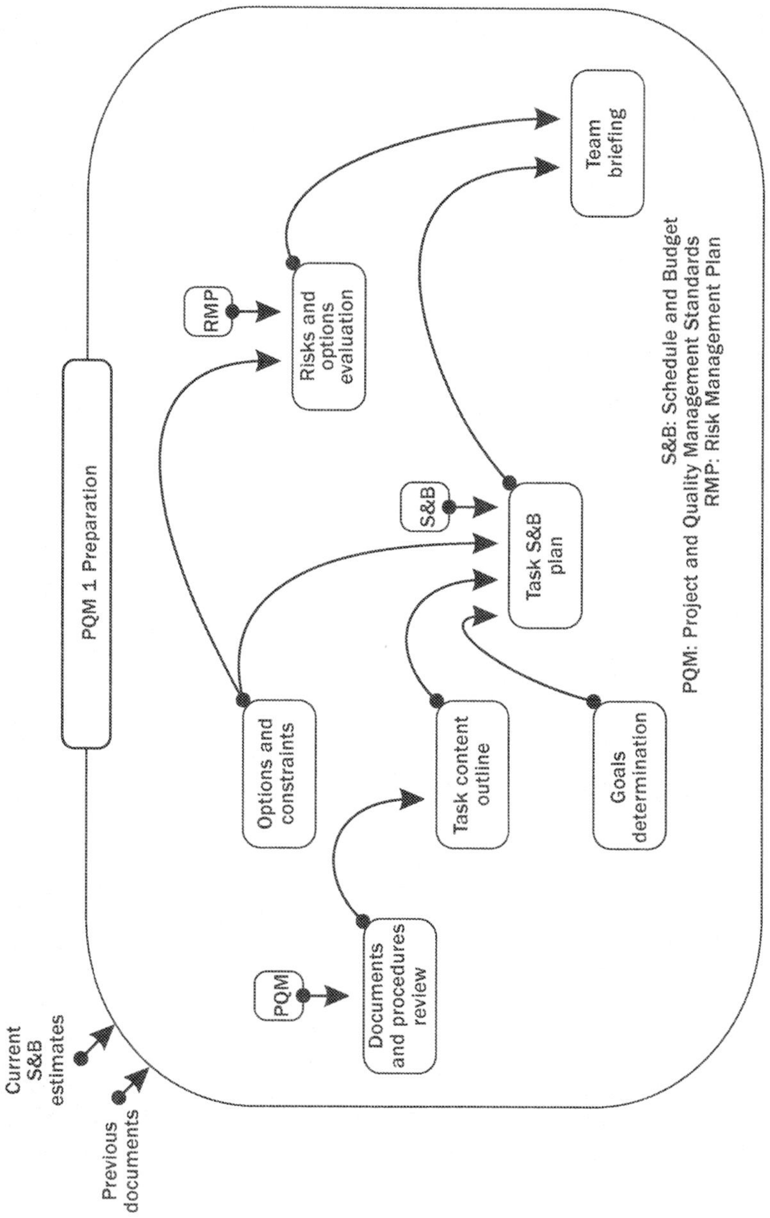

Technical options may include different ways to approach the technical challenges of the stage, different methods to employ or different features to try. Constraints may include equipment issues such as availability.

Managerial options include deciding upon the number or type of staff to deploy on the stage, deciding upon the timing and phasing of samples, prototypes and client meetings and deciding upon the target level of functionality and explicit documentation required of the stage products. Constraints may include schedule issues such as forthcoming public holidays or staff leave, budget issues such as current cash flows and organisational political issues such as the need to maintain the support of sponsors and other stakeholders.

After deliberation and discussion, the effects of the options and constraints are fed into the step of risks and options evaluation, and the preparation of the stage schedule and budget plan.

The goals of the stage – technical and managerial – should be clearly determined. These help to focus on the options and constraints of the stage, and the preparation of the stage schedule and budget plan.

The stage schedule and budget plan can now be developed in detail, and this plan comprises the major management outcome of the preparation for the stage. Schedules and budgets are discussed below.

The risk management plan (a product of the project plan stage if the project has moved into the design phase, or of the feasibility report stage if the project is still in its analysis phase) is reviewed as part of the risks and options evaluation step, and the risks relevant to the stage are considered and any necessary action planned.

Finally, the project manager arranges for the staff involved in the stage to have a team briefing, at which they are appraised of the current state of the project and its current budget, schedule, goals and risks. Relevant documents from earlier stages are reviewed and discussed.

Development

Figure 15.6 illustrates the project and quality management tasks during the development of the technical products for a stage.

During development the technical staff prepare and then inspect, review and/or test samples and/or prototypes of the materials relevant to the stage. From there, the draft products of the stage are prepared and reviewed.

As work progresses on the stage's products, the project manager is responsible for the following.

- Tracking the project's schedule and budget (discussed in more detail below).

Figure 15.6 Development

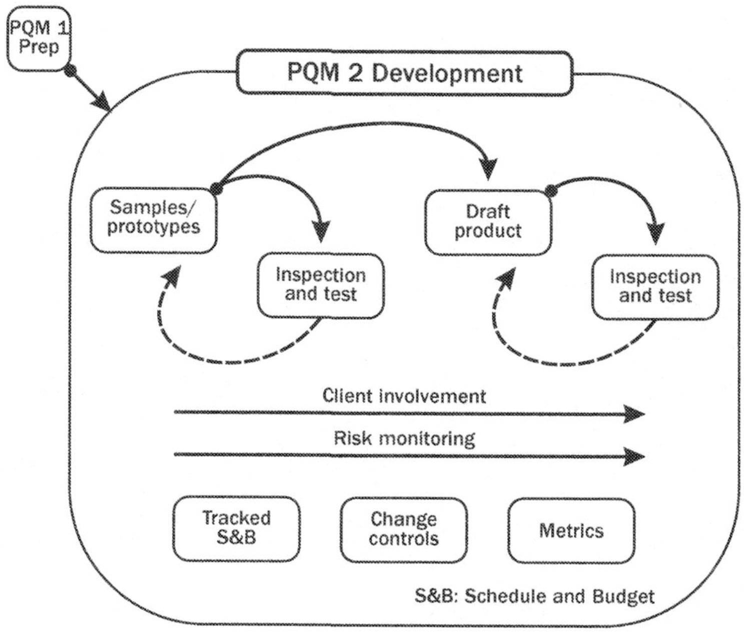

- Monitoring the risks and ensuring both that identified risks are under control and that previously unidentified risks are attended to. Risk analysis is discussed as part of the project plan stage (Chapter 7).
- Managing the quality activities of inspection, review and testing. Inspection and review are discussed in Chapter 14 on quality management; testing is discussed in Chapters 12 and 13 dealing with the stages of production and pilot.
- Involving the customer as necessary to ensure an acceptable product is delivered. The major outcomes of customer involvement are changes to the project; managing these changes is discussed below.
- Tracking key defined measures – metrics – of the project's and product's quality and development. Metrics are discussed below.
- Prioritising and authorising the requests for design and content changes, which will come from both team members and the customer. Change control is discussed below.

Delivery

The stage products must be formally agreed by the customer and signed off (Figure 15.7).

Post-mortem

After the delivery of the stage products and customer sign-off, the project manager undertakes a post-mortem of the stage, usually in consultation with the team members. Using the metrics gathered, the results from the product inspections and feedback from the customer sign-off, actions are planned to improve the development processes involved in the stage (Figure 15.8).

Figure 15.7 Delivery

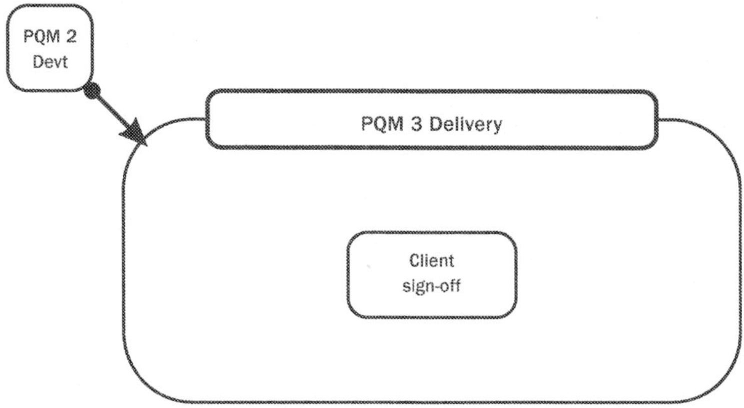

Figure 15.8 Post-mortem

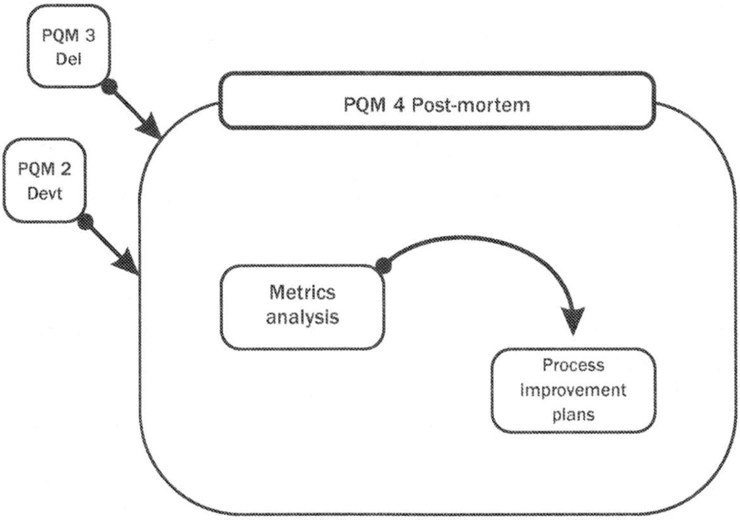

Estimating

The problem of estimating is the problem of answering the question 'what is the size of this project?' in terms of time and money. The 'size' of an e-learning system is usually measured as 'hours of study time', and there are a number of rules of thumb about the number of development work-hours needed to produce one hour of study time. A project that involved the development of an e-learning session involving an hour of study time using text-based materials and an expository treatment would generally be a very modest ELSYE project, perhaps 20 work-hours of development time, even where the development team included an e-learning designer, a subject matter expert and a technical writer. On the other hand, the same project of an e-learning session of an hour of study time when treated through the use of a fully interactive video involving numerous different simulated consequences of decisions made would be a substantial project, perhaps requiring 2,000 work-hours of development time. The usefulness of 'study hours' as a measure of an ELSYE product's size is that it scales up reasonably well when larger projects *of the same type* are considered. For example, the text-based expository project would take about 200 hours of development time if there were materials for ten hours of study time to be developed.

Published sources of specific techniques of estimating that are applicable to ELSYE projects are very few; Gery (1987) is one of the most accessible.

Budgeting

A simple ELSYE project budget is illustrated in Table 15.1, where the major headings of personnel, equipment and expenses are generally all that is necessary. For larger projects these cost categories may be broken down by project phase, as illustrated in Table 15.2.

Table 15.1 **Simple ELSYE project budget**

		£000
Personnel	Project management E-learning design E-learning programming Graphics design	1 5 10 2
Equipment	Authoring software Multimedia PCs	3 6
Expenses	Customer meetings SME meetings	1 1

Table 15.2 **ELSYE project budget by phase**

		FEA	ID	DD	Production	Pilot
Personnel	Management	0.1	0.2	0.3	0.3	0.1
	Design		1.5	2.5		1.0
	Programming	1.0		2.0	8.0	2.0
	Graphics			0.5	1.5	0.5
Equipment	Authoring software				3.0	
	Multimedia PCs	6.0				
Expenses	Customer meetings	0.2	0.2	0.2	0.4	0.2
	SME meetings	0.2	0.2	0.6		0.1

Much if not most of an ELSYE project's budget is measured by the amount of effort needed to design and develop the e-learning materials. The measure of project effort is in work-hours, work-days, work-weeks and so on. Personnel costs are estimated from the work-days taken by each activity. Note that work-days of effort are quite distinct from calendar days of elapsed time; each activity in fact requires an estimate of both. For example, the activity 'design e-learning strategy' might involve two e-learning designers for a total of 20 work-hours, but take ten elapsed days to complete because of allowances for meetings with customers, internal reviews and other work in which the designers are also involved. The activity 'code and test e-learning module' might involve two e-learning programmers for a total of 30 work-hours, but be completed in two days. The elapsed time estimates of ten days and two days are relevant for the project schedule, while the effort estimates of 20 and 30 work-hours are required for the project budget.

The cost of a project team member derives from the cost of employing them spread over the number of days they are expected to be chargeable to a project. The number of days they are chargeable to a project is based on the number of working days in the year, taken to be 260, less public holidays, personal holiday allowances and provision for sickness, yielding perhaps 220 days per year. These days are then reduced by the expected utilisation of the staff member, usually 80 per cent for technical staff and between 20 per cent and 60 per cent for supervisors and managers.

Employment costs consist of salary plus overhead provision. In some budgets the overhead provides only for direct overhead costs such as National Insurance contribution, pension, company car and so on, and would range from about 20 per cent of salary cost for junior staff to about 50 per cent for senior technical staff and up to 100 per cent for senior managerial staff. In other budgets the overhead provides for indirect costs as well, where office furniture, heating, lighting and telephones, management costs and so on are included. Such direct and indirect overheads would generally add between 50 per cent and 200 per cent to basic salary costs.

For example, an e-learning designer might earn £30,000 as a salary. Pension, NIC and a small company car might increase the direct costs of employment by, say, 40 per cent to £42,000. At 80 per cent expected utilisation in a working year of 220 days, 176 days, the daily cost of the designer would be about £240. If the design activities involved ten work-days, the project budget would show £2,400 as the cost of e-learning design.

Equipment costs represent major and capital project costs, not only for equipment but for items such as software tools, buildings and furnishings and so on. Expenses and consumables costs represent minor and/or revenue expenditure such as travel and stationery.

Scheduling

Each project activity has an estimated duration. The activity's duration is expressed as calendar or elapsed time; for example, four weeks, or three days. Note the distinction here with the activity's estimated effort, which is expressed as a number of work-weeks or work-days. If two staff are assigned to a two-work-week activity, it would be scheduled to take one elapsed calendar week. The number of staff assigned to an activity is known as the activity's head-count, and the key problem of scheduling is to decide on an appropriate head-count for each activity. The head-count, or level of resourcing, translates the effort needed by an activity into a schedule for its completion. The later section on estimating ELSYE project sizes provides some guidelines on establishing head-count levels at the various phases and stages of project development.

Milestone charts

Simple projects can be scheduled using a milestone chart, illustrated in Figure 15.9. The project is broken down into a

Figure 15.9 Milestone chart

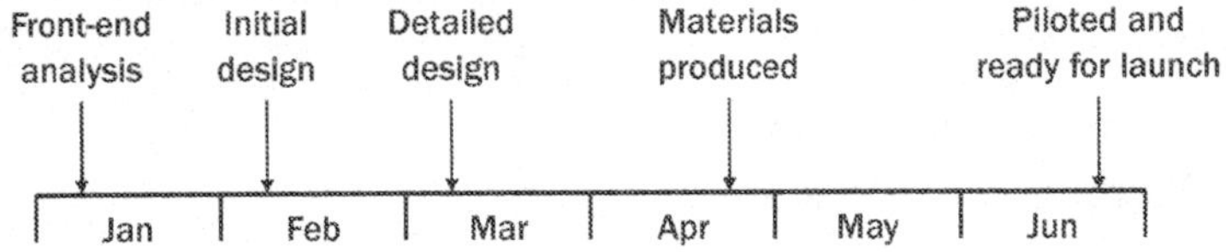

Figure 15.10 Gantt chart example

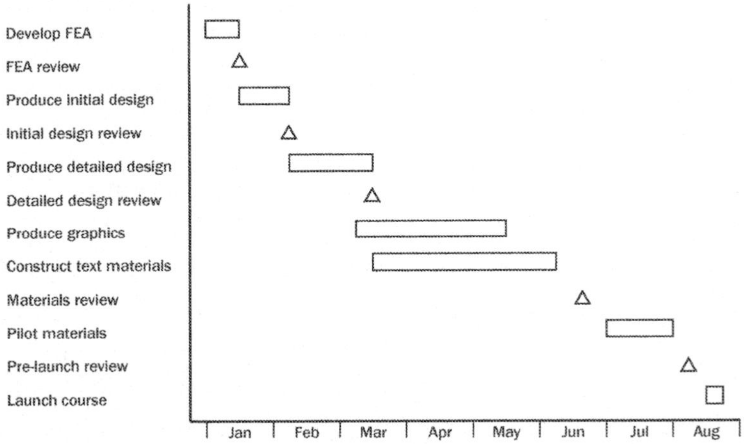

number of end products or deliverables, and the delivery of a product, called a milestone, is shown on a timeline.

A milestone chart is adequate for up to about six milestones, a period up to a few months and the work of one or two staff.

Gantt charts

For scheduling medium-sized projects, the Gantt chart is a suitable technique, illustrated in Figure 15.10. The project is broken down into a set or series of activities. The exact number of activities depends on the project: complex projects will have many activities, simple projects few. A sensible Gantt chart would need to have at least six or more activities; any fewer and a milestone chart would suffice. As a guideline, it is desirable to have each activity taking between two and ten working days of elapsed time for effective day-to-day project control, so Gantt charts begin to be useful for projects expected to take more than about one calendar month. The activities should be chosen to represent 'natural' units of work, and attention should be given to involving broadly similar amounts of effort in each of the various activities. This means that activities should not show great variability in effort or duration. For example, a plan which involved three activities of one, two and 100 days would be unsatisfactory, while 18, 27 and 58 days would be more acceptable. The earlier activities, at least, should be constructed to allow the first few to be completed within the first 10 per cent or 15 per cent of the project, enabling an early progress check to be made of the accuracy of the later duration estimates.

Each activity is represented as a bar against a timeline, where the start of the bar shows the activity's expected start date and the length of the bar shows the activity's expected duration in elapsed or calendar time. Activities are shown in the order in which they are expected to be tackled. Overlap between the bars is common, showing that more than one activity is in progress at any one time. Where one activity must follow another, its start date would be set to the end date of the activity it must follow.

Activities may be grouped together to form project phases or stages. Again, it is useful for the first stage or phase to involve no more than 20 per cent of the project, so that an early progress check can reveal the beginnings of schedule slippage or cost over-run. Activities can also be decomposed into sets of sub-activities when finer detail and more control are required.

The project plan should make provision for quality by explicitly scheduling the quality assurance (QA) activities to be employed. QA procedures are designed to measure and ensure conformance to requirements and standards. These typically involve the inspection and review of samples and products, so there will be a number of activities shown as 'Review...', 'Inspect...', 'Report on...', 'Meeting with...' and so on. Meetings and reviews are shown on a Gantt chart as activities with zero (nominal) duration, using a special symbol such as the triangle shown in Figure 15.10.

CPM and PERT networks

More sophisticated project schedules involve CPM (critical path method) or PERT (project evaluation and review technique) activity networks. A simple CPM chart is illustrated in Figure 15.11.

A CPM chart is used in addition to a Gantt chart when there are a variety of dependencies between activities: that one activity must finish before another can begin, that one activity must finish or be finished when another activity finishes, that one activity can only start once another has

Figure 15.11 CPM or PERT chart

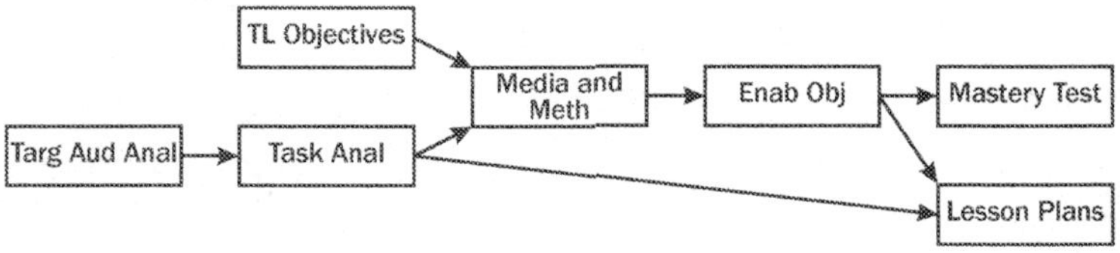

started, and so on. Such dependencies do not normally arise in ELSYE projects that produce conventional materials, but may well arise in multimedia projects requiring specially produced video footage or audio tracks. CPM and PERT charts are best constructed using appropriate computer software applications, and are not discussed further here.

Budget tracking

It is useful for the project budget to be presented with the costs broken down according to the cost categories for each of the project stages or phases. Project cost is expressed in monetary terms, and comparing actual costs incurred against budgeted costs monitors the project budget. Actual costs usually exceed the budget, and the result is called *over-run*. The extent to which the project as a whole is overspent is expressed as an over-run percentage. For example, a 125 per cent budget over-run on a £100,000 project indicates a final cost of £225,000.

The essential component of budget tracking is the comparison of projected costs with those budgeted. Expenditure on equipment and expenses is usually straightforward to log and track, while personnel costs are usually tracked through the use of timesheets. An example of a timesheet is shown in Figure 15.12.

Project team members note the hours spent on their various activities on their weekly timesheets. These hours are transferred to a budget tracking form, usually implemented as a spreadsheet. An example is shown in Table 15.3, illustrating the necessary management information required for all but the most complex of

Figure 15.12 Example timesheet

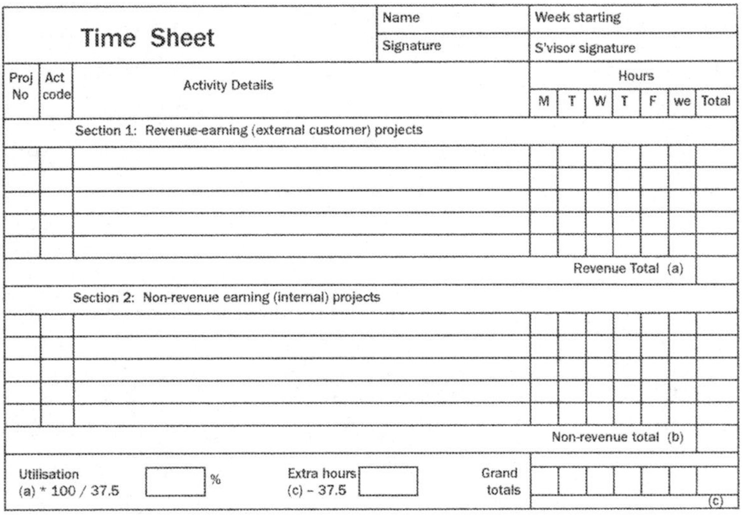
Time Sheet
Name
Week starting
Signature
S'visor signature
Proj No
Act code
Activity Details
Hours
M T W T F we Total
Section 1: Revenue-earning (external customer) projects
Revenue Total (a)
Section 2: Non-revenue earning (internal) projects
Non-revenue total (b)
Utilisation (a) * 100 / 37.5 %
Extra hours (c) – 37.5
Grand totals
(c)

Table 15.3 Budget tracking spreadsheet

		Project management	Design	Graphics	Production	Total
	Charge rate	400	250	250	200	
Budgeted	Work-days Cost	5 2,000	20 5,000	4 1,000	60 12,000	89 20,000
Projected	Work-days Cost	5 2,000	25 6,000	8 2,000	80 16,000	118 26,000
Variance	Work-days Cost	0 0	(5) (1,000)	(4) (1,000)	(20) (4,000)	(29) (6,000)
Actuals/ done	Work-days Cost	2 800	20 5000	8 2000	0 0	30 7,800
To go	Work-days Cost	3 1,200	5 1,000	0 0	80 16,000	88 18,200

projects. The project manager revises the projected person-days as needed, and reports on the variance between budget and projection to senior management.

Schedule tracking

A project schedule is expressed in terms of calendar time, and progress is measured by comparing the actual amount of time taken so far in activities completed and milestones reached against the original schedule plan. In most organisations the time taken so far is measured through the use of personnel timesheets. Activities often take longer than originally scheduled (although this does not necessarily imply they use more work-hours), resulting in what is called schedule *slippage*. The degree to which the whole project is behind schedule is expressed as a percentage of schedule slippage. For example, 25 per cent slippage in a 12-month project indicates a finish after 15 months.

Periodically (often weekly) the project schedule must be updated, usually along with the project budget, otherwise it quickly becomes outdated and thus of little use for project management purposes. For a Gantt chart, below each activity's originally planned bar is shown the current situation. Activities that have finished have their actual start and end dates shown, and the whole bar is shaded to show completion. Activities in progress have their bars shown with actual start dates and current best estimated end dates, with a suitable part of the bar shaded to show the degree of completion of the activity. Activities which have yet to start are shown with current best estimates of both start and end dates on an unshaded bar. An example of a Gantt chart showing schedule tracking is illustrated in Figure 15.13. The dashed line down the centre of the diagram represents the 'as at' date.

Metrics

Product quality assurance and continuous process quality improvement require measurements of the products and

Figure 15.13 Schedule tracking example

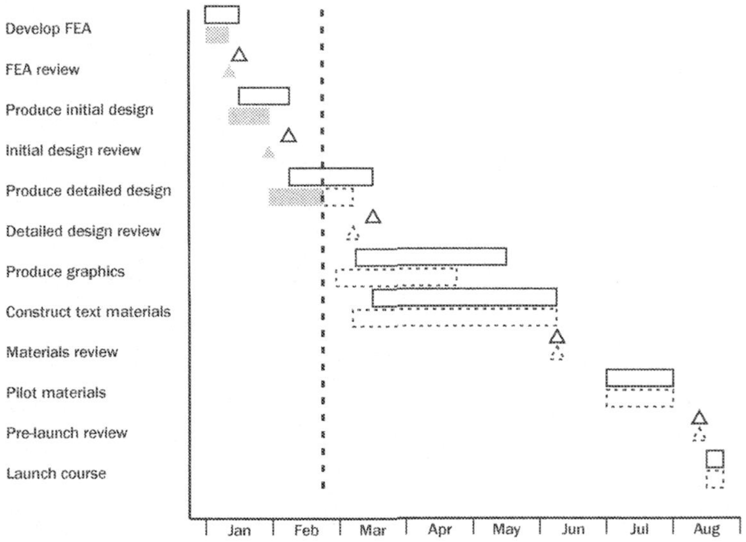

processes in order to demonstrate the success of planned changes and improvements. Measurements of product and process quality are called metrics.

There are no standard measurements of ELSYE product or process quality, in the same way that there are standard measurements, for example, for project size (hours of study time) and project effort (work-hours). However, a common measurement method is to count the number of defects revealed by the inspection and review processes, where a defect is defined as a single non-conformance to a specified requirement or standard. The target is usually a small number of defects found (and corrected) at the pre-delivery inspections, with zero found post-delivery.

Inspections should develop and use measures of the defectiveness of the products inspected, while quality improvement should develop and use measures of the

Table 15.4 Example metrics for inspection

Metric	Measure
Documents inspected	Pages
Defects logged	Numerical count
Defect density	Defects per page
Time spent on inspection	Hours
Detection rate	Defects per hour
Cost of inspection	Money
Cost per defect	Money per defect
Inspection rate	Pages per hour
Time spent in rework	Hours
Cost of rework	Money
Rework rate	Defects per hour
Cost per reworked defect	Money per defect
Defect severity	Rating
Average defect severity	Average rating
Cost of materials inspected	Money
Cost to find and fix materials defects	Money (cost of inspection plus cost of rework)
Cost inflation due to defects	Percentage of cost to find and fix defects to cost of materials inspected

effectiveness of the analysis, design, production, piloting, evaluation and product inspection processes.

Example metrics for the inspection process are illustrated in Table 15.4.

Change control

The most significant problem for most projects, particularly those which actively seek customer involvement and input, is the management of the changes brought about by 'improvements' to the project, changes of mind by the customer, 'new ideas' from the marketing staff and so on.

One of the most significant decisions that a project manager makes is how to deal with requests or demands for changes to the project. As mentioned earlier, a 'one-hour study time' e-learning session could take between 20 and 2,000 work-hours of development, depending upon its design. Apparently innocuous changes to a design could, and usually do, have disproportionate consequences.

The key concept in change control is that changes must be managed, not just 'happen'. The management of change requires a baseline in the first place – a clear statement of what the project currently involves and is projected to involve in terms of functionality (what the e-learning materials and systems do), schedule and budget. Then one or more changes are considered and their impacts on functionality, schedule and budget are assessed. The changes are arranged in a priority order according to current concerns, and the project management decides which of the changes are accepted into a revised baseline and which are not to be implemented at this time.

Project team roles

Although the discussion of this chapter may seem to be more concerned with larger ELSYE projects and substantial organisations whose only mission is the production of e-learning materials, the principles are equally applicable to the in-house development of a very short course by just one member of staff. In such a case, the single member of staff needs to undertake all of the development and management roles, clearly a very tall order indeed, and so even a very modest in-house course would be greatly improved by some input from outside experts who possess the skills required (Table 15.5).

Project management generically involves planning, organising, staffing, directing and controlling, as illustrated in Table 15.6. Project management in the ELSYE life cycle is, in principle, not much different from general project management, and all of the general activities of Table 15.6 apply. Because of this, only certain features of project management are discussed in this chapter and elsewhere; the remaining components of a project manager's armoury of knowledge and techniques are treated by a large number of texts devoted exclusively to the subject.

Structuring a project team

It is a little unusual to consider the strictly managerial issue of the structure of an organisation in a text on the engineering of e-learning systems, but the problem, not often recognised, is that a project team structure that is fixed for the entire project may not be maximally effective. The discussion of this section is applicable only to projects involving more than one person. Figure 15.14 illustrates the four main kinds of project organisation: product-oriented, function-oriented, 'strong' matrix and 'weak' matrix.

A product-oriented project organisation is composed of teams working on different parts of the product. For the development of e-learning materials, for example, there might be staff whose job is to produce textbooks or workbooks, while other staff produce computer-based teaching (CBT) programs.

A function-oriented project organisation is composed of teams working on different parts of the development process. For the development of e-learning materials within

Table 15.5 **Project roles**

Role	Duties
Customer	Requests and approves project Reviews deliverables and products Single customer contact signs off deliverables and products Negotiates priorities and changes
Stakeholders	Contribute to project definition and evaluation
Project manager	Defines budgets, schedules, QA procedures Obtains commitment and agreement on staffing, stage deliverables, responsibilities Establishes priorities, negotiates changes
Subject matter expert (SME)	Provides content Provides input on e-learning and graphic design Reviews and signs off technical accuracy of products
E-learning designer	Undertakes front-end analysis, initial design and detailed design Reviews and inspects products Designs and conducts evaluations
Writer/editor	Produces and reviews text Defines standards for text Reviews products
E-learning programmer	Implements courseware Reviews products
Graphic/media designer/producer	Produces graphics, video, audio Defines standards for look and feel Provides input on e-learning design Produces storyboards Reviews products
Administrator	Coordinates stage products and materials production Liaises with contractors Distributes materials Coordinates inspections, reviews, pilot and evaluation materials Coordinates change requests

Table 15.6 Generic project management activities

Activity	Detail
Planning	Develop project aims and goals Formulate strategies, policies, procedures and rules Prepare budgets and time and resource schedules
Organising	Define and structure tasks Establish project organisational structures Create posts, define responsibilities and authority Obtain required resources
Staffing	Select staff Orient new staff Train and develop staff Appraise staff
Directing	Provide leadership Supervise Delegate Motivate Coordinate and facilitate communications Encourage creativity, innovation, options and alternatives Resolve conflicts
Controlling	Set performance standards Establish monitoring and reporting systems Measure, monitor and review results Initiate corrective action Reward and discipline

such an orientation, for example, there might be a team of e-learning designers who pass designs on to the graphics team for graphics production and on to the programming team for the computer programming of CBT.

For both product- and function-oriented organisations, the teams are relatively fixed in structure and comprise full-time members of staff. Such organisations are appropriate to a section, department or company whose full-time mission is the continuous design and development of e-learning systems.

Figure 15.14 Four kinds of project organisation

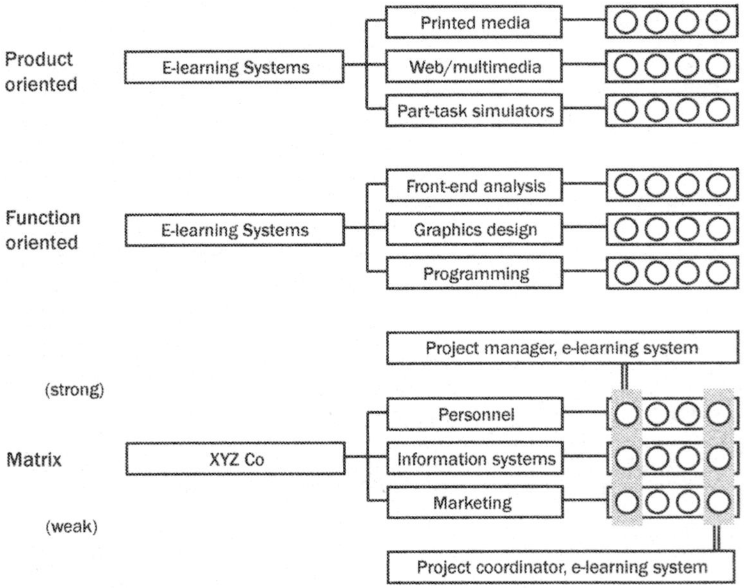

A matrix-oriented project team organisation, on the other hand, draws the staff for a project from other sections or departments in the company, or from other companies, usually because the project is a one-off. Staff work part-time on the project, interleaving their project work with their other 'normal' company work. Two varieties of a matrix organisation may be distinguished, depending upon the authority given to the project leader. Figure 15.14 illustrates one team drawn from the example departments under a 'project manager', and another team under a 'project coordinator'.

A 'strong' matrix organisation involves a project that is headed by a project manager fully authorised and resourced to design and develop the e-learning system required. A 'weak' matrix organisation involves a project coordinator whose brief is limited to bringing together the

Figure 15.15 Suitability of various project organisations

	Product oriented	Function oriented	Weak matrix	Strong matrix
Analysis	●	●	●●	●
Design	●●	●●		●●
Production	●●			●
Customer involvement	●			●●
Long duration	●			●
Complex technology	●	●	●	●●
High risk	●	●	●●	●●
Many staff			●	●●

● Possibly suitable ●● Highly suitable

project team members as necessary in order to achieve the project goals. While a 'weak' matrix organisation may seem impossibly weak to achieve a robust outcome within acceptable timescales, it does have its place at a certain point within the development life cycle, as shown in Figure 15.15.

The point of the discussion of these various project organisations is made in Figure 15.15, where the suitability of the organisation of the project team is related to both the phase and other significant features of the ELSYE project.

During the analysis phase of an ELSYE project, the weak matrix form of project organisation is most suited. During the design phase any form *other* than the weak matrix is most suited, while during production a product-oriented organisation is most suited. The implications of this are as follows.

First, for *one-off e-learning projects*, the strong matrix form of organisation is highly suitable, particularly if it can be evolved from a weak matrix organisation that would be effective at the start of the project, in the analysis phase.

Second, where a section or company is in the business of *full-time e-learning project design and development*, a product rather than a functional organisation is indicated. This is rather contrary to current common practice in the UK, but it points to more of an outward-looking and market-oriented concern with the product and the customer's satisfaction with the product than an inward-looking concern with staff job demarcations.

Finally, even where full-time e-learning projects are organised on product lines, attention should be given to the benefits of a matrix approach to individual projects where certain features are significant, such as high risk or extensive customer involvement, as illustrated in Figure 15.15.

Principles of organisational power and politics

The following discussion draws heavily on three texts: Sauer (1993), Pfeffer (1993) and Block (1983).

Table 15.7 Decision-taking situations

		Goals agreement	
		Yes	No
Means agreement	Yes	Rational decisions	Compromise
	No	Judgement	Political decisions

Organisational politics

Whether there is agreement or not on goals, and agreement or not on the means appropriate for reaching those goals, gives the four decision-taking situations shown in Table 15.7. In most organisational circumstances there is neither uniform agreement on goals nor agreement on the means to achieve whatever goals there may be. Most organisational problem situations are therefore inevitably political.

Since an ELSYE project is essentially a technical activity staffed by technicians, it needs to operate within situations where, ideally, project decisions are made on rational grounds. This means, ideally, securing agreement among all participants on both the goals of the project and the means of achieving those goals. Where these agreements prove problematic, the role of the project manager is, on the one hand, to insulate the project team from such external problems and their political consequences and, on the other, to foster and maintain consensus internally and within the project team itself.

Power

For this discussion, power may be seen as the ability to secure favourable political decisions for the project under consideration.

The fundamental source of power generally lies in the control of resources – information, decision process, materials or services, money and personnel – upon which others are dependent. The effect of this dependency on the party who lacks the resource, and hence the amount of power wielded by the party who controls the resource, depends on two broad issues.

- The importance of the resource to the party who lacks it. A project is more affected the more it needs the resource in order to make satisfactory progress.
- The discretion of the party controlling the resource over its allocation. An organisation, group or person has more power the more control they have over how and when a resource is distributed to others.

From the point of view of a project, the significance of its dependency upon a resource depends on three concerns: the resource's immediacy, substitutability and pervasiveness.

- *Immediacy* refers to the timescale of dependence. The control of a resource that is not really needed for another six months does not provide much power, while the control of a resource that is urgently needed confers significant power. Similarly, a project may not currently be greatly affected by the lack of a resource only needed in six months' time, but might be effectively terminated by the lack of a resource needed tomorrow.
- *Substitutability* refers to the extent to which some other resource can be used in place of the scarce resource. The control of a resource for which many other alternatives can easily be found does not confer much power. Similarly, a project may not be affected by the lack of a particular resource from a particular supplier if an

alternative can be found, in the form of either an alternative resource or an alternative supplier.

- *Pervasiveness* reflects the extent to which a necessary resource is required throughout all the stages or components of a project. Arranging matters so that a scare resource is only absolutely needed for a small part of the project reduces dependence upon the resource and restricts the power that accrues to that resource's controller.

Exercising power and political influence

The extent to which power is in fact used to make political decisions depends on a number of factors:

- an actual scarcity of resources, or an actual limitation of information or access to decision-making processes, among parties who are interdependent;
- the issues involved being deemed important;
- a distribution of power among the participants;
- the ability and willingness of those with power to exploit it.

Where some or other of these factors do not apply to a particular situation, it is more likely that decisions are made in ways other than the obvious or explicit exercise of power. And, because the obvious or explicit use of power between people is commonly considered vulgar, other means of exercising power are usually sought. Characteristically, this involves moving the decision-taking situation of Table 15.7 out of the 'political' box and into one of the other three boxes. This in turn involves seeking consensus among the parties on goals, or on the means of achieving such goals as may be agreed.

Exercising power and political influence thus involves two major activities:

- unobtrusively gaining legitimacy for decisions, influence, actions, or the premises on which decisions might be taken;
- unobtrusively building support and alliances for a favoured position.

These are quintessentially political activities, undertaken where there is little agreement on goals or on the means to achieve whatever goals there may be. It is important for the prospective project manager and the current technical team member to appreciate and ponder this essentially social nature of organisational politics.

A well-executed system diagram should show the conflicts and alliances between those involved, and hence where the exercise of power and political influence might be expected. It should also show where the project is located within its context, and hence the likely support or resistance it might expect.

In order to resist the exercise of power against a project, it follows that a project manager needs to undertake an analysis of the resource requirements of the project and of the points where the project is subject to review. In the case of project resources, the project manager needs to ensure low immediacy, high substitutability and low pervasiveness, and in the case of project review or decision points, the project manager needs to acquire as much control as possible of the review criteria, procedures, options and information about the project.

The greater the consensus about values and goals in the subgroup, the more effective and coherent the action in a power struggle. As noted earlier, a project manager seeks to foster and maintain consensus within the project team.

What counts as important can be negotiated. A project manager has a number of tactics and strategies available by which the relative importance of favourable project aspects can be emphasised and unfavourable aspects can be de-emphasised.

Finally, the abilities required for the successful exercise of power include hierarchical position, articulateness, stature and credibility, diagnostic and problem-solving skills, social tact and subtlety, knowledge of organisational rules and self-belief. Apart from the position within the organisational hierarchy, the project manager has a considerable measure of control over these personal abilities. Where a new project team is being formed, these are the traits to be sought in its project manager.

Tactics of organisational power and politics

Table 15.8 provides a summary of various strategies and tactics that commonly occur in organisational politics. The table can be used as a simple 'spotter's guide', more actively as a defensive guide, or ultimately as an offensive guide for the committed.

Planning for organisational power and politics

During feasibility the prospective project manager constructs a system diagram and a plan for dealing with the inevitable organisational politics that will arise during the project. The following procedure may assist in the development of such a plan. The approach taken here is to pay particular attention to two aspects of the project: project support, and project reviews or assessments.

Table 15.8 Tactics of organisational politics

Technique	Specific tactics
Control the agenda	Both what is on it and the order of the items Items off the agenda are labelled non-issues, and may be decided without scrutiny Present the weaker of two related proposals first: this airs positions and principles and softens opposition Present contentious proposals later; time is usually short and members will agree to almost anything to get away
Influence which alternatives are taken seriously	Definition of acceptable alternatives narrows the likely outcome into favoured options Select beforehand the few to be considered from the many Have an 'expert' make an 'objective' selection
Label decisions, criteria or facts	Avoid a political situation by labelling a decision or an alternative as unimportant Construct a desirable political situation by labelling a decision or an alternative as particularly important
Influence the evaluation criteria	Influence the dimensions, constraints or premises on which alternatives are to be evaluated Set the norms, standards, beliefs or values to be used in arriving at any judgement; this is often tantamount to making the decision Claim or assert some 'rule' or higher 'policy' which needs to be respected during the decision process (usually quite easy and simple to do, and the claim is always very difficult to challenge; a challenge implies bad faith, or may show the challenger as not *au fait* with higher thinking or the latest or most expert view)
Control information about alternatives or decisions	Provide biased or only supportive data Leave the opposition to research problems Keep all information secret Only release information selectively Control information flows: from whom or where it is sourced, and where it goes
Ensure room for manoeuvre	Keep statements as vague as possible, non-measurable, non-specific, non-committed Use verbal, undocumented communication, avoid writing decisions down Keep options open as long as possible Avoid 'big' decisions: break down a big,

Table 15.8 **Tactics of organisational politics (*Cont'd*)**

Technique	Specific tactics
	contentious, impactful decision into a series of small, minor changes, each of which can be quickly and easily implemented without need for consultation or discussion
Build coalitions and alliances	Build external constituencies who can demand involvement Build internal alliances, negotiating or bargaining for support Promote 'unobvious' persons who owe their position to you and will thus support you
Coopt uninterested or opposing parties	They will receive privileged information and be constrained to behave 'appropriately' They will be subject to conformance pressure and self-justification They will be labelled as, and expected to be, cooperative There are risks of loss of secrecy and loss of control
Use outside experts	Only if you control them They legitimate what is being said
Build consensus and shared views	Meet socially, informally Discuss and communicate Take opportunities to propagandise achievements
Promulgate your views	Use guise of seeking consensus Use guise of consulting on what is best for organisation or stakeholders
Use appropriate symbols	Employ rituals, ceremonies and settings to legitimate, claim, establish or display power Act symbolically; send messages by acting in certain ways Arrange signals of power: larger desks, thicker carpets, bigger cars, different mail arrangements, your own secretaries, sitting at the head of tables, a permanently reserved table in staff dining room, etc.
Use appropriate language	Meanings, significance and perceived meanings and significance are in a state of constant common negotiation and interpretation in any group of social actors

Table 15.8 Tactics of organisational politics (*Cont'd*)

Technique	Specific tactics
	Employ written or verbal interpretations to legitimate, claim, establish or display power Claim, assert and occupy the high ground: what is in best interests of department, organisation, customer, or whatever Seek commonality in approach, interpretation, language, goals Communicate by using words more for their emotional impact and connotation
Control assessment	Avoid assessment or evaluation if possible Conduct and communicate your own assessment to forestall external assessment Provide measures of input only Deflect attention to the amount of worthy effort which is being put in to process this input Avoid providing process or, especially, outcome measures
Control assessment process	Specify or influence the criteria to be used Specify or influence the standards, norms, beliefs or values used in judgement Specify or influence the procedures to be followed Specify or influence who will carry it out Specify or influence the timing Specify or influence the people to be spoken to Specify or influence where it takes place Specify or influence the terms of reference
Enhance others' dependency (and perceived dependency) upon resources you control	Attempt to ensure their immediacy, non-substitutability and pervasiveness Make the resources deliberately scarce Make alternatives impossible
Reduce your dependency on resources you do not control	Find alternatives Make them less important (and define them as not important) Limit and localise their use Stockpile them
Collect the control of resources into instruments you control	Committees Allies Experts and consultants External constituencies

1 Identify the goals and anticipated impacts (pay-offs) for the supporters of and stakeholders in the project and of the project members themselves. Embed these in the system diagram. Consider a private copy of the diagram (accurate and honest) and a public copy (appropriately edited for language and content).

2 Particularly assess the impact of the project on supporters and stakeholders in terms of the immediacy, pervasiveness and substitutability of the project's deliverables and services. In other words, assess the power that the project provides, when complete, to its supporters.

3 Assess the environment in terms of the formal organisational power and management structure (including committees) and procedures. Assess the informal social and private organisational alliances (friends, non-friends, enemies, influencers, those with delegated authority, allies, information channels, patrons and their protégés). Note these on the system diagram.

4 Assess the actors' historical tendencies in behaviour as well as their beliefs, values, perceptions, attitudes and motivations. Add these tendencies to the system diagram.

5 Identify the funders, fixers and power-brokers, and the competing demands on supporters' support. Assess the importance of the project to its supporters relative to their other interests and enterprises.

6 Identify and categorise the project problems: obstacles to delivery of quality products on time and within budget; disagreements with concept, approach or content; assessments, evaluations and reviews of the project; reasons for denial of approval or favourable review.

7 Plan to control and influence evaluation reviews and the actors' expectations of these reviews. Influence and control evaluation effects, timescales and timing, criteria and process, and information access, flow and content. Keep in mind that settling the questions to ask is tantamount to deciding the outcomes.

8 Develop an evaluation plan and attempt to own the evaluations as much as possible.

9 Develop solutions to project problems by devising solution scenarios and then identifying and evaluating their probable consequences. Attend to minimising flaws in the ELSYE development process itself. If possible, absorb within the project itself the flaws and problems that do occur. Attend to the support and resource requirements of the project. Make the project's products or outcomes as non-substitutable, pervasive and immediate as possible.

10 Consider a formal role of 'support manager' in the project team who will manage project support and supporters in a political context.

References

Avison, D. and Fitzgerald, G. (2006) *Information Systems Development*. London: McGraw-Hill.

Block, R. (1983) *The Politics of Projects*. New York: Yourdon Press.

Bloom, B.S. (1956) *Taxonomy of Educational Objectives*. Boston, MA: Addison-Wesley.

Bloom, B.S. and Hastings, J.T. (1971) *Handbook of Formative and Summative Evaluation of Student Learning*. New York: McGraw-Hill.

Boehm, B. (1981) *Software Engineering Economics*. Englewood Cliffs, NJ: Prentice-Hall.

Buckley, R. and Caple, J. (2007) *The Theory and Practice of Training*, 5th edn. London: Kogan Page.

Checkland, P. (1999) *Systems Thinking, Systems Practice*. Chichester: John Wiley.

Checkland, P. and Scholes, J. (1999) *Soft Systems Methodology in Action*. Chichester: John Wiley.

Clark, R.C. and Kwinn, A. (2007) *The New Virtual Classroom*. New York: Pfeiffer.

Clark, R.C. and Mayer, R.E. (2003) *E-Learning and the Science of Instruction*. New York: Pfeiffer.

Clark, R.E. (1983) 'Reconsidering research on learning from media', *Review of Educational Research*, 53(4): 445–59.

Clark, R.E. (1994) 'Media will never influence learning', *Journal of Educational Technology Research and Development*, 42(2): 21–9.

Crosby, P.B. (1995) *Quality Without Tears: The Art of Hassle-Free Management*. New York: McGraw-Hill.

Dick, W., Carey, L.M. and Carey, J.O. (2004) *The Systematic Design of Instruction*, 6th edn. New York: Allyn & Bacon.

Gagné, R.M., Wager, W.W., Golas, K. and Keller, J.M. (2004) *Principles of Instructional Design*, 5th edn. New York: Wadsworth.

Gery, G. (1987) *Making CBT Happen*. Boston, MA: Gery Associates.

Hofstadter, D.R. (2000) *Gödel, Escher, Bach: An Eternal Golden Braid*. Harmondsworth: Penguin.

Humphrey, W. (1990) *Managing the Software Process*. New York: Addison-Wesley.

Laurillard, D. (2001) *Rethinking University Teaching: A Conversational Framework for the Effective Use of Learning Technologies*, 2nd edn. London: Routledge Falmer.

Mager, R.F. (1997) *Preparing Instructional Objectives*, 3rd edn. Atlanta, GA: Center for Effective Performance.

Merrill, M.D. (1994) *Instructional Design Theory*. Englewood Cliffs, NJ: Educational Technology Publications.

Merrill, M.D. (1999) 'Instructional transaction theory (ITT): instructional design based on knowledge objects', in C.M. Reigeluth (ed.) *Instructional Design Theory and Models: A New Paradigm of Instructional Theory Vol. II*. Mahwah, NJ: Lawrence Erlbaum Associates.

Molenda, M. (2003) 'In search of the elusive ADDIE model', *Performance Improvement*, 42(5): 34–6.

Pfeffer, J. (1993) *Managing with Power: Politics and Influence in Organizations*. Boston, MA: Harvard Business School.

Pirsig, R.M. (1999) *Zen and the Art of Motorcycle Maintenance*. New York: Vintage.

Pressman, R.S. (2004) *Software Engineering: A Practitioner's Approach*, 6th edn. London: McGraw-Hill.

Sauer, C. (1993) *Why Information Systems Fail: A Case Study Approach*. Henley-on-Thames: Alfred Waller.

Index

Printed in Dunstable, United Kingdom

91343007R00199